LOVE & CONFLICT

LOVE & CONFLICT

A Covenantal Model of Christian Ethics

JOSEPH L. ALLEN

UNIVERSITY
PRESS OF
AMERICA

Lanham • New York • London

Scripture quotations in this publication unless otherwise noted are from the
Revised Standard Version of the Bible, copyrighted 1946, 1952, © 1971, 1973
by the Division of Christian Education of the National Council of the Churches
of Christ in the U.S.A., and are used by permission.

Scripture quotations noted NEB are from The New English Bible. © the
Delegates of the Oxford University Press and the Syndics of the Cambridge
University Press 1961, 1970. Reprinted by permission.

Library of Congress Cataloging-in-Publication Data

Allen, Joseph L.
Love & conflict : a covenantal model of Christian ethics /
Joseph L. Allen.
p.   cm.
Originally published: Nashville : Abingdon Press, © 1984.
Includes bibliographical references and index.
1. Christian ethics.   I. Title.   II. Title: Love and conflict.
BJ1251.A37   1995   241—dc20   94–38273 CIP

ISBN 0–8191–9763–7 (pbk. : alk. paper)

 The paper used in this publication meets the minimum requirements of
American National Standard for Information Sciences—Permanence
of Paper for Printed Library Materials, ANSI Z39.48–1984.

To Mary David,
partner in the special
covenant of marriage

Contents

PART I: Model, Standard, and Conflict

   The choice of a model
   Covenant ideas in the Bible
   The nature of a covenant relationship
   Two types of covenant relationships
   The significance of a covenant model
      for Christian ethics

   Discerning the standard
   God's covenant love
   Human covenant love

   Conflict and the concept of prima facie duty
   Reinhold Niebuhr on conflict
   Covenantal participation in conflict
   The problem of priorities

PART II: Covenant, Conflict, and the Problem of Priorities

   The meaning of love for self
   Priority between the interests of self and others

Preface

This book has grown out of the interrelation of two convictions. The first, the significance of which has increasingly impressed me in recent years, is that faithfulness to one another in our various relationships, also expressible as loyalty, steadfastness, or other terms, is central to a Christian outlook on moral action. That belief finds expression in what follows in the use of a covenant model of human relationships and in the concept of "covenant love" as the basic moral standard of Christian ethics.

The second conviction is that conflict is an inescapable feature of life, in several senses: conflict among moral claims, conflict among the interests of various people and groups, and conflict as struggle over those interests. Conflict is not the only side of the matter; it is never separable from some degree of harmony. But it is conflict especially that poses moral problems. Even so conflict is not simply evil, nor is harmony simply good; it depends upon what kind of conflict or harmony. Both are ambiguous.

The reality of conflict is highly significant for ethical reflection. Without conflict in these senses we would not encounter moral perplexities. Perhaps we would not even be moral agents. Because of conflict, though, we must choose among alternative claims and interests and groups. For this reason it will not suffice in ethics simply to identify standards

9

and to talk about how we ideally ought to relate to one another. Christians already know that they should love one another, although they would benefit from further reflection about what that means. But even with more insight into their most basic moral standard, Christians would continue to face difficult decisions about what love requires under various kinds of conflicts.

This book seeks to speak both to the meaning of the standard of love in Christian ethics, to the problems posed by conflict, and to the bearing of both of these realities upon our special moral relationships. The first part of the book explores the basic concepts underlying the book: covenant relationships, how we are to understand the basic moral standard of Christian ethics, and conflict in its various senses. The reality of conflict forces us to resolve in some fashion or other the problem of identifying priorities among the various moral claims upon us.

Part 2 inquires into four kinds of moral conflicts: (1) those that arise between the self's interests and those of other persons, (2) conflicts that occur because we belong simultaneously to various covenants, (3) conflicts over how to distribute justly the benefits and burdens of social life, and (4) conflicts between the interests of wrongdoers and of those whom they wrong. The objective in this part is to see how a covenantal interpretation of Christian ethics can help us identify priorities amid each of these types of conflicts.

In part 3, I deal with the interrelation of covenant love and conflict by discussing three important types of special covenants: marriage, political community, and the church. Other covenants would be well worth exploring, but limits of space and time prevent treatment of them here. With each of these three types of covenants, I am asking (1) what it implies to interpret this special relationship as covenantal, and (2) what would be an appropriate kind of response, given this interpretation, to some types of conflicts that one characteristically encounters in this special relationship.

In the preparation of this volume I am indebted to a large company, only a few of whom I can mention here. In my work in Christian ethics and on this book in particular, I have received continual insight and support from the faculty, students, and administration of Perkins School of Theology. Their often probing questions about my ideas, as well as their constructive proposals, have aided my thinking in countless ways. The work of writing was much assisted by two periods of research leave provided by deans Joseph D. Quillian, Jr., and James E. Kirby. Colleagues at Perkins and elsewhere who have read sections of the manuscript and have offered valuable comments include Harold Attridge, Frederick Carney, Victor Furnish, Paul Ramsey, Charles Reynolds, James Ward, James White, and Charles Wood. I have learned much from their observations, even though at various points I have persisted in what one or another of them judged to be errors. My friend and fellow inquirer into things ethical, Mac McPherson, may not remember the remark he made one day in Bridwell Library that suggested to my mind a major line of development that I had not considered previously. Several members of the Society of Christian Ethics have assisted by their questions and suggestions. Although I am the grateful recipient of the help of all these persons and more, I remain responsible for all the book's inadequacies.

Sally Snow, Mary Ann Marshall, and Terry Smith together have typed and retyped the manuscript and probably hope that it will remain in the form in which they last typed it. Bob and Joyce and David have assisted in many ways by their presence, their affirmation, and their appreciation for the subject. Most especially Mary David, to whom the book is dedicated with love and affection, has combined patience and an unobtrusive but steady encouragement and confidence that the work has been worthwhile.

December, 1983

PART I

MODEL, STANDARD, AND CONFLICT

1

A Covenantal Model of the Moral Life

The Choice of a Model

One of the fundamental ingredients of any ethical theory is its model or conception of how moral selves are related. Sometimes ethicists adopt a model without announcing to their readers (or even to themselves) that they have done so, but the model's influence over their theory is no less pervasive. The choice of a model for the moral life sets the framework within which that writer explores each moral question. It is best to give explicit attention to a judgment of that significance.

A model of the moral life has to do with how moral selves *are* related, and not merely nor primarily how they ought to be related. Therein it offers an answer to the question, What is going on? which, as H. Richard Niebuhr points out, is a question prior to the more obvious one, What shall I do?[1] It answers this prior question first at the level of the observable interrelations of moral selves in their physical and social context. At this level Niebuhr asserts, for example, that all moral action has the character of response to action upon us. It is not, he says, merely "making" something, as a sculptor or shoemaker would do, nor is it merely obedience to law. It is the response of selves to selves.

The second level of answer to What is going on? that a model provides, whether explicitly or implicitly, is the ontological, the level of assertions about the ultimate ground and meaning of the moral life. Macbeth is drawn by his despair to the ontological level: "Life is a tale told by an idiot, full of sound and fury, signifying nothing." From a radically different viewpoint Augustine is answering the same kind of question when he writes, "Thou hast formed us for Thyself, and our hearts are restless till they find rest in Thee."[2] Whatever the answer, elaborate or simple, reflective or intuitive, it is concerned at this level with the most basic questions of the moral life. Is there any meaning to moral action at all? If so, what, and why? *Is* there even a moral life, rather than merely the interactions of B. F. Skinner's human animals wholly conditioned by the environment? Because ethics must work with a model of some kind, it is inseparable from metaethics, that is, from reflection upon the ultimate justification of our moral judgments. A model of the moral life is a way of pointing to the connections between normative ethical reflection and its metaethical foundations.

Such a model provides assistance (or resistance), therefore, for our moral understanding. Judgments about what kind of persons we ought to be and what we ought to do presuppose some model of our relationships with one another and with the ultimate ground and meaning of things. The model significantly affects the content of these judgments; it gives direction and shape to our moral decisions. Our model may be a source of motivation for moral action (or may undercut it), but in any event it also influences our moral conclusions. It is desirable then to adopt a model that will adequately represent what the moral life is like.

Because the ethical position presented here seeks to be appropriate to the Christian confession that Jesus Christ is Lord, the model in terms of which I shall be working in what follows is one that is presupposed in that confession. It is a model in which all moral relationships are understood to be *covenant relationships*. I shall shortly explain what this means. For the moment suffice it to say that understanding ourselves to be in covenant with other people involves believing that we and they belong to the same moral community; that in this community each person matters in his or her own right and not merely as something useful to the society; that we all participate in the moral community by entrusting ourselves to others and in turn by accepting their entrusting; and that in the moral community each of us has enduring responsibility to all the others.

To work from this model is to reject some other models. At least it is to reject them as adequate conceptions of the moral life as a whole, even though they may validly point to certain features of human relationships. It is to reject any *individualistic* model, that is, one in which moral selves do not belong essentially together, but are merely a collection of separate individuals. This assumption of essential separateness is much more important than a further point on which its holders disagree—whether the individual selves are egoistic or altruistic.

To work from this covenant model is also to reject *some contractual* ideas as adequate conceptions for the whole of the moral life—those, for example, in which the social contract is seen as a relationship only of bargaining (explicit or implicit) in which the rights and obligations of each person are limited to what has been agreed to, or would be agreed to, in the bargain. The terms *covenant* and *contract* can each mean many things, but where this is what is meant by *contract*, it is not the kind of model I have in mind when I speak of *covenant*.

Finally it is to reject *part-whole* models of the moral life— models in which the individuality of each person is lost in the whole. These are models in which the moral life is pictured as the interacting of many cogs in a machine, rather than of selves in a community. These models affirm the essential relatedness of each part; but what is related is no longer a number of selves, nor is the whole a community, for where the individuality of the members is lacking, the whole cannot be a community, but only a construction of some kind, like a building or a computer.

In contrast to all these other kinds of models, the covenant model that follows pictures persons as both essentially social and yet with individuality and accountability as moral agents. We can rebel against our social relationships, but we cannot divest ourselves of all of them. Similarly we can deny our responsibility and seek to lose ourselves in the whole, but in spite of all denials we remain accountable selves, and society is possible only because that is true. To be social and to be a centered, individually accountable self are not alternatives; each requires the other.

There are many possible covenant models. In this chapter I shall set forth the outlines of the one that underlies this book. I shall consider first some of the ways a covenantal model is present in the Bible and how such a model helps the writers convey their proclamation. Second, on that basis it is possible to identify more precisely the meaning of *covenant* as the idea will be used here. Third, I shall need to distinguish between two types of covenant relationships in order adequately to express a Christian understanding of the kinds of covenants in which we stand. Let us begin, though, by turning to the presence of covenant ideas in the biblical proclamation.

Covenant Ideas in the Bible

Covenant is a central theme in the Bible. By that I do not mean what Eichrodt[3] maintains about the Old Testament— that covenant is *the* central theme. Nevertheless it is indeed important in both testaments and can shed considerable light upon biblical understandings of God's action and of the moral life. It provides a unifying theme in the midst of the multiplicity of the Bible.

Covenant in the Old Testament

Covenants in the Old Testament between God and the people all share certain characteristics. First, they are (unlike some human-to-human covenants) between parties of unequal status. Second, God initiates each covenant and sets its terms; they are not negotiated. Each covenant is therefore a reflection of God's power and grace—God's power, in that nothing external to God's will requires the covenant or dictates its terms; instead, in covenanting God creates a new thing, a covenant community where none existed. God's grace is present in that though nothing requires covenanting, God nevertheless sees fit to create a covenant, to the benefit of the people. Third, although God initiates each covenant, the people must still decide whether they will accept it. Their freedom is not destroyed by God's initiative, and yet it is severely circumscribed in that if they were to refuse God's offer of a covenant, they would be rejecting an act of grace.

Even with this common core there is no single covenant tradition or single meaning of the covenant, but a continual process of reinterpretation of the various traditions. I shall discuss two main groupings of covenant tradition and then some of the ways the latter prophets developed their ideas.

1. *The promissory covenants with Noah, Abraham, and David.*[4] A "promissory covenant" is one in which God performs an act of self-limitation through a solemn promise, but in which there is no mention (or only marginal mention) of obligations upon the human parties to the covenant. Instances of promissory covenants are God's covenants with Noah (Gen. 9:8-17), with Abraham (esp. Gen. 15 and 17), and with David (II Sam. 7). Whatever was the chronological order of the traditions, God's covenant with Noah stands earliest in the biblical text as we have received it. One thing about this covenant calls for special note: it is with Noah and his descendants, that is, with all future human beings. More than that, it is with "every living creature." Here is a covenant not with people chosen from among others, not even only with people, but with the whole array of living creatures. This universal covenant is now theologically part of the background for the covenant with Abraham.

In the Genesis 15 strand of tradition of God's covenant with Abraham, several features stand out. (1) Genesis 15 stands within a wider account in which the theme of promise and fulfillment is prominent. The note appears in Genesis 12:2-3: "And I will make of you a great nation, and I will bless you, and make your name great. . . ." (2) God comes to Abraham (Abram) unexpectedly and not because of any merit on Abraham's part. (3) God promises Abraham an heir (he has none, and he and Sarah are old), descendants as numerous as the stars, and "this land" as their land. Although the earliest tradition may have seen this promise as entitlement to a small area around Hebron in Judah, the promise eventually came to be seen as including the whole of Israel at its greatest reach. (4) Through a solemn covenant ceremony God vows to keep the covenant. (5) No obligations upon Abraham are mentioned in this strand of the tradition.

Because of these features, the Abraham covenant represented in all stages of Hebrew and Jewish history the dependable graciousness of God—gracious because freely given, and dependable because based on God's solemn pledge. For the Yahwist, writing in the tenth century B.C., this covenant points to the success of the empire of David and Solomon. For the Deuteronomic writers of the sixth century, it becomes a covenant not only with Abraham but also with Isaac and Jacob, and as such the revelation of God's election of Israel, whereby Israel became a chosen people. It comes to stand as the basis of the Jewish hope in the midst of the exile. Still later the Priestly writer (in Gen. 17) stresses that this covenant is "everlasting"; that circumcision is the sign of membership in the elected community; and that not only are they God's people, but also "I will be their God" (v. 8). This last feature can be interpreted as the obverse side of their being the elected people: elected to worship God; elected not simply as a political entity but as a people of faith.

In God's covenant with David (II Sam. 7), we again have a promissory covenant. God promises to establish the Davidic line forever (v. 13) but places no explicit obligations on the human partner. The Davidic covenant is also described as unconditional and everlasting (vv. 14-16). When the king sins, he will be chastened, but the covenant will not be ended—"I will not take my steadfast love from him" (v. 15). Here, as in the Abraham covenant, is the assertion of an absolutely dependable promise of God. The chief purpose of this covenant account is reflected in the reference in verse 12: it is a covenant not only with David but with David's lineage, especially Solomon. The Davidic covenant functioned in later Hebrew-Jewish history to legitimate the Davidic succession and to provide the assurance of a stable rule.

Later, the success of David's reign became another reason for looking back to this covenant. The time of David and Solomon had been the time of the united kingdom and of the greatest extent of Israel's boundaries. So in a later time of troubles, Isaiah expresses his hope for the fulfillment of God's promise in this covenant:

> For to us a child is born,
>   to us a son is given;
> and the government will be upon his shoulder,
>   and his name will be called
> "Wonderful Counselor, Mighty God,
>   Everlasting Father, Prince of Peace."
> Of the increase of his government and of peace
>   there will be no end,
> upon the throne of David, and over his kingdom,
>   to establish it, and to uphold it
> with justice and with righteousness
>   from this time forth and for evermore.
> The zeal of the Lord of hosts will do this. (Isa. 9:6-7)

Still later, at the end of the exile in Babylon, that anonymous prophet we call Second Isaiah declares a word of reassurance, based on this same Davidic covenant, and simultaneously turns its meaning outward to the nations Israel is to serve:

> Ho, every one who thirsts,
>   come to the waters;
> and he who has no money,
>   come, buy and eat!
> Come, buy wine and milk
>   without money and without price.
> Why do you spend your money for that which is not bread,
>   and your labor for that which does not satisfy?
> Hearken diligently to me, and eat what is good,
>   and delight yourselves in fatness.
> Incline your ear, and come to me;
>   hear, that your soul may live;

and I will make with you an everlasting covenant,
  my steadfast, sure love for David.
Behold, I made him a witness to the peoples,
  a leader and commander for the peoples.
Behold, you shall call nations that you know not,
  and nations that knew you not shall run to you,
because of the Lord your God, and of the Holy One of
  Israel, for he has glorified you. (Isa. 55:1-5)

Like the Abrahamic covenant, the Davidic one functioned in the exilic and post-exilic periods as a reminder of the steadfast love of God for Judah and as a source of hope that the dire troubles of those times would someday be replaced by a return to the greatness of the time of David. Much of the messianic hope that developed in Judaism over succeeding centuries centered around the figure of David. The Messiah would be a fulfillment of the promise made by God in the covenant with David.

2. *The covenant at Sinai-Horeb.*[5] Because the Ten Commandments are so often lifted from their context and taught in isolation, we need to remind ourselves that their context in both locations (Exod. 19:1–20:21 and 24:3-8, and Deut. 4:44–6:3), as the texts have come to us, is a covenant framework. Not only does the term *covenant* introduce both passages (it occurs both in Exod. 19:5 and Deut. 5:2), but also the form of both is that of a covenant, though differing in details.[6] The Exodus account includes near its beginning (19:8) a pledge of obedience by the people and concludes with a solemn oath and ceremony of sealing the covenant (24:3-8). The Deuteronomic account is placed within the covenant form of the whole book of Deuteronomy; it reminds the people of God's covenant with the patriarchs, and in the same breath it stresses that the decisive covenant is not that earlier one, but this present one in which the commandments are given (5:3).

The Sinai-Horeb covenant is sometimes called a "law covenant" in the sense that, in contrast to the Abrahamic and Davidic promissory covenants, it makes demands upon the people and seems to put less emphasis upon God's promises.

Yet it is important to qualify this characterization. It is not as though this law covenant did not have to do with grace. God's grace toward the people pervades both the giving of the commandments and the people's attitude toward them. In both accounts the commandments are given in the context of grace. In Exodus 20:2, the announcement of who gives the covenant is simple: "I am the Lord your God, who brought you out of the land of Egypt, out of the house of bondage." The God who commands is the God of the Exodus, the God who has delivered you, and deliverance precedes the commandments. In Deuteronomy the God who commands is the same God who made a self-binding covenant with Abraham and Isaac and Jacob, and, as the book endlessly repeats, "brought you out" (from servitude in the land of Egypt) "with a mighty hand and an outstretched arm." The Israelites' attitude toward the commandments was one of immense gratitude. The law was to them a great gift, not a burden, for it was what gave shape and meaning to the people, in that it revealed God's will. As von Rad expresses it, "Israel understood the revelation of the commandments as a saving event of the first rank, and celebrated it as such."[7]

Conversely God's grace appropriately expresses itself in the law. For the people to be in covenant with their God is for them necessarily to stand under the requirements of God's will. Thus the specific commandments express the covenant relationship between God and the people. To abstract the commandments from this covenant context is to lose their spirit and much of their meaning.

The first commandment is the center of the covenant. "You shall have no other gods before me" is the fundamental requirement of the covenant relationship between God and the people. God requires absolute loyalty from the people. To break this commandment, to commit idolatry, is not simply to transgress an isolated or arbitrary requirement; it is to deny the whole covenant relationship, to reject the framework in which the commandments are given. Lest the people misunderstand, the Deuteronomist turns the prohibition into a matter of positive inner loyalty (6:5): "You shall love the Lord your God with all your heart, and with all your soul, and with all your might." Even slightly to qualify this love is to break the first and fundamental commandment and so to break the covenant. The other commandments of the first table likewise express this covenant relationship.

The requirements of the second table have to do with the conduct of life in the covenant community—not a special "religious life," but fundamental social relationships. There too the covenant is decisive; God rules over every aspect of human life. Our sense of the Israelites' being in a covenant community may be somewhat diminished as we read the commandments today, because to us the "you" in each command may be misread to refer only to individuals one by one. For Israel, while the individual is responsible to obey, the "you" refers first of all to the people as a community. The second table states negatively the basic requirements of peace and right relationships in the covenant community; it prohibits dishonor of parents by children, murder, adultery, theft, false witness, and covetousness as incompatible with a rightly ordered covenant community. For the Hebrews the fruit of a just covenant community is genuine peace—*shalom:* not merely the absence of violence, but communal wholeness, fellowship, and the proper balance between competing claims.

The relationship of covenant and commandments in the Sinai-Horeb traditions is striking. In both accounts covenant is the context within which the commandments are given. In the Exodus account the commandments are in no wise a condition for the covenant to come into effect; rather, the covenant is made, and as a part of it come the commandments. Similarly in Deuteronomy there are repeated appeals to the gratitude of the people: God has "brought us out of Egypt with a mighty hand"; therefore, obey his commandments. As von Rad puts it, "The obedience which Deuteronomy demands is in no sense the prerequisite of election. The order is rather the reverse."[8] What appears in the Sinai-Horeb covenant is the expression of God's active, living will for the people within the framework of God's covenant love. Obedience to the law is the appropriate response of the people in covenant both with God and with one another.

3. *The prophets and covenant.* In the prophets we see the continuation of the process of reinterpretation of the idea of covenant. Their ideas about covenant appear primarily in imagery and terms that presuppose it, rather than in the explicit use of the Hebrew word for covenant, *berit.* The well-known passage from Micah 6:8 illustrates this point: "And what does the Lord require of you but to do justice, and to love kindness, and to walk humbly with your God?" In Hebrew the basic concepts of the passage are all covenantal. "Justice," *mishpat,* is the ordinary Hebrew term for the kind of behavior required by the covenant; "to love kindness," *hesed,* refers specifically to the love that is expressed within a covenant, whereas another word, *'ahabah,* means love where no covenant is present; "to walk humbly with your God" says in effect "to conduct life as a vassal would toward his lord," that is, again in a covenant relationship.[9]

Where the pre-exilic prophets speak judgment upon the people, that judgment makes sense only against the background of the Sinai covenant, for that is what the people have disobeyed. The prophets do not intend to teach a new morality, but rather to call the people back to loyalty and obedience to the covenant. This is certainly true of Amos, in whom the note of condemnation is almost unqualified. One passage will illustrate both the centrality of the Sinai covenant for his prophecy and how he interprets God's covenant:[10]

> You only have I known of all the families of the earth;
> therefore I will punish you for all your iniquities. (3:2)

The word *know* here does not mean simply "be acquainted with," but rather "recognize," "be loyal to," "be intimate with." But the conclusion is what marks off Amos's thought from the easy hopes of his time. Whereas his contemporaries are thinking, "We are in covenant, and therefore we shall receive special favor," Amos draws the opposite conclusion: "Therefore I will punish you for all your iniquities." To be in covenant is to be held responsible, not to be indulged.

The Sinai covenant is likewise the context of the prophecy of Amos's contemporary, Hosea. In the imagery of chapters 1–3, he likens the covenant between God and Israel to a marriage and the disobedience of the people to the unfaithfulness of a wife who becomes a harlot. But though the people's sin cannot be overlooked or indulged, Hosea speaks of a response more profound than the unqualified judgment Amos proclaims. God's love for the people is like that of the harlot's husband who goes and buys her back out of harlotry, bids her no longer be disloyal, and loves her again as his wife (chap. 3). Such is the steadfastness of God's love for the covenant people, Hosea declares, that God will renew the covenant even with those who have struck at its very foundation by worshiping other gods.

Like Amos and Hosea, Jeremiah over a century later sees the people's woes to be a result of their disobedience, and he declares judgment upon their disloyalty in equally vivid terms. Their wrongdoing is so persistent that he asks whether they are even capable of obeying. The problem is not merely a conscious and intentional desire to disobey, but somehow, in their hearts, an *inability to obey*. "Can the Ethiopian change his skin or the leopard his spots? Then also you can do good who are accustomed to do evil" (13:23). If the problem is of this depth, it will not suffice to condemn disobedience and call for obedience, as had Amos, for the people cannot obey. Nor can they remain loyal even though God forgives them and renews the covenant with them, as Hosea had prophesied. It is from this view of the problem that Jeremiah arrives at his prophecy of the new covenant:

> Behold, the days are coming, says the Lord, when I will make a new covenant with the house of Israel and the house of Judah, not like the covenant which I made with their fathers when I took them by the hand to bring them out of the land of Egypt, my covenant which they broke, though I was their husband, says the Lord. But this is the covenant which I will make with the house of Israel after those days, says the Lord: I will put my law within them, and I will write it upon their hearts, and I will be their God, and they shall be my people. And no longer shall each man teach

his neighbor and each his brother, saying, "Know the Lord," for they shall all know me, from the least of them to the greatest, says the Lord; for I will forgive their iniquity, and I will remember their sin no more. (Jer. 31:31-34)

Note several things about this passage. First, it presupposes the Sinai covenant—"my covenant which they broke." The requirements of that covenant are not to be forgotten; that covenant is presumably the law that will be written upon their hearts. Thus the *content* of the requirements of the new covenant is to be no different from the one they broke. The grace of the new covenant will not annul or displace the law of the earlier one.

Second, a brief phrase occurs that is easy to overlook: "my covenant which they broke, *though I was their husband*, says the Lord." Jeremiah here uses Hosea's image, and in so doing he evokes the same sense of intimacy of the covenant between God and the people and the same awareness of the pain God experiences from their disobedience.

Third, what will be new in the new covenant will be the way in which God's will is made known in the covenant relationship. God will change their very hearts, so that they have the will to obey, so that they "know"—recognize, are loyal to—the Lord without external teaching. No more exhortation will be necessary; their inmost inclination will be loyalty to the covenant.

Finally, the new covenant, like the renewal envisioned by Hosea, will be accompanied by forgiveness. That will be essential to the relationship, lest it be stained by the accumulation of past guilt. Yet Jeremiah means to portray forgiveness as essential in an even deeper sense. Note that the passage reads: "They shall all know me, . . . *for* I will forgive their iniquity, and I will remember their sin no more." Jeremiah here speaks of God's forgiveness as a way of explaining *why* they will know him in their hearts. What happens in God's forgiveness, given this connecting term *for*, is much more than a legal transaction of canceling past iniquities. What happens is that forgiveness renews the relationship between the covenanting partners. That is the central reality of a covenant. If so, the very act of God's forgiving is what writes the law upon human hearts, so that they are no longer the kind of people they were before. Here then is Jeremiah's hope for a new age.

These are only a few of the many instances of the prophets' use of the idea of covenant. This process of reinterpreting the covenant continues in later Old Testament writings, for it is God's covenant that gives identity to the people.

Covenant and the New Testament

It is not surprising that the process of reinterpretation of the covenant continues in the New Testament, because the Old Testament writings are the Scriptures for the first-century Christians. These early Christians use many different ways of explaining the meaning of God's action in Jesus Christ; covenant is one of those ways. The New Testament writers accept the Hebrews' way of talking about the God-human relationship as covenantal, and they accept much of the meaning ascribed to it. For them, however, Jesus Christ has become the center and culmination of God's gracious action. The meaning of God's covenant with Israel must now be reinterpreted through Christ. Let us see some of the forms this reinterpretation takes.

1. *Identification of Jesus with the promises of the Old Testament.* At many points in the New Testament—especially in the Gospels—the writers identify Jesus with God's promises to the people and thus by implication with the covenant. He is described as "the son of David, the son of Abraham" (Matt. 1:1), born "in the city of David" (Luke 2:11), and the offspring of Abraham (Gal. 3:16). The Gospel according to Mark sees him as a "light to the nations," as Second Isaiah had declared, for at his last cry the curtain of the temple is rent that divided Jew from Gentile (Mark 15:38; cf. Eph. 2:14). Precisely at this moment a Roman centurion—a Gentile—is moved to declare, "Truly this man was the son of God" (Mark 15:39). When the disciples of John the Baptist ask Jesus whether he is the one who is to come, the reply, according to Matthew, is that "the

blind receive their sight and the lame walk, lepers are cleansed and the deaf hear, and the dead are raised up, and the poor have the good news preached to them" (Matt. 11:5)—direct references to Isaiah 35:5-6; 42:7; and 61:1—passages that promise these very deeds from God. In the very title, *Christ*, the New Testament witnesses are declaring him to be the Messiah, the promised one of God—in effect, the one in whom the promises of the covenant are to be fulfilled.

What is of theological significance to Christians today in these passages is the basic outlook they express—that in Jesus Christ is the fulfillment of the prophecies and promises of God—and not the method the writers use to try to prove their case, which is often a method of seeing Jesus Christ as the fulfillment of every word and phrase of the Old Testament, rather than of the inner meaning of the history declared therein.[11] Their method does not, however, diminish the significance of their belief that God's covenant proclaimed in the Old Testament is rightly to be reinterpreted in terms of Jesus Christ.

In the New Testament allusions to the Old Testament idea of covenant, the term *covenant* (Greek *diathēkē*) itself does not ordinarily occur. This is characteristic of how most of the New Testament writers draw upon the idea—by using its imagery rather than the term itself. The major exception is the Letter to the Hebrews, where the term frequently appears. Much more illuminating for our purposes, though, are the ideas of Paul, who occasionally uses the word but more often assumes the idea.

2. *Paul and the idea of covenant.* In II Corinthians 3, Paul distinguishes between "the old covenant" and "a new covenant" as a way of explaining what has happened through Christ. God has "made us sufficient as ministers of a new covenant," he writes (3:6), "not of letter, but of spirit, for the letter puts to death but the spirit gives life."[12] By "letter" or "written code" (RSV), he appears not to mean the Old Testament as a whole, for he has just alluded approvingly in 3:3 to Jeremiah's prophecy of a new covenant written on the heart, nor does he mean simply the Old Testament law, for

elsewhere he says that the law is spiritual (Rom. 7:14), but he means the law seen as a human achievement, as a means to righteousness.[13] By "spirit" he means here God's power revealing grace and giving us the possibility of living rightly.

If here Paul is labeling as "old covenant" the law viewed as a human achievement, then we can understand why in this passage he does not see the relation of this "old covenant" and the new covenant as one of promise and fulfillment. Rather it is one of inadequacy and replacement. The faults of the law taken as a means to works-righteousness are too great; the new covenant cannot complete it but must replace it.

Yet in other passages Paul has another meaning in mind for the old covenant. In Galatians he relates the work of Christ to the promise to Abraham. Referring to the promises "to Abraham and his offspring" (3:16), he asserts that Abraham's offspring (stress upon the singular) is Christ. To be in Christ, through faith, is to be "sons of God" (3:26). That is how he can declare: "There is neither Jew nor Greek, there is neither slave nor free, there is neither male nor female; for you are all one in Christ Jesus" (3:28). But his idea is not yet complete; we must continue to the next verse to see his full point: "And if you are Christ's, then you are Abraham's offspring, heirs according to promise" (3:29). Here Paul affirms that, in covenant terminology, God's covenant with Abraham includes all who have faith in Christ and is not a matter of biological descent or external social characteristic.

Similarly in another passage Paul uses the Abraham covenant tradition in a favorable sense to explain his meaning. He writes that Abraham, when confronted with God's promises, "believed God, and it was reckoned to him as righteousness" (Rom. 4:3—Paul's rendering of Gen. 15:6). The promise itself came, therefore, not by works of the law, for the covenant with Abraham preceded the giving of the law at Sinai, "but through the righteousness of faith" (4:13). The heirs of the covenant, then, are not such because of works of the law, but through faith. From this idea Paul can move to his affirmation in 5:1: "Therefore, since we are justified by faith, we have peace [that quality of a proper covenant relationship] with God through our Lord Jesus Christ."

In Romans 4, as in Galatians 3, Paul understands God's covenant with Abraham to be closely related to the new covenant in Christ Jesus. In receiving God's promise by faith, Paul maintains, Abraham received what really mattered—he was reckoned righteous. So much is this the case that Paul makes no distinction between the faith by which Abraham trusted God and the faith that comes through Christ. Far from replacing the old covenant in *this* sense of the term, or even completing it, for Paul the gospel of Christ confirms it. The relationship between old and new covenants depends for Paul upon the meaning he ascribes to the old. Here God's covenant with Abraham serves Paul as a way to explain the meaning of the gospel.

3. *The Lord's Supper as participation in the new covenant.* In several New Testament writings the Greek term for covenant appears in connection with the Lord's Supper: I Corinthians 11:25, Mark 14:24, Matthew 26:28, and in some manuscripts, Luke 22:20. Paul's wording in the Corinthians passage is "This cup is the new covenant in my blood." The wording suggests that the early church tradition that Paul is quoting alluded to Exodus 24:6-8, in which Moses ratified the covenant between God and Israel by throwing blood against the altar and then upon the people. For this tradition the death of Christ is the ratification of the new covenant (probably a reflection of Jeremiah's prophecy of a new covenant). To celebrate the Lord's Supper is to proclaim his death "until he comes" (11:26). By this interpretation, participation in the Lord's Supper signifies participation simultaneously in the new covenant and in the body of Christ (10:16-17).

4. *Naming the testaments.* The centrality of the idea of covenant for Christian faith, as for Jewish faith, is later perceived by Irenaeus and his late-second-century contemporaries, who are the source of the enduring names for the two parts of the Christian Scriptures. Following Paul and the Letter to the Hebrews,[14] these theologians declare that Jeremiah's prophecy of a new covenant has become a reality in Jesus

Christ. No longer is this merely a hope; the new covenant has come. Irenaeus and others speak of the apostolic writings as the "books of the *kainē diathēkē*"—of the new (or fresh) covenant. What they mean by the term is not merely a book, but a living reality that these writings declare. This phrase then comes to be generally accepted as a title, and before long it is used to refer to the book rather than to its message, and similarly with the books of the old covenant. Through accidents of translation, the title comes to us in English as "testament" rather than "covenant." Yet "covenant" conveys much more adequately what these writings declare: that in Jesus Christ God has decisively brought about a new covenant, a new relationship with the people.

The Nature of a Covenant Relationship

Let us inquire now how we can express the meaning of the idea of covenant in a way appropriate to the early Christian proclamation of Jesus Christ. The term *covenant* can refer either to the act by which a certain type of interpersonal relationship comes into being or simply to the relationship itself. It is primarily in the latter sense that I shall use the term here. A covenant is a relationship that (1) *comes about through interactions of entrusting and accepting entrustment among willing, personal beings; (2) as a result, the parties belong to the same moral community and have responsibility to and for one another as beings who matter;* and (3) *their responsibility in the relationship endures over time.*

1. A covenant relationship comes about through interactions of entrusting and accepting entrustment. A covenant is not simply a biological relationship, like that of brother and sister, though a biological relationship may for other reasons also be covenantal. Nor is it merely happenstance, as geographical proximity may be. Rather a covenant comes into being as people, whether they are closely related biologically or geographically or not, entrust themselves to one another and correspondingly accept one another's entrustment.

Whatever form the covenanting transaction takes, it always involves an act or acts through which we entrust ourselves in some identifiable respects to someone else, along with a corresponding act or acts through which the other accepts our entrusting and therefore becomes obligated to us. Whether the entrusting-accepting entrustment relationship can be one-way, or whether it is always reciprocal, is a difficult question. We can say, though, that ordinarily it is reciprocal in some respects.

Entrusting is to be distinguished both from trusting and from being trustworthy, though they are closely related. To be trustworthy is to be one upon whose words and acts of commitment others can rely. To trust someone is to judge that the person is trustworthy and inwardly to orient ourselves accordingly. To entrust is not merely to trust in the inner sense of being *disposed* to entrust ourselves to the other, but actually to place ourselves or something we value in the other's hands. Some degree of trusting is ordinarily present when we entrust, though we might entrust ourselves to another even when the degree of trust is very low, simply because we have no acceptable alternative at the time. To entrust is to take a risk—to risk that we might be betrayed. When and how to take the risk are matters of judgment.

In spite of the uncertainties of entrusting, it is impossible to live in society without in many ways entrusting ourselves to others, even if with reservations. Consider some of the ways we commonly entrust ourselves: we put ourselves or what we value in the hands of doctors, food packagers, automobile mechanics, teachers, students, employers, newspaper editors, drivers who might be careless and kill us, and even casual passersby on the sidewalk. In a parallel way we accept the entrustment of countless others who take similar kinds of risks with us. This is not necessarily an uncritical entrusting, but we have neither the resources nor the inclination to check out all the relevant features about the other before we take a risk. Life would become unworkable, and social communities could not endure.

Not only social conventions, but human life itself requires a preparedness to trust, at least to some extent, and thereupon to entrust. Erik Erikson describes the first stage of life in terms of "basic trust vs. basic mistrust,"[15] when the child, it is hoped, comes to experience some "consistency, continuity, and sameness of experience" in its outer environment, as well as within. A weakness of basic trust leads to severe psychological difficulties. Indeed its total absence is incompatible with continued life.

As acts of entrusting are essential to the origins of covenants, so also are acts of accepting entrustment. Accepting entrustment is done in many ways. Dennis J. McCarthy describes the great variety of forms that were used by the ancient Israelites to symbolize the creation of a covenant: "an exchange of gifts, the shaking of hands, the eating of something together, oath, and a host of other things, could be used to form covenantal relationships."[16] When Jacob was leaving his father-in-law Laban after many years of labor, those two distrustful tricksters made a covenant together that they would not harm each other and that Jacob would not ill-treat his wives, Rachel and Leah, Laban's daughters (Gen. 31:43-54). As a witness to their covenant they set up a stone as a pillar, apparently as a symbol that God was witness to the covenant, and Laban offered these words sometimes used in our day as a benediction, but then an indication of his lack of trust except for their covenant: "The Lord watch between you and me, when we are absent one from the other."

Both the fact of covenanting and the content of the obligations thereby undertaken can be conveyed either by words or in other ways. Donald Evans explains this in his study of "performative language"—words that are in effect deeds:

> Sometimes an institutional act can be performed not only verbally but also non-verbally. I acknowledge status by bowing or saluting; I welcome by shaking hands; I bless by laying on of hands; I marry by mingling blood; I command by pointing; or I mourn by rending garments. Each action, like a performative utterance, has a performative force.[17]

A commitment need not be made in words. "Will you do this for me?" one asks, and the other may simply nod, indicating commitment to do so. Or an officer asks for a volunteer to undertake a dangerous mission, and a private stands up, picks up his equipment, and departs without a word. The content of the commitment has been verbalized by the one making the request.

Yet the content of covenant obligations may not be stated in words by *either* party. Imagine a driver, Sam Smith, who, risking more than he ordinarily ought to nowadays, stops to pick up a hitchhiker, Jack Jones. Jones gets in, saying, "I'm trying to get to St. Louis." "That's where I'm headed," Smith replies, and off they go. Neither has verbally requested or promised anything, but only described his situation or intentions. Yet each has implicitly entrusted himself to the other, and in response each has implicitly accepted the entrustment. The driver has implicitly committed himself to take appropriate care in driving, not to harm the passenger, and perhaps more; the hitchhiker has implicitly committed himself at least not to harm the driver.

It might be rejoined that neither the driver nor the hitchhiker necessarily intends any such commitment. Either one might enter the relationship intending to take advantage of the other. Yet what is most fundamental to their interaction is not the end-goal each seeks, but that each intends to enter the relationship. In this respect each party to a covenant must be a willing, intending being. Whether each has intended to commit himself to the other is beside the point. By intentionally entering the relationship, each has performed an *act* that is commissive, whether or not accompanied by commissive words or commissive intentions. By stopping and accepting the hitchhiker as a passenger, the driver has implicitly accepted some responsibility for him; and the hitchhiker has done likewise. Implicitly they have communicated their trustworthiness. If they did not intend to be trustworthy, their actions were deceitful. But that would not prevent their brief relationship from being covenantal. I might enter into a covenant intending from the start to be unfaithful to it, but it would be no less a covenant and I would be no less obligated within it. It is the committing *act*, whether in words or not, together with the intention simply to be related, and not the intention to be trustworthy, that is essential to the origin of a covenant relationship and to the members' being obligated within it. To say that the members are obligated by their commissive acts is not to say that they necessarily "feel committed," but that there have been outer acts that have obligated them to one another. The same would be true had they explicitly promised. It would be possible for each to promise verbally without intending to keep the promise, but their false intention would not make it any less a promise, nor would they be any less obligated.

We can think of many examples of people who accept entrustment without fully verbalizing their commitments, and who thus covenant with others: parents who bring a child into the world; a minister who counsels a couple about their marriage; a person standing on the street who is asked for directions by another; a dentist who tells you a tooth needs filling. Sir W. D. Ross points to this phenomenon, though he does not call it covenantal, when he writes that some prima facie duties arise from "the implicit undertaking not to tell lies which seems to be implied in the act of entering into conversation . . . or of writing books that purport to be history and not fiction."[18]

William F. May declares that "the fact of indebtedness constitutes the chief reason for using the term 'covenant,'" and that therefore "responsiveness to gift characterizes a covenant."[19] Let us see the sense in which this is true and how it is related to entrustment transactions. It is directly true of the Abraham and Sinai covenants and the new covenant in Jesus Christ, all of which involve the bestowal of priceless gifts. All these covenants show God's grace and God's covenanting to be inseparable. Yet acts of entrusting and accepting entrustment among human partners may or may not directly come about through giving and accepting gifts. What is directly conveyed may be not gift but responsibility, as the Jacob-Laban covenant illustrates. Likewise in his acceptance of the hitchhiker's entrustment, the driver has accepted not a gift but an obligation in the presence of the other's risking. Even so, gift and indebtedness stand in the background of all such transactions, as in the fact that the driver even has a car and can drive. That background feature of covenants is May's point. In a specific entrustment transaction, gift and indebtedness may not be prominent. Yet all who accept others' entrustment do so against the background of their own indebtedness to others and ultimately to the gracious God.

2. When two or more persons enter into a covenant relationship, they thereby create and enter into a new moral community, or at least they enter into a community to which they did not previously belong. Part of what this implies is that they have moral responsibility *to*, and not only *for*, one another, that they are answerable to one another. But to belong to the same moral community carries with it a more basic implication: the recognition by each that the other has worth, that each matters for his or her own sake, and not merely that each is useful. Each member of any covenant is obligated to and for the other members themselves, and is not merely obligated to the extent of the letter of the commitments explicitly made.

This is the understanding conveyed in biblical covenant accounts, though without any explicit theory of human worth. We see it, for example, in the Deuteronomist's concern for the orphan, the widow, the sojourner, and the servant (e.g., Deut. 5:14-15; 10:18-19); in Amos's indignation that those with whom God has made covenant would "sell the righteous for silver, and the needy for a pair of shoes" (2:6b); and in Jesus' teaching that "as you did it to one of the least of these my brethren, you did it to me" (Matt. 25:40b).

In contrast someone might maintain that various human relationships are purely external morally, obligating only to the letter of the verbal agreement, and that such relationships imply no further obligation to or for the other parties to the agreement themselves. Consider that you as a private individual are selling a used car. A buyer appears, hears what you have to say about the car, checks it out to some extent, and the two of you agree upon a price that seems reasonable. After the sale, though, the buyer discovers that the car is in far worse shape than had been communicated. Let us assume that you have not told any lies in the process of selling the car and have not intended to misrepresent its general condition. You did not know that the car was in such bad shape; you might or might not have suspected it. Do you have any further moral responsibility to the buyer? Would you even if the law said you had no further *legal* responsibility? In large part one's answer will depend upon the model of the moral life from which one is working. Are you and the buyer members of the same moral community or not? If the assumption is that you are not, and yet if somehow the transaction has been fully legal, one might argue that this is the end of the matter as far as the seller's moral responsibility goes. But if the two of you are fellow covenanters together, then that is not the end of the matter. The obligation to be fair may well call for some adjustment in the price, even after the sale; at least whether it does is not immediately to be ruled out of rational discussion. Perhaps the point can best be made if we imagine that you sold the car to your best friend. Would any of us then not adjust the price after the discovery had been made? The moral is not that we should sell used cars only to strangers. It is rather that strangers are also covenant members, however difficult it is for us to think of them fully in that way. To enter into transactions of entrusting and accepting entrustment is to belong to the same moral community in this serious way—that the other person matters, and is not merely a convenience.

3. The parties to a covenant thereby come to have *enduring* responsibility to one another. The responsibility may endure for a shorter or longer time, but it continues throughout the life of that covenant. It is not merely that covenant responsibilities are the sort that take a long time to perform (such as caring for a child), though they may be. Nor is it only that they must be performed over and over again (caring for the child again each new day), though often they must be. The point is that in a covenant we must accept responsibility over time for the effects of our behavior upon the other covenant members.

"This is our child; therefore, we must accept responsibility now and in the days to come." Moral relationships in covenant always extend over time; they are not temporally atomistic, as though tomorrow one could wipe the slate clean and start over again. Tomorrow the parent will still be parent of that child. Ten miles down the road the driver will still be the one who picked up that hitchhiker. Because covenant responsibility is enduring, the virtue of faithfulness is an essential requirement of covenants.

In brief a covenant relationship is one with these three characteristics. Let us look now at two different kinds of covenants, to both of which we all belong.

Two Types of Covenant Relationships

The Inclusive Covenant

From a Christian standpoint the whole of humanity is to be understood as one covenant community. One might say, after the fashion of the covenant with Noah, that the inclusive covenant is with all living creatures, but if so one needs to be careful what is meant. It is not as though nonhuman living things actually covenant; they neither entrust nor accept entrustment. One might dispute that, pointing to the tameness of animals like dogs, cats, and sheep, or the loyalty of a dog or a horse. Yet however admirable these traits are, they do not reflect moral decisions. A dog is *trained*—conditioned—to obey and be loyal; it does not *decide* these things in the sense that human beings can. In that sense dogs do not covenant, let alone turtles, paramecia, or pine trees. Yet the inclusive covenant has to do with all living creatures, whether they can covenant or not, in that it affirms their value as God's good creatures and places on human beings the responsibility of caring for them.

The act whereby the inclusive covenant has come into existence is God's act of covenanting, an expression of God's intention in creation, decisively declared in Jesus Christ.[20] The Christian proclamation is that God has created all people to live in covenant with God and with one another. Therefore Paul declared his message to the Gentiles, not only to the children of Israel; for the same reason Christians are called to "make disciples of all nations" (Matt. 28:19), for in Jesus Christ they know that all persons alike are God's children. What has originated the inclusive covenant is not some intentional agreement that we have made, as though prior to that we were not in covenant. The relationship is rather like that of a child to its parents. The child exists in that special covenant relationship before it ever knows it; normally it entrusts itself to its parents' care preconsciously and later comes to have special responsibilities toward them and toward its siblings. Similarly all human beings are members of God's inclusive covenant whether they consciously agree to it or not, and in this covenant they have responsibilities to and for one another whether they agree to them or not.

In this sense the inclusive covenant exists prior to human agreement. Yet in another sense it awaits human trust and loyalty before it is fully present. In the first sense it is brought into existence not by human willing but by God's will. Human beings cannot legislate the inclusive covenant out of existence; they can only decide whether they will accept it or not. All are intended by God for the inclusive covenant, whether or not they consciously affirm it. It is God's trustworthiness rather than human trust and loyalty that constitutes the inclusive covenant. In the second sense, though, the inclusive covenant is an eschatological hope. Because of human rejection of one another and of God, even in the midst of human companionship and dependence upon God, the inclusive covenant is not fully realized. Even so there is always present in one way or another in our lives the witness to our mutual belongingness. We are told, for example, that in the midst of the theory and practice of *apartheid* in the Republic of South Africa, the story of a black woman's sufferings has moved even some right-wing white supremacists to realize that blacks too are persons.[21] It is a realization that cannot be completely blotted out, for it is written on our hearts, even if our minds have been conditioned to reject it. The inclusive covenant as original reality and eschatological hope stands in judgment upon the brokenness of all human communities and calls us to believe that it can be more fully realized.

The inclusive covenant is the most fundamental human relationship. Yet it is not the only morally significant type of human relationship, nor is it the only type of covenant community.

Special Covenants

A special covenant is a relationship of entrusting and accepting entrustment between two or more parties that arises out of some *special* historical transaction between the members and not only from their participation in the inclusive covenant.

There are many different kinds of special covenants. The category includes both small, intimate, primary-group relationships, such as a family, and large, impersonal, secondary groups in which we may not even know who all the members are, such as a nation-state. It includes groups that differ greatly in their duration, from brief encounters of strangers who may never see each other again ("I'll watch your shopping cart while you go look for your little girl") to the permanence pledged in marriage—"Till death us do part." It includes groups about which individual members exercise great freedom in choosing whether to belong, as with clubs and other voluntary associations, and groups to which the individual has come to belong through no personal choice (e.g., a child's belonging to this family rather than that) and from which it would be difficult to withdraw (e.g., one's country). Finally it includes groups in which we entrust ourselves to others in only a few respects, as when we take a car to a mechanic for repairs, and groups in which the entrustment is over a wide and not fully specified range of concerns, as in a marriage.

Our moral responsibilities are heavily and consciously shaped by our special covenants. This fact is reflected in such phenomena as ceremonies of initiation with accompanying requirements upon the members, and formal standards of professional ethics for various occupations. It is expressed in the Protestant Reformers' doctrine of vocation, with its belief that we are called by God to perform the duties of our various offices. Even though the inclusive covenant is our most fundamental relationship, special covenants have their own significance for the moral life.

The Differences and Similarities Between the Two

The inclusive covenant and special covenants differ in three respects: in their origins, their membership, and their rights and responsibilities.

1. *Different origins.* We have seen that the origin of the inclusive covenant is in God's act of covenanting, which is expressive of God's intention in creation. In contrast we enter into special covenants only through some special interaction. This interaction always involves specific human acts of entrusting to these people (known and unknown) and accepting their entrustment, whether with full verbal explicitness or not.

2. *Different membership.* All persons are members of the inclusive covenant without regard to age, sex, racial or ethnic membership, nationality, special covenants entered into, or other characteristics that differ from person to person. In contrast the membership of a special covenant is always limited to the parties to the special interactions that bring it into existence and bring later members into it. Only those who have entered with each other into the appropriate actions of marital entrusting and accepting entrustment are members of a particular marriage; only those inducted are members of a given club; only the parents' own children, natural or adopted, are those for whom they are parents.

Some special covenants have limited membership in principle, as in the case of a marriage, a business contract, or a club. Some others have limited membership in the weaker sense that not everybody does in fact belong. It is conceivable that a special covenant might come into being that includes all people living at a given time—a world-state, for example, or an inclusive religious institution. That is highly unlikely, though, and even if it were to occur, the group would remain a special covenant because of its limited functions and how people had come to belong.

3. *Different kinds of rights and responsibilities.* All moral rights, whether in the inclusive covenant or in special covenants, arise within a community and reflect the relationships of the community. Rights are therefore always social rather than individualistic matters, however differently some theorists have interpreted them. In the inclusive covenant the rights that all possess and that correspondingly all ought to respect are *human rights*—rights rooted in what it means truly to live in society as a human being and thus belonging to all human beings as such. These rights are not conventional—not created by human choice; they exist as moral rights whether socially recognized or not. The responsibilities that correspond to human rights are owed to every person and ought to be honored without discrimination. A weak, little-esteemed individual, for example, an impoverished little girl in a Mexican village, should receive the same consideration at law, when hungry, or when in trouble along the wayside, as any powerful or highly prestigious person such as, say, the president of General Motors, simply because both are human. The inclusive covenant thus requires basic justice, which necessitates that we treat like cases alike and unlike cases differently without regard to the names of the individuals. This is what human rights are about, apart from the difficult question of what human rights there are.

The rights of special covenants, on the other hand, are *special rights*, rights that arise out of some special interaction and belong only to the parties to that interaction. The corresponding responsibilities likewise belong to those parties and not to every human being as such. Each spouse has rights and responsibilities toward the other that differ from her or his rights and responsibilities toward all other people. Similarly a child has a right to expect certain things of its parents that it cannot justifiably expect of all adults. A citizen with a grievance may have a right to legal redress against the party that has committed the wrong, but not against simply anybody.

Along with these differences there are also some important similarities between the inclusive covenant and special covenants:

1. In both types of covenant, we are obligated to respect the worth of the other members and to treat them as ends and not merely means, whatever their usefulness or uselessness. Otherwise we would not be accepting our obligation in the face of the other's entrustment to us.

2. In both types we have the obligation to be concerned for the needs of the other members. It is through the thwarting of our needs that we are harmed as persons; and the hope that our needs and interests will be met, or at least taken seriously, accompanies our entrustment of ourselves to one another. Even so what constitutes a relevant need will differ from one kind of special covenant to another; the need with which we go to a doctor is not the same as that with which we purchase a car.

3. Both kinds of covenants require faithfulness from all their members, even though what constitutes faithfulness depends in some respects upon the kind of covenant. Jesus' statement of the double love commandment (cf. Matt. 22:37-39) includes within the meaning of *agape* love the requirement of faithfulness to God ("love the Lord your God with all your heart, and with all your soul, and with all your mind") and to all persons ("love your neighbor as yourself") within the inclusive covenant. At the same time from a Christian perspective any special covenant likewise requires an appropriate kind of faithfulness—love for the neighbor to whom we have chosen, or for whom we have been chosen, to be specially related. The kind of faithfulness that is appropriate is not the same for every special covenant, and yet what is appropriate is not simply whatever we choose to think. Faithfulness in marriage understandably takes a form especially related to sexuality, though not reducible to it. Faithfulness in church membership is especially related to that church's norms

concerning its proclamation. Faithfulness toward one's country has especially to do with the use of political power in the pursuit of justice. All these kinds of faithfulness raise issues that are not at all simple; I shall discuss some of them at greater length in part 3 of this book. However those issues are resolved, though, faithfulness of an appropriate kind is properly a requirement of every human relationship. Faithlessness in any covenant is a rejection of that covenant relationship and of the other members.

Although we can distinguish between the inclusive covenant and special covenants, we cannot separate them. We are always in both at once, and ordinarily in several types of special covenants at once. Furthermore it is only through our participation in our various special covenants that we are able to express concretely our participation in the inclusive covenant. There is no way to do so except by special transactions—by entrusting ourselves to certain identifiable people and accepting the entrustment of specific people. At the same time, say, that we are in a special covenant with fellow citizens in the same city, whereby they and we have certain special rights, such as to the city government's services, we and they also have human rights as members of the inclusive covenant. The city's ordinances may in part be designed with an eye to these human rights. Our humanness is thoroughly interwoven with all our special relationships. The purpose of the distinction is not to invite the claim that these two types of relationships can ever be separated. It is rather to assist us to see both dimensions as they are constantly present in all our relationships.

Through awareness of the inclusive covenant, we recognize that God is the center of the moral life and that it has a unity amid our several special loyalties. The most basic assertion for the moral life, as seen in terms of Christian faith, is that God has brought into being an inclusive covenant. Through awareness that all our special relationships are covenantal and that none of them is outside the inclusive covenant, we recognize that we are called in every special relationship to express our loyalty to the members of the inclusive covenant.

The Significance of a Covenant Model
for Christian Ethics

The biblical use of the idea of covenant, with and without the explicit terms meaning "covenant," enables the writers of both the Old and New Testaments to express their understanding of God's character and action, as well as of human relationships under God. A covenant model would therefore appear to be especially appropriate as a framework for Christian ethical reflection. For several reasons it readily lends itself to expressing the ethical significance of the proclamation of God's reconciling work in Christ.

1. A covenant model expresses the essential *socialness* of human life. It presupposes that every aspect of life is lived out of our belongingness with others in the human community. Through others we receive our being and all our resources for continuing to be. We are always dependent upon others and must entrust ourselves to them if we are to live at all and if we are to find what it is truly to live well. This model declares that we are social in the further sense that in every aspect of life we stand responsible to and for all other people to whom we are related. We are among those to whom others entrust themselves; we are thereby their trustees, as they are ours. A Christian covenant model points beyond the socialness of our relationships with other persons to God as the center and ground of our being, the One by whom the human community is brought into being, is called to reconciliation amidst its unfaithfulness, and has the continual hope of becoming one true community.

2. At the same time a covenant model enables us to express the Christian awareness that each member of the covenant community has a value not reducible to his or her usefulness to the whole group; each has what has been called a *worth*. The essential socialness of our lives does not eliminate our individuality. Socialness understood in this way is fully compatible with the uniqueness of each person and with the worth of each as an end in the sight of God. Not only is it

compatible, but the nature of a community conceived as covenantal is such that it fosters this individuality. A covenant is rightly understood as a community in which each person's true fulfillment is to be found in the common good, and in which the good of the community is to be found in the enhancement of the true well-being of each and all of the members.

3. This model, especially with its distinction between inclusive and special covenants, enables us to take seriously the *historical* fabric of the moral life, both of the individual and of the community, without losing our recognition of the moral unity of all people under God. Each person has her or his own configuration of special covenants, not identical with that of any other person, as distinctive as one's fingerprints and not interchangeable with anyone else's: special obligations to this spouse, these parents or children, employer, employees, fellow citizens, and so on. Each configuration is the reflection of that person's unique history and especially of the events of that life that are these specific moral transactions.

The same is true of communities. Each community develops special dependencies and special responsibilities over time that other communities do not have, even if they have relationships of a similar type. An oil-producing country has special obligations concerning that oil that are different from those of other countries. The community of those who speak English has a special responsibility for the preservation of English literature. A company that uses a dangerous chemical in its activities has special obligations toward people who might be harmed by it, as well as toward other living things.

The history of the moral life (and not only its universal features) is significant in Christian ethics because each person matters in God's sight. It is only through that history, including the present, that we can know what anyone's special rights and special obligations are. This means that for a covenant model the members of the moral community are never interchangeable units, as they would seem to be on principle in a utilitarian calculus of the greatest balance of good over evil. Our history accompanies us throughout the moral life, revealing our identities as moral selves.

It is because history is morally significant in a covenant model that the moral life has continuity over time. What we did yesterday matters as we seek to discover what we should do today. We do not come new to every situation. Instead we come bringing with us many moral responsibilities that we have incurred in the past. They continue to be claims upon us, often for many years, even though God offers us freedom in each new moment from the burden of our past sin so that we may respond rightly to them. To recognize obligations incurred in the past is to confess that one has a name, that one is this person and not some other. It is to declare that life can have integrity, that each of us is one person and not merely a succession of moments. This is how it is possible to be responsible for past deeds. The sense of responsibility, for which any serious ethic will seek to account, can be explained in terms of a covenant model's sense of moral continuity over time.

This is the model with which I shall work in the pages that follow. The first need at this point is to analyze what the biblical proclamation of God's covenant implies about the shape of the moral life. That is the subject of the following chapter.

2

The Standard of Covenant Love

Discerning the Standard

The Function of a Standard

Four assertions will help to explain the idea of a basic moral standard. (1) It refers to a fundamental quality that should be present in all the moral life. (2) That quality should be present both in moral selfhood and in moral action. (3) A basic standard functions as a criterion or test of subsidiary moral judgments and actions. (4) It reflects, at least in Christian ethics, a perspective upon what is ultimately real and significant.

1. A basic standard is fundamental to moral judgment; it has to do with all aspects of life. An example is the principle of utility as it functions within utilitarian ethical theories: in all our actions we should seek to produce the greatest possible balance of nonmoral good over nonmoral evil for the whole world.[1] Another is the categorical imperative of Immanuel Kant. Of his several formulations of it, this one is clearly a moral and not only a logical standard: "Act so that you treat humanity, whether in your own person or in that of another, always as an end and never as a means only."[2] In Christian

ethics the love command in one or another of its expressions has often been treated as a standard in something like the sense here.

A moral standard like any of the above is to be distinguished from all kinds of subsidiary moral norms and judgments. There is no situation in which the quality which the most basic standard prescribes should not be present. It is, as Frederick Carney has expressed it, "context-invariant,"[3] or in Gene Outka's characterization, "it is (a) applicable to everyone unrestrictedly, (b) and on every occasion so that it is always relevant."[4] Utilitarians would assert this of the principle of utility, Kantians of the categorical imperative, and many Christians of the love command. Subsidiary moral judgments, on the other hand, always have to do with some less inclusive aspect of the moral life. A rule, for example, is a moral norm that prescribes or prohibits or permits some type of action in a certain kind of context: for example, "Do not break a promise." It is, to use Carney's term, "context-variant."

In what respect, though, are rules context-variant? Certainly they are as to *relevance.* The rule that one ought not to break a promise is relevant only to contexts in which someone has actually made a promise. But are rules also context-variant as to *bindingness*? Even where the rule about promises, for example, is relevant, ought we to follow it regardless of the circumstances? Surely not; there are contexts in which it is justifiable to break a promise. But is that the case with all rules? Are any rules absolute—always to be kept? It is best if we are cautious at this point. Most rules are not absolute; that is, for most rules there are some contexts in which it would be justifiable from a Christian standpoint to break them. But are they all that way? Would it, for example, ever be justifiable to torture someone? or to commit rape? It is not unreasonable to suppose that some rules ought never to be broken. If so, rules may or may not be context-variant as to bindingness, but they always are as to relevance. In contrast, to have a basic moral standard, at least where there is only one, means both that it is always relevant and that one ought always to conform to it. In fact, unlike any kind of rule, it would reflect a misunderstanding even to *ask* whether we could justifiably break it. Our basic standard is relevant to and binding in all situations.

2. A basic moral standard is fundamental both to moral action and to moral selfhood; the same standard is rightly to be expressed in both regards. Concerning moral action it serves as a *moral principle*. In that form one might say, "Always *act* so that this quality is present in the action": that is, so as to produce the greatest possible balance of good over evil, or so as to conform to the categorical imperative, or so as to show love. Concerning moral selfhood it serves as a *standard of virtue*. In this way one might say, "Always be the kind of person who is disposed in this way, who has this kind of character": that is, always be disposed to seek the greatest possible balance of nonmoral good over nonmoral evil, or have the kind of character that always values rational humanity as an end, or always be a loving person.

Here I am making the limited claim that the same standard should be expressed in both these aspects, not that our standard of virtue is to be derived from our principle, nor the reverse. However distinguishable these two aspects of morality—being and action—are, they are not logically separable. To have conflicting standards for these two aspects is morally unjustifiable even if it can actually be done. If, for example, our standard of virtue required that we were always to be disposed to treat others as ends and not means only, but our principle of action were to permit us to treat others as mere means, there would be no integrity in our understanding of the moral life. At the very least our standard of virtue and principle of action must be congruent. They must logically "fit." That means they must not require responses that are irreconcilable, or even responses that are unrelated. The loving person, for example, ought always to act on the principle of love, understood in a way congruent with what it means to be a loving person. This is a version of the philosophical idea that the relation between virtue and obligation should be one of complementarity.[5]

3. A basic moral standard functions in an ethical system as a

criterion or test for subsidiary moral judgments and actions. Ought one to keep or to break a particular promise? The test is whether breaking it under the circumstances of this case expresses a valid basic standard. If not, then it ought to be kept. Ought each of us to be the kind of person who is disposed to keep promises? The test is whether being that kind of person is compatible with the basic standard stated in terms of moral selfhood. By definition a basic standard takes precedence over any rule or other subsidiary judgment. If a rule conflicts with the basic standard, the latter is to be followed and the former is to give way. Basic standards are to govern rules. Following rules independently of or contrary to a basic moral standard is the essence of legalism. Legalism is not necessarily present if we use or follow rules, or even if we judge that some rule ought always to be followed (it might always express our basic standard), but only if we make our judgment to follow the rules independently of or contrary to our basic standard.

A basic standard is not a source from which we can deduce all the right moral answers, but is rather a test for the moral answers we are considering. Rules and particular moral decisions are derived through an interplay between our basic standard and the morally relevant circumstances; they are not merely deduced from one or the other. We might be confident of our basic moral standard but still not sure what would express it in some particular situation—in the choice between two political candidates or the treatment of a certain dying patient or the punishment of a criminal.

4. Our basic moral standard is inseparable from our understanding of what is ultimately real and significant in life. It is not an arbitrary norm that could as readily have been something else. Rather it is rooted in our metaethics, in our body of explanation for how our most basic moral judgments can ultimately be justified.

In Christian ethics, however it may be with other ethical positions, this metaethical justification takes the form of a theological explanation, which in turn is rooted in the Christian proclamation about God's action revealed in Jesus

Christ. This is why one Christian ethicist after another rightly says that Christian ethics is a theological discipline. If someone were to present an interpretation of the basic standard of Christian ethics—of what love means, say—in a way entirely detached from theological reflection upon the Christian proclamation of God's action and of human life as we are created, have fallen, and are offered redemption through Jesus Christ, the result would not be Christian ethics at all, even though the standard would have the same name and might sound similar in content. No longer would it be possible on Christian grounds to explain why love should be the basic standard and not something else. Nor could we on Christian grounds explain why love should be understood one way rather than another.

Our basic standard must then be seen as a part of our whole theological outlook. It is rooted in judgments about the nature and action of God, humans, the nonhuman creation, and their relationships to one another. Because our basic standard is that part of our theological outlook that is formulated as a test for moral selfhood and moral action, it constitutes an important link between an answer to the question, What is ultimately going on? and responses to the question, What ought we to be like and to do in these concrete situations? On the side of metaethics, a change in our basic standard would reflect a change in our understanding of God and of human beings. On the side of specific moral judgments, such a change would often lead to profoundly different moral conclusions.

The Understanding of God as the Source of the Basic Standard

All adequate theological reflection, including theological ethics, revolves around the subject of God. Numerous theological-ethical positions recognize this: for example, Barth's theological ethics of the command of God, Bultmann's idea of radical obedience to God, Reinhold Niebuhr's concept of sacrificial love that expresses the *agape* of God, Paul Ramsey's principle of obedient love that is measured by God's righteousness and God's kingdom, James Gustafson's conviction that a moral act is one "of fidelity to God and of honor to

God,"[6] John Howard Yoder's "messianic ethic" in which the Christian decides in terms of God's action in bringing the kingdom, Stanley Hauerwas's study of character "in terms of the tension between God's action and man's response which is at the heart of Christian existence."[7] For all these different approaches Christian ethics is *theo-logical* in the literal sense of the word.

Yet in our moral reflection we as Christians often do not see how the reality of God actually bears upon the moral life. It becomes a theoretical assumption rather than a functioning reality. It is not enough to declare *that* the reality of God is the foundation of the moral life for Christian ethics; we must also say *how* that is the case.

Let us look at three ways of speaking of God's relationship to moral action: moral action (1) as response to the action of God, (2) as obedience to the command of God, and (3) as patterned after the being and action of God. Any one of these three can be a valid approach to Christian ethics. I believe it is desirable to combine all three.

1. *Christian ethics as the ethics of response to God's action.* This approach is the most general of the three and is presupposed by the other two. Although almost every theological ethic reflects it, H. Richard Niebuhr's work speaks about it most explicitly. Niebuhr interprets moral action as *fitting response* to the action of God.[8] God stands at the center of all being as One who creates, governs, and redeems us. Human beings are always answering to God's action. Unlike a teleological ethic, as he understands it, in which moral action is seen as a seeking after the good, or a deontological ethic, in which it is obedience to law, for Niebuhr, "Responsibility affirms: 'God is acting in all actions upon you. So respond to all actions upon you as to respond to his action.'"[9]

What for Niebuhr would make an action fitting rather than unfitting? His answers to this question, though valid as far as they go, are very general and not fully satisfactory. It would be action that responds to prior action of others but that also anticipates others' reaction, and action "in a continuing community of agents," not action "as an atomic unit."[10]

Criteria like these seem right, and yet our action might meet them and still not be fitting—irresponsible even if responsive. Elsewhere Niebuhr offers additional suggestions: we must love what God loves;[11] we must respond to the one God as integrated selves;[12] we must act with a universal responsibility because all creatures are God's;[13] we must be merciful because we render account to God-in-Christ;[14] we must "reduplicate" the deed of Christ.[15] These judgments are unexceptionable in Christian ethics. Yet they assume more than the idea of response by itself; they suggest that we should in some sense imitate God's action.

In Christian ethics all human action ought indeed to be understood as response to God's action, as Niebuhr maintains. Yet if we are to identify the content of a fitting response, we must say more than this.

2. *Christian ethics as the ethics of obedience to God's command.* There are many different kinds of divine command theory. Some theories abstract the question of God's command from God's characteristics,[16] but that procedure raises unnecessary questions, such as whether if God were to command cruelty, we ought to obey. We cannot rightly judge as Christians how to understand the command of God apart from reflection upon the proclamation of Jesus Christ as revelation of God's nature. The fundamental question for any Christian divine command theory, as for Christian ethics generally, must be "Who is God?"

Karl Barth, who seeks to state his theological ethic in terms of the divine command, clearly believes that the divine command must be seen in close relation to the divine being or action. For Barth the law is the form of the gospel; the command is the expression of God's grace. "The divine claim never stands alone," he writes. "On the contrary, it is always the form, or shape, or garment of grace. . . . Conversely, the grace of God never stands alone. . . . The gracious God wills to be respected and loved and feared as the Lord of man."[17] Theological ethics is for him a response to the divine action in grace.

Sometimes Barth seems to suggest a plurality of divine

commands: for example, "There is no divine claim in itself. There are only concrete divine claims."[18] Actually, though, he strongly affirms the oneness of the divine command, speaking repeatedly of "the divine claim" and "the command of God," rather than primarily of divine claims and commands. Although the divine command expresses itself in relation to many different situations, in all of them, Barth says, it demands complete human loyalty and wills human liberation. Its unity-in-continuity is more fundamental than its pluralism.

Yet anyone who seeks to determine what God commands faces the temptation to identify the command of God with the fallible judgment of some person, as perhaps of some biblical figure. We must show how we are to guard against, for example, attributing to God's will Paul's assertion, "The women should keep silence in the churches" (I Cor. 14:34a), or the judgment that God commanded Joshua to kill the Israelite Achan and his family because of Achan's sin (Josh. 7:10-26). If we are to distinguish the divine command reflected in the Christian proclamation from human misinterpretations of it, we must, like Barth, focus upon the divine being and action. Isolated from the other two approaches, divine command theory is misleading; yet we must still seek to determine what is God's command.

3. *Christian ethics as patterned after the being and action of God.* This approach considers God as example: divine exemplar theory. At many points writers in both the Old and New Testaments reflect this idea. Not only are the Hebrew people to obey the God who brought them out of the land of Egypt; how they are to obey is sometimes stated in terms of God as example:

Remember the sabbath day, to keep it holy . . . ; for in six days the Lord made heaven and earth, . . . and rested the seventh day. (Exod. 20:8, 11)

You shall be holy; for I the Lord your God am holy. (Lev. 19:2)

[God] executes justice for the fatherless and the widow, and loves the sojourner, giving him food and clothing. Love the sojourner therefore; for you were sojourners in the land of Egypt. (Deut. 10:18-19)

New Testament writers often enjoin those who believe in Christ to pattern their lives after God's own action.

> You, therefore, must be perfect, as your heavenly Father is perfect. (Matt. 5:48)

> Love your enemies and pray for those who persecute you, so that you may be sons of your Father who is in heaven; for he makes his sun rise on the evil and on the good, and sends rain on the just and on the unjust. (Matt. 5:44-45)

> Be merciful, even as your Father is merciful. (Luke 6:36)

> All this is from God, who through Christ reconciled us to himself and gave us the ministry of reconciliation. . . . So we are ambassadors for Christ, God making his appeal through us. (II Cor. 5:18, 20)

> Therefore be imitators of God, as beloved children. (Eph. 5:1)

> Beloved, let us love one another; for love is of God, and he who loves is born of God and knows God. . . . Beloved, if God so loved us, we also ought to love one another. (I John 4.7, 11)

There is no self-conscious or explicit divine exemplar theory in these writers' minds. Yet appeals like these are not at all foreign to the biblical proclamation. The writers are declaring that God is the ultimate standard in terms of whom human morality is to be judged, that God is in an important sense the pattern for all human selfhood and action.

Divine exemplar ideas have often appeared as a minor theme in the writings of Christian theologians. Nevertheless we can see them, and not only in obscure thinkers or unimportant issues. Luther's eloquent call for the Christian to be Christ to the neighbor also expresses the idea of the imitation of God: "Just as our neighbor is in need and lacks that in which we abound, so we also have been in need before God and have lacked His mercy. Hence, as our heavenly Father has in Christ freely come to our help, we also ought freely to help our neighbor through our body and its work, and each should become as it were a Christ to the other."[19]

In a comment on Matthew 5:48, Calvin both accepts the idea

of patterning one's life after God and at the same time carefully qualifies it:

> *You shall therefore be perfect.* This perfection does not mean equality, but relates solely to resemblance. However distant we are from the perfection of God, we are said to be *perfect, as he is perfect,* when we aim at the same object, which he presents to us in Himself. Should it be thought preferable, we may state it thus. There is no comparison here made between God and us: but the perfection of God means, *first,* that free and pure kindness, which is not induced by the expectation of gain;—and, *secondly,* that remarkable goodness, which contents with the malice and ingratitude of men.[20]

Among twentieth-century theologians we can find instances of divine exemplar thinking in, for example, passages by H. Richard Niebuhr cited above, Reinhold Niebuhr's choice of God's sacrificial *agape* as the ultimate standard for human action, Anders Nygren's guiding assumption that God's love is what human love should be like, and Paul Ramsey's stress upon God's righteousness as the measure of human morality:

> The important point to see is the unanimity with which men of the Bible applied a supernatural measure to all obedient love. How to care for the resident alien is known from God's care of the sojourners in Egypt; the meaning of human justice from the redemptive righteousness of God; how to be perfect from God's care for the just and unjust, the good and evil alike; the meaning of Christian love by decisive reference to the controlling love of Christ.[21]

Although many instances of the idea of God as example can be found, it is ordinarily more used than noted or explained. We need then to explain some of the logic of the idea.

Divine exemplar theory presupposes the idea of response to God's action. It also seeks to be obedient to God's command. Yet it is different from theories of response or obedience to command that do not determine the content of the response and of the command on the basis of reflection upon the character and action of God. From a Christian standpoint there can be no conflict between God's command and God's nature, for God is one, and God's command can only express God's inmost nature. The issue how to proceed is over the question of how best we can *know* the content of God's command and of our fitting response. Where we are uncertain, it may be helpful to resort to the idea of God as example; even if we are not in doubt, the idea helps to explain why God's command is what it is. Divine exemplar theory refers us behind commands stated in Scripture or tradition to the nature of the God who commands, behind the law to the gospel in which it is rooted.

Yet *can* we pattern ourselves and our action after God? We are both like and unlike God. The likeness is expressed in the idea that we are created in the image of God. The unlikeness is twofold: the inherent limitation of human powers and the sinful corruption of those powers. Concerning the first unlikeness, the power of God incomparably surpasses ours in every respect. Concerning the second, we stand under the judgment of God's righteousness because of our sin, our willful corruption of created human possibilities. Both these differences are so marked that we might well wonder whether it can be meaningful to say that we should pattern our selfhood and action after God's.

Yet the biblical writers, while aware of these two kinds of differences, nevertheless spoke of imitating God, as we have seen, and they had good reason to do so. That reason has been expressed in the affirmation that we are created in the image of God. Whatever our created limits and however pervasive our sin, God's righteousness remains the measure of our fitting response, and God's love the source and criterion of human love. This is possible only because we are in God's image. Our limits and our sin qualify the conditions under which we are to pattern our lives after God, but they do not negate the obligation to do so.

It is appropriate, then, to understand the relation of God to the basic moral standard in all three of the ways discussed above: (1) We ought always to understand the moral life as response to God's action. (2) We ought in all moral action to be obedient to God's command. (3) We can and should understand the basic standard of Christian ethics—the fundamental content of a fitting response and of God's command—as patterned after the being and action of God.

The following discussion of that basic standard concentrates upon the third of these, while accepting the other two. It seeks first to identify from the Christian proclamation certain essential and fundamental features of God's character and God's action toward us. On the basis of that analysis, it then proposes a parallel understanding of the basic standard of human morality. My thesis is threefold: (1) *that God's being and action, as presented in the Christian proclamation, is to be understood as always and everywhere expressive of covenant love*; (2) *that the sense in which human beings are in the image of God finds its culmination in the capacity to enter into covenant with God and with one another*; and (3) *that following the pattern of God's being and action, the pattern of human selfhood and action should be one of covenant love.*

God's Covenant Love

The writers of the Old Testament declare that God has covenanted with the chosen people and that God wills to be their God and for them to be God's people. For them, and not only for the New Testament writers, God is a God of love. They designate this love by two different Hebrew words, each for a different relationship. The term *'ahabah* refers to love that is unconditioned by covenant, the "election-love" of God, who freely chose to make covenant with the people. The term *hesed*, on the other hand, refers to love within covenant and thus love that includes faithfulness to covenant; the Revised Standard Version appropriately translates this term as "steadfast love."

The New Testament writers proclaim that in Jesus Christ, God has fulfilled the covenant with the Hebrew people as it ought really to have been understood, as one "written on the heart" and as not confined to the biological descendants of Abraham, Isaac, and Jacob, but offered to all who have faith. Through God's revelation in Jesus Christ they too declare God's love, which they express in the Greek term *agape*. This term connotes the meaning of both the above Hebrew words. On the one hand, similar to the Hebrew 'ahabah, God's agape has freely created a new covenant and has freely elected a people to that covenant. "Once you were no people but now you are God's people" (I Pet. 2:10a). And like the meaning of the Hebrew hesed, God's agape is God's faithful love for the covenant people. Nothing at all, Paul writes, "will be able to separate us from the love of God in Christ Jesus our Lord" (Rom. 8:39). God's agape is both covenanting and loyal to covenant. Covenant love is God's constant orientation toward humankind.

If we are to understand God's covenant love as the standard for human morality, we must attempt to identify its various characteristics. God's love is not a simple idea, and we must avoid the temptation to see it merely as something like the human emotion we call love. Instead we must attempt to state the meaning of God's love as it is implied in the Christian proclamation, both in the New Testament and in the Old as interpreted from a Christian standpoint.

Using this method, we can identify six characteristics of God's covenant love: God (1) binds us together as members of a covenant community, (2) affirms the worth of each covenant member, (3) extends covenant love inclusively, (4) seeks to meet the needs of each member of the covenant community, (5) is steadfast, and (6) is reconciling.

1. *God binds us together as members of a covenant community.* In covenanting with us, God creates a covenant community and causes us to be members of it. God creates us as social beings, capable of covenanting and in need of it. In the creation story of Genesis 2:4b and following, the comment, "It is not good that the man should be alone" (2:18), is not at all casual. It leads to the story of Adam and Eve and of their "one flesh" relationship. This phrase speaks of marriage, but the story of the creation of Adam and Eve, as many exegetes have interpreted it, is concerned with more than marriage—it is concerned with the social nature of human life.

God covenants with a people, not merely with individuals. The Hebrews understand God's covenant with Abraham to be with them as a people, not merely with one man, for they are the descendants to whom God has promised the land (cf. Gen. 15:5, 13, 18). Similarly they interpret the covenant with David as not merely with the king, but through him with his lineage and with the people (cf. esp. II Sam. 7:10), as the latter prophets assume in their references to the covenant with David. Likewise in the New Testament the new covenant is with the community of faith in Jesus Christ, not merely with individuals one by one. There may be an individualistic faith, but it is neither Jewish faith nor Christian faith; some covenant somewhere may be declared that is limited in scope and significance merely to God and one person, but that is not the proclamation with which the Bible is concerned.

God's covenant is social because God's creation is social,[22] in the sense that we become *selves* (to be contrasted with mere biological beings with human genes) only in community. Through the entrustments and acceptances of a community, we learn a language. In dialogue with a community, using its language and reflecting upon its experience, we learn interpretations of the meaning of our lives and respond to these interpretations in belief and disbelief. Our consciences develop only in a community and thus only in the presence of a shared morality of some kind, and we receive that morality before we ever come to reflect upon whether what we have received is exactly as it ought to be.

Furthermore, in covenanting with us, God calls us to be social in the further sense of being responsible to and for our fellow covenant members. The covenant at Sinai commands that as a requirement following from the covenant relationship the people are to maintain peaceful and just relationships with one another. As we have seen, the commandments follow from the grace of God's deliverance of the people from oppression and gracious covenant with them. God's love for the covenant people is inseparable from God's requirements upon them, so that they may know what it is truly to be a *people*, and thus loyal to one another as an expression of their loyalty to God.

2. *God creates and affirms the worth of each covenant member.*

62

Worth refers here to the goodness of our being as persons, a kind of "nonmoral value," to use William Frankena's term,[23] that is, the goodness of anything, such as a life or an experience of pleasure, distinguishable from anyone's good will and good character (one's "moral value"). To say that God affirms the worth of each is to say that God affirms each person for that person's own sake, that person's own true well-being, and not only as a means to the well-being of other creatures. Our worth is not simply any kind of nonmoral value; it refers to our goodness as ends, not merely as means. We *are* all means, whether in the way we would wish or not, to the intentions and interests of other people, and God also affirms each of us as a means. Farmers can be means to others' having enough to eat, parents to their children's development and happiness, teachers to students' education, and this is desirable; it expresses their callings. But God affirms each of us as an end and not merely a means.

It is essential to speak this way if we are to express in our day the meaning of God's covenant love. The idea that God affirms each person as an end and not only a means is not merely a Kantian idea grafted onto theological ethics. (Historically it may have been the reverse—a Christianly derived idea that Kant separated from its theological roots to be the central principle of his moral philosophy.) The idea is so important to Christian ethics that to overlook it today would be to misread the spirit of God's covenanting. It is our *being* as covenant members that matters most fundamentally in God's sight; our being as persons precedes whether we are morally good and whether we are useful. God desires our moral goodness, our faithful participation in the covenant, but for our own sakes, and not only as means to the good of others. So it is that when the prodigal son declares to his father, "I have sinned against heaven and before you; I am no longer worthy to be called your son," the father responds, "Let us eat and make merry; for this my son was dead, and is alive again; he was lost, and is found" (Luke 15:21, 23-24).

There is in the Bible no theory of human worth, nor any abstract assertion that God loves each person as an end.

Nevertheless not to speak this way in our day, with our self-conscious distinction between means and ends, is to miss something that the biblical writers intend to say about God. Because God has created us and entered into covenant with us, we must therefore be said to matter to God in a most serious way. This is what is being said when it is declared that we have worth. In Christian theology human worth has its source in God's creating and covenanting action. It does not refer to anything self-sufficient, self-authenticating, or prior to the God-human relationship. From a Christian standpoint *worth* is a relational term. It is completely compatible with the earlier point, that God covenants with us as members of a covenant community. Worth in this context means worth-as-bestowed-by-God and thereafter worth-as-recognized-by-God. At the same time that God affirms us in the covenant community, God affirms *each* of us, and not simply the community as a totality. It is not only the whole that matters, but each member as a participant.

This idea helps us to see a level of meaning we might otherwise miss in various biblical passages that speak of how God loves us. Hosea calls it to our minds in his picture of God's love for Israel, a love so deep that God seeks to bring the people back from idolatry as a husband would ransom an unfaithful wife. God cares for the people, Hosea also says, as a parent does for a child: "When Israel was a child, I loved him, and out of Egypt I called my son. . . . How can I give you up, O Ephraim! How can I hand you over, O Israel!" (11:1, 8*a*). The same idea helps us to see what is meant in the New Testament when God's love toward each person is portrayed as like that of a shepherd who goes to find his lost sheep, and having found it, calls in his friends and neighbors and says, not simply because of the sheep's monetary value, but because it is *this* sheep, "Rejoice with me, for I have found my sheep which was lost" (Luke 15:6). Of such worth is each person in God's sight that to act compassionately "to one of the least of these" is to do it to Jesus himself (Matt. 25:40). "The least of these" does not mean "least in God's sight," but "least in the eyes of the world," "least in our customary valuations." The "least" are the disadvantaged, the unsuccessful, the outcast: a retarded child, an illiterate street-dweller in an Asian city, an aged invalid whose daily needs must be met by others, a murderer on death row. Whatever persons are "least" in the eyes of the world, nevertheless God affirms their worth. God seeks to bring them back to be what they were created to be—fully affirmed and affirming members of the covenant community.

This means that God loves us for what God has created us to be, and not because we merit that love. Thus Paul writes: "While we were still weak, at the right time Christ died for the ungodly. Why, one will hardly die for a righteous man—though perhaps for a good man one will dare even to die. But God shows his love for us in that while we were yet sinners Christ died for us" (Rom. 5:6-8). God's love does not wait for our obedience. Its measure is that "Christ died for us."

Anders Nygren is correct in two respects when he maintains that God's *agape* is "indifferent to value."[24] First, it is offered without regard to differences in moral value. Neither a morally good character nor any accumulation of good works merits it. Second, it is offered without regard to various kinds of *nonmorally* good characteristics that a person may inherit or acquire or develop, such as wit, charm, skill, intelligence, or education. God's love is indifferent to these good qualities, even though God finds satisfaction in human well-being.

Nygren erroneously overgeneralizes his claim, however, to include all senses of value. The one fundamental sense in which God's love is not indifferent to value is that God is not indifferent to each person's worth. In that respect God's love is directed toward value—value that God has already bestowed on us by creating us as beings intended for covenant. But that is a type of value that rules out differences among persons. Merit is based on what people differentially have or accomplish with what they have, either morally or non-morally. It is, as Gregory Vlastos says, a "grading concept," one on the basis of which individuals can be ranked and rewarded accordingly.[25] God's covenant love is directed toward worth, not merit. It is mistaken to say, as Nygren does, that God's love is "unmotivated,"[26] for then it would be unintelligible and arbitrary. Instead it is unmotivated by anything apart from God's own action. It is motivated by the worth that God has bestowed in the act of creating.

Three further comments help us see the meaning of God's affirmation of our worth:

a. God values each person *individually*, even though as one who can be a person only in community. In the covenant community each person is an end-point of God's valuing. The faithful covenant community that God seeks is not one in which each individual is lost in the whole, but one in which the good of each is affirmed in relationships of peace and justice.

b. God values each person *irreplaceably*, however replaceable each of us may be as a means to some good end. Someone might say to the shepherd in the parable, "Forget about that sheep; I'll get you another one." The shepherd might well reply, "There is no such thing as 'forgetting' one of my sheep. I could get another, but it would not be *that* one." Likewise if a child dies, the parents might thereafter have another child. That might make them feel better, but it would not be the same child, and they would be fully aware of that difference. Such is the worth of each person in God's sight. No other person can ultimately be substituted for the being of any one of us, though substitutions of means are quite conceivable.

c. God affirms all persons *equally*. If we are merely considering usefulness or merit, human equality is a fiction. Whatever quality people contribute for any purpose, they do so unequally. On all such qualities they can theoretically be ranked or graded. Even if we are considering the contribution that each one's life makes to the satisfaction of God, they will not be equal, because the faithful and upright person is surely more satisfying to God than the faithless and the evildoer. What is equal is not God's satisfaction gained from the contemplation of each, but that God has created each alike for covenant. God is therefore equally committed to each, however unequally they contribute to God's satisfaction. In this sense God's love is just.

Human beings have a *kind* of worth for God that is different from that of other creatures, though each of them has its own kind of worth in God's sight. Human worth arises from the distinctiveness of the kind of creature God has here created. In his creation story the Priestly writer declares that human beings, as distinguished from other creatures, have been created "in the image of God" (Gen. 1:26, 27; cf. 9:6). Christian theologians have used this term to express what it is about human beings, as contrasted with other creatures, that is like God, although they have differed about what this quality is. A judgment about this issue goes to the root of the question of a basic moral standard in Christian ethics.

In Kantian ethics the basis on which each person has worth is that each is rational. The foundation of the categorical imperative is that "rational nature exists as an end in itself,"[27] and Kant is not alone in this emphasis. Christian theologians, however, have ordinarily interpreted the *imago Dei* to be something more than rationality. Thomas Aquinas did say, reflecting the influence of Aristotle, that "man is said to be to the image of God by reason of his intellectual nature." Nevertheless he went on to speak of the image as present "inasmuch as man knows *and loves* God perfectly."[28] Without intellect we would not be in God's image, he says; thus we image God *by reason* of intellect. Yet the image itself, as Aquinas understands it, is not simply intellectual capacity as such, but one's knowing and loving God.

In his classic discussion of human nature, Reinhold Niebuhr adds another dimension to the idea of the *imago Dei* when he interprets it as the human capacity for self-transcendence.[29] Alone of all creatures the human self has the capacity to "stand outside itself" in the imagination and to make both the external world and itself the object of its knowledge. Therefore the self must choose its own total end. Niebuhr sees this capacity as the crux of human spirit, the quality that it shares with God and that distinguishes it from other creatures.

Yet we must go a step further. The self is not only rational and not only transcends itself, but as one who must choose its own total end in a community of others who do likewise, it has *the capacity to enter into covenant with God and with other human selves.* The capacity for self-transcendence provides not only the possibility for gaining perspective upon one's life, but also for committing oneself steadfastly to others. The apex of the *imago Dei* is then the capacity for covenant, a capacity that is possible because the self also has the capacity for rationality and for self-transcendence. This is the sense in which, in Karl Barth's words, creation is "the external basis of the covenant," and covenant is "the goal of creation."[30]

The capacity for covenant is then an essential feature, created by God, through which each person individually, irreplaceably, and equally has worth as an end, and not only as a means. Out of love, God creates us capable of entering into covenant and capable then of mirroring God. This is to say that God creates us for steadfast community with God and with one another.

These first two characteristics of God's covenant love are presupposed in the other four, as we shall see.

3. *God extends covenant love inclusively.* There are no boundaries to the persons to whom God extends covenant love. At times Old Testament writers express an inclusive understanding of God's love, but most often the conception is of a love directed especially toward the children of Israel. In the New Testament God's love is extended to all persons without restriction. Even in the earliest church, though, this belief was accepted only after a battle. Paul had to convince Peter and the church at Jerusalem that it was legitimate to preach the gospel to the Gentiles and to receive them into the church without circumcision, the sign of God's covenant with Abraham. Paul's victory in that conflict permanently fixed the church's position in principle (even if often not in practice) in favor of inclusiveness.

Two issues are raised by this concept of God's inclusive love. One concerns the relation of the church to love's inclusiveness. Those whom God loves are not only those within the church— those who have (presumably) committed themselves self-consciously to the new covenant in Jesus Christ. They have indeed recognized and responded to God's love as revealed in Jesus Christ. But God's covenant love is intended for and offered to all persons, and not only those who respond in this way. The church recognizes this in its understanding that it is to "make disciples of all nations" and in its decisive condition for church membership (confessing Jesus Christ as Lord, not membership in some social category). We must make a distinction in principle between *the church*, the community that responds positively and self-consciously to the new covenant in Jesus Christ, and *the inclusive covenant*, those to whom God's love is extended—that is, all persons without exception.

The second issue concerns the relation of God's love for human beings to God's love for nonhuman creatures. What I have said thus far presupposes a distinction between God's love for humankind, which is covenant love, and God's love for all other creatures. God's love in the broadest sense is not limited to human beings, but is directed toward all creation. Nevertheless to speak of God's *covenant* love is to speak of a love directed toward creatures capable of covenant, that is, toward human beings. Love toward those who can covenant has its own characteristics and its own problems to face that are not present where the other is not a covenanting being. Only covenant love can evoke a consciously covenanting love from the other; only covenant love encounters the problem of the creature who will not accept it; only covenant love involves the question of forgiveness and the reestablishment of community. This implies no diminution of God's love for nonhuman creatures, but simply emphasizes that the nature of God's love is always appropriate to the creature loved.

4. *God's covenant love seeks to meet the needs of the members of the covenant community.* Because for God each person matters as a member of the covenant community, God seeks to meet each person's true needs. For the Old Testament writers God's care for the people is continually being expressed: for example, in delivering them from bondage in Egypt, providing manna in the wilderness, making known the law to provide a structure for their lives as a people, giving them the promised land, declaring God's judgment upon those who oppress the needy, and calling the people to repentance. The conviction that God seeks to meet our needs continues in the New Testament.

Although God is aware of all the things we need (cf. Matt. 6:32*b*), the preeminent need God is meeting, these writers declare, is deliverance from the bondage of sin into participation in God's inbreaking kingdom. The writers declare God's need-fulfilling love when they announce, as in Mark's gospel, that "the time is fulfilled, and the kingdom of God is at hand" (1:15), or that, in Paul's words, "God was in Christ reconciling the world to himself" (II Cor. 5:19). The healing narratives not only express the writers' conviction that Jesus is the promised Messiah in whom the blind see, the lame walk, lepers are cleansed, the deaf hear, the dead are raised, and the poor have the good news preached to them (Matt. 11:5). They declare the message that God continually seeks to meet the deepest human needs, that God's love is compassionately extended toward all the unfortunate of the world.

To say that God's love is need-fulfilling calls for some answer to the question of what people need. A theory of human needs is one aspect of a theory of human nature. As soon as we speak of "being human," we find it necessary to distinguish between a sense of the term that is mere human existence, and a higher sense designated by some such phrase as "truly human" or "human fulfillment." This distinction is assumed in various New Testament passages, as, for example, in Matthew 6:25 ff.:

> Therefore I tell you, do not be anxious about your life, what you shall eat or what you shall drink, nor about your body, what you shall put on. Is not life more than food, and the body more than clothing? . . . Your heavenly Father knows that you need them all. But seek first his kingdom and his righteousness, and all these things shall be yours as well.

The passage does not imply that the necessities of physical life are unimportant, nor that meeting them is wrong, but that their importance is to be seen in terms of the centrality of God's kingdom; they cannot be rightly appraised outside that context. Indeed in the parable of the last judgment (Matt. 25:31-46), those on the "right hand" are commended for meeting just such needs. What people most need is God's kingdom and God's righteousness, and that in turn gives significance to physical needs while preventing them from assuming an ultimate importance.

We can express the highest priority need, the ultimate human need for God's kingdom and God's righteousness, in terms of covenant. What people need, in and beyond every other need, is to live loyally in covenant with God and with one another, to live in that fellowship with God and their fellows in which they can truly be themselves. God's giving the covenant relationship is a humanizing gift. It represents the possibility that we can live in true fellowship with one another on the foundation of faith in God. God does not work salvation merely one-by-one, nor in abstraction from community, nor by relieving us of concern for our fellows. Salvation is essentially social—the restoration of true participation in the faithful covenant community. Here is the fulfillment that truly liberates. Here is the need that surpasses all others in importance and at the same time renders meeting other needs significant. Final satisfaction of this ultimate need is an eschatological hope. We can never identify some visible human community at a certain time or place as the fulfillment of the covenant hope. Yet through God's grace this hope can continually be embodied, partially but significantly, in the midst of human life in society. Therefore faithful actions are significant even though they are not perfect in every way, even though their social effects pass away, and even though people do not fully appreciate them.

Lower priority human needs—proximate needs—gain their significance from the contribution that meeting them makes to true humanness in a true covenant community. We ought not to try to choose between ultimate and proximate needs, but to see the former as requiring concern for the latter in their proper place. Food is important, both because starving is individually painful and destructive and because the starving person is not free for fellowship in covenant. Health is important, both because ill health is in itself an evil for that person and because the one who is ill is to that extent hindered from full participation in the covenant community, though participation in other respects might continue. So also with other proximate needs; for example, for work, rest, or relief from acute anxiety. Unless proximate needs are met at least minimally, persons are harmed and community in covenant is hindered. God's covenant love seeks our fulfillment both ultimately and proximately.

5. *God's covenant love is steadfast.* God is faithful to covenant, offering love even when the people waver and are faithless. This characteristic of God's covenant love is readily suggested by the very meaning of a covenant, a relationship in which the parties have enduring responsibility to one another. To keep a covenant requires committedness over time: not momentary concern, but enduring loyalty; not occasional beneficence, but dependability.

The story of the Abraham covenant, as we have seen, is one in which God pledges dependability to Abraham by taking a vow. The Davidic covenant is to be maintained regardless of David's misdeeds. In Hosea's declaration God is faithful in spite of Israel's idolatry. Throughout the Old Testament the idea of the covenant functioned to assure Israel of God's dependability. As Eichrodt observes, "Because of this [God's covenant] the fear that constantly haunts the pagan world, the fear of arbitrariness and caprice in the Godhead, is excluded. With this God men know exactly where they stand; *an atmosphere of trust and security* is created."[31] The idea is not that, being dependable, God can be manipulated. On the contrary, God's love expresses itself in quite unexpected ways, including in the form of judgment. But the Israelites voice the assurance that in all its forms God's action expresses love. Therefore the Old Testament speaks of God's *hesed*, steadfast love, as the measure of human love.

So also the New Testament assumes and declares the dependability of God's love. The father awaits with steadfastness the return of the prodigal son and receives him; at least as strikingly, the father declares to the elder son: "Son, you are always with me, and all that is mine is yours" (Luke 15:31). The

Christian witness is that we can be assured of God's love in every circumstance.

The steadfastness of God's love is a reflection that what is fundamental to the covenant is the relationship between the parties and not merely the fulfilling of certain external stipulations. Because the lives of the covenant members extend over time, God's love for them endures.

6. *God's covenant love is reconciling.* This characteristic reveals to us the difference between God's covenant and a merely legal transaction. In the latter, if one party breaks the agreement, the other ordinarily has no more legal obligation to it and is free to terminate the relationship. Because God's covenant expresses an enduring concern for all persons, when people break the covenant through their disloyalty, God seeks their repentance and their acceptance of forgiveness, so that the covenant relationship can be restored and the people made whole again.

So it is that Jeremiah's vision of a new covenant is one, as we have seen, in which the people will know the Lord, "for I will forgive their iniquity" (Jer. 31:34). God's forgiving love will bring the community back into a right covenantal relationship. This is what Paul declares God has done in Jesus Christ, "that while we were yet sinners Christ died for us" (Rom. 5:8).

Forgiveness must be distinguished from indulgence. To indulge someone is to overlook the person's misdeeds, to be overly lenient, to suggest that the wrongdoing does not really matter. Indulgence takes place without any repentance on the part of the wrongdoer. To forgive is an utterly different concept. It is not merely to blot out the sin of the other. It is to recognize the sin but to extend the possibility of reconciliation in spite of the sin—the possibility of repentance and change. So in the parable the father not only extends love to the resentful elder son but also desires that he change. Indulgence is a bookkeeping transaction that concentrates upon the wrong and seeks to erase it. Forgiveness is a personal transaction that seeks the sinner's transformation and return to full acceptance in the covenant community.

God seeks to forgive us, not simply to indulge us by overlooking our disloyalty. Accepting forgiveness is painful in that it requires confession and repentance. That might not take place, or might not for a long time. Yet the Christian proclamation is that God steadfastly forgives and seeks to receive us back into full fellowship in the covenant community. That God's love is reconciling is the full measure of God's faithfulness; it is the capstone of the love of God.

These are six characteristics of God's covenant love. We might be able to identify other characteristics of God's love, though I suspect that they would be extensions of those discussed above. The heart of the matter is God's relationship with the covenant people. God initiates, sustains, and continually renews the covenant relationship. This is the morally relevant answer to the question, What is going on? It is the first word of Christian ethics. What we ought to do is to be determined on the basis of this word, in response to God's action, in obedience to God's command, and in patterning our being and action after God's insofar as that is humanly possible. The basic standard of Christian ethics is to be derived in this way from our understanding of the character and action of God.

Human Covenant Love

It is impossible to discuss human covenant love apart from a discussion of faith, with which it is a unity. It is from faith in God that our covenant love arises and through faith in God that it is sustained, both by God's grace. Indeed faith and love are not two separable things at all, but two ways of speaking of the orientation that we ought to have toward God and neighbor in response to God's covenant love.

Faith as the Right Human Response to God

In a religious sense of the term, *faith* (including love as inseparable from it) can be defined either generically or normatively. Generically it refers to any orientation of trust and loyalty concerning what is of ultimate significance in life. In this generic sense everybody has some kind of faith. Normatively the term refers to a *right* orientation of trust and loyalty. From a Christian standpoint normative faith is the self's right response and relationship to God and neighbor.

H. Richard Niebuhr has defined faith generically as the attitude and action of "trust in that which gives value to the self" and "loyalty to what the self values."[32] Normatively it is on the one hand trust, "the passive aspect of the faith relation," confidence in God, and confidence therefore in the meaningfulness of life. On the other hand, it is loyalty or faithfulness, "the active side" of faith, fidelity to God's "cause." We can express Niebuhr's idea of faith in covenant terms: faith as trust is the acceptance of God's covenant with us; as loyalty it is active commitment and participation in the covenant community. In this latter, active sense faith is virtually synonymous with love. Covenant love is faith's commitment over time in the covenant community.

Faith as trust and loyalty necessarily involves belief, and not merely as "the secondary form of faith,"[33] as Niebuhr describes it. To trust is impossible unless we believe that the object of our trust has a certain character—for example, that God is dependably loving. In a parallel way loyalty presupposes a belief that the community to which we are loyal includes certain members with certain types of claims upon us. Change the beliefs and we change the character of our faith.

Because of this element of belief, faith not only *motivates* moral action, but also *shapes* it. It shapes action as we make belief-judgments about questions like these: (1) whether we are essentially or only incidentally members of a community in our relationship to God, (2) whether individual human beings have any ultimate significance, (3) who belongs to the covenant community, (4) what we should seek for those we should love, (5) how enduring the covenant community and its claims are, and (6) whether it endures even in the midst of the members' disloyalty. Answers to these six questions, which correspond to the six characteristics of God's covenant love discussed above, constitute matters of belief, and different answers would lead to different moral judgments. It is therefore not merely the case, as the philosopher Stephen Toulmin has expressed it,[34] that "ethics provides the *reasons* for choosing the 'right' course: religion helps us to put our *hearts* into it." It is true that faith in God (rather than "religion") involves putting our hearts into right action. But the bearing of faith upon action is greater than this. In Christian ethics how we understand God's action in Jesus Christ not only motivates, but it governs the shape of the basic moral standard for all moral action. Faith is the root of loving action both as it shapes our understanding and as it moves our wills.

Faith's opposite, sin, is also to be understood in covenant terms. Like faith, sin in its most fundamental meaning is an orientation toward God—a pervasive distortion of the self and not merely a number of evil acts. Sin is the distorted condition of the self from which evil acts arise. To extend H. Richard Niebuhr's analysis of faith, sin is the orientation of distrust in God and disloyalty to God's cause. In covenant terms it is the distrust of God's covenant love and the rejection therefore of God's covenant community. It is placing our trust in something other than God—some creature—as what gives value to the self. It is loyalty (of a sort) to some portion of the community over against the rest. In this latter sense sin is also the opposite of love.

Sin finds expression in responses counter to the six characteristics of God's covenant love. Whereas God covenants with us as members of a covenant community, the sinful self wishes not to be indebted to or responsible to and for others but to live as an uncommitted, uninvolved individual. Second, whereas God affirms the worth of each covenant member, the sinful self affirms people for the benefit it can receive from them and thus judges them on the basis of some set of merits, fancied or real. In the third place, the sinful self is exclusive about those who are to be loved; it relegates some to the category of outsiders, people who do not really matter. Its god is a tribal god. Fourth, the sinful self is not open to the other's true need, except as that need coincides with its own objectives or compulsions. It is unable to hear the other's cry, but fits every communication to what it already expected to hear. Fifth, the sinful self is unreliable; either it commits itself only to be found wanting, or it is unwilling to commit itself at all lest more be demanded than it is willing to give. Finally, it accepts a condition of alienation from others, perhaps even with relief, because its self-understanding depends largely upon having some group of persons whom it is against.

Conceptually faith-love and sin are mutually exclusive opposites. In actual life, though, they intermingle in the same self. Yet becoming a faithful self in a loyal covenant community stands both as a human possibility through God's grace and as a judgment upon unfaith. It points to the need and possibility of reconciliation with God, with one another, and with oneself in a moral life in which the operative standard is covenant love.

Covenant Love as the Basic Moral Standard

As an expression of faith in the covenanting God, we ought always to respond with covenant love toward God and all God's creatures. Following a divine exemplar method, we can express the meaning of human covenant love in terms of the six characteristics we have identified in God's covenant love.

1. To have covenant love is always to see self and others as essentially belonging together in community. It is to know that we and they have come to be selves only through participation in communities, and that we constantly stand responsible to and for other people under God. In covenant love there are no "self-made people," no ultimate "loners," no uncommitted. In our time the call to "fulfill yourself" continually tempts, but it is not the call that Christian faith makes. Instead its call is to vocation, to pursuit of one's various roles as ways of being faithful toward one's fellows. True fulfillment comes only to those whose objective is not really fulfillment, but faithfulness to God's covenant. That faithfulness is always social, never the egoistic or isolated pursuit of our own individual good, never mere concern for our own personal perfection.

2. To have covenant love is to affirm the worth of each covenant member, to regard each as someone who matters individually, irreplaceably, and equally. It is to recognize each one's humanity under God, each one's sacred worth. A test of love is whether we ultimately affirm alike as human beings the outcasts and failures of society along with its contributors and achievers—the heroin addicts, the Willy Lomans, the retarded children, the senile, along with the Mozarts and Lincolns and Einsteins. An even more stringent test is whether we affirm equally the gross evildoers along with their victims and responsible citizens generally: James Earl Ray along with Martin Luther King, Jr.; the Nazis as well as the Jews they murdered—the wrongdoers, but not the wrong deeds. This is what is required in the teaching, "Love your enemies and pray for those who persecute you" (Matt. 5:44).

3. To have covenant love is to include every category of person in the covenant community and therefore in those we affirm for their own sakes. Love permits no chauvinism of any kind. It makes no ultimate distinctions among persons—fellow citizens/aliens; believers/unbelievers; male/female; black/brown/yellow/red/white; young/old; educated/uneducated. It has no ultimate category of "out-group," but only an in-group to which all persons belong because God has elected all to covenant. All this is true however much we need to distinguish for provisional, justifiable, and nonchauvinistic reasons between types of human offices and functions, as Paul did between the many members of the body of Christ (I Cor. 12; Rom. 12:4ff.).

Covenant love does indeed make a distinction between human beings and nonhuman creatures, but that does not permit irresponsibility toward the nonhuman world. The opposite is the case. Because human beings alone among God's creatures can covenant and can have moral obligation, we carry responsibility for nurturing and caring for the nonhuman environment as a community that, like us, receives God's boundless love.

4. To have covenant love is to seek to meet the needs, both

ultimate and proximate, of each person. It is to be prepared, like Sir Philip Sidney as he lay dying of his battle wounds, to give his mug of water to another soldier as bad off as he.[35] It is to be disposed, like the soldier in J. O. Urmson's example,[36] to throw his body upon a live grenade so that his fellow soldiers will not be blown to bits—even though he could argue that one of *them* should do so, or that he has no special duty to do it, or that they are not an especially meritorious bunch for whom to be sacrificing himself.

5. To have covenant love is to be faithful in our commitments to others, both in our ultimate commitment to all members of God's inclusive covenant and in our special covenants with this or that person. There are some in our time who mistakenly view liberation as the opposite of commitment. To them, to be "liberated" is to be free from obligations. To the contrary, our past pledges and actions do obligate us in enduring ways in the future. To be faithful is to be people on whose word others can depend, and more crucially, on whose *being* others can depend. To be faithful is to be willing to return to the scene of our past deeds and stand accountable for them—as the good Samaritan was when, having left the injured man with the hapless innkeeper (who had not planned on being a good Samaritan), he then added, "I will repay you when I come back" (Luke 10:35)—for he planned to return. To be faithful is to accept responsibility over time for the effects of our actions upon others, and to return to care for those others. It is not the case morally that we come new to every situation. We come into each moment bringing along our accountability and past commitments to others. It is not that these commitments can never be changed, but changing them is morally permissible only under certain types of circumstances that we do not fully control, and not merely for whim or change in our personal preferences. Of all the characteristics of covenant love, this one is the most neglected today in the moral argumentation and the rationalizations of our popular morality. It is currently not fashionable in many quarters, fortunately, to be a bigot, that is, to exclude some people from

the category of human being; and let us give thanks, insofar as this is the case. But it is often very fashionable and the topic of elaborate efforts at self-justification to be faithless to past commitments. So little today is the meaning of covenant love grasped, that some do not see that faithfulness is essential to true affirmation of the being of the other person. Faithfulness—enduring loyalty—is a necessary expression of covenant love, even as God's love never ceases. Human preferences and affections change, often beyond our power to control, but covenant love is not merely an affection. It is a commitment to the being of the other to whom God has already unalterably made commitment.

6. To have covenant love is to seek reconciliation wherever alienation exists. It is never to be content with the breakdowns of community that continually occur in our midst, through others' fault and through our own. It is never to be too proud to confess our responsibility for those breakdowns, or too stubborn to accept the other who, however haltingly, seeks to convey to us a wish to reestablish fellowship. This is not a naïve belief that efforts at reconciliation will always be understood and received; often they will not. Nor is it the indulgence that overlooks the other's (or our own) wrongdoing in order to preserve a surface harmony. Surface harmony is often to be preferred over open strife, but true reconciliation is as different from the one as from the other, and requires far more of us.

These are the characteristics of human covenant love, each one patterned after God's love for the covenant people. Again there may be other characteristics that we can discern, though they are probably only extensions of these six. What is important is not the sixfoldness or the order, but the whole picture of the moral life that together they provide. They portray what it is to be a person of trust and loyalty toward God in our relationships with others. Likewise they describe the basic principle by which all our moral action is to be tested for its rightness or wrongness.

These six characteristics call to mind many kinds of moral claims upon us: many persons who as our fellow covenanters are ones to and for whom we stand responsible, many needs that these people have. If life were such that these claims never came into conflict with one another, then the study of ethics would call for little more than identification of a basic standard. In reality, though, moral claims are in continual conflict, so that what it means to follow this or any other basic moral standard is not fully clear. We move now to examine this phenomenon of conflict and what it implies for Christian ethics.

3

The Conflict of Moral Claims

Conflict and the Concept of Prima Facie Duty

Covenant love is a demanding standard. It obligates us to
every person and to other creatures as well. Furthermore it
obligates us to each of the many needs of every person. Each
need constitutes a moral claim upon others in the sense of
"something that could be claimed with justification,"[1] not
merely something that people assert as their desire or their
due. Moral claims in this sense have an objective quality about
them; they are not reducible simply to our desiring or claiming.
The term refers to anything in a relationship that creates
obligation on the part of one or another of the parties, such as a
need, a past commitment, or a moral right. We live in the midst
of a multitude of moral claims and thus in an intricate web of
obligations.

The problem is that we cannot possibly meet every claim.
The many claims conflict with one another, so that often if we
are to serve one claim, we must forgo serving another. None of
us individually has the option of meeting every moral claim
upon us; more significantly, no society has that option either.
The phenomenon of conflict of moral claims creates serious

difficulties for the moral life, difficulties which call for us to move beyond simple moral injunctions to moral judgments that will take the reality of conflict adequately into account.

The first rule of John Wesley's Methodist societies illustrates the difficulty. The members of the societies were "to evidence their desire of salvation, first, *by doing no harm*, by avoiding evil of every kind, especially that which is most generally practiced."[2] Wesley had some serious evils in mind, such as "the buying and selling of men, women, and children with an intention to enslave them," "returning evil for evil," and "doing to others as we would not they should do unto us"; and it was of great importance then, as it is now, to seek to introduce into the lives of Christian people a discipline of life appropriate to their faith. Yet the words I have italicized above call for more refinement today than Wesley saw the need of in his time.

What does it mean to *harm* someone? In legal terminology today a *harm* has a broader meaning than Wesley seems to have had in mind. Joel Feinberg has explained its meaning by distinguishing between a harm and a *hurt*.[3] To harm others is to injure their interests in some way, as perhaps by damaging their property or their reputation or by interfering with some activity that they seek to enjoy. To have an interest in this sense is to stand to benefit in some way, and an object of an interest is, in Feinberg's words, "what is truly good for a person whether he desires it or not."[4] In contrast, to hurt others is to cause them physical or psychological pain. A person might be harmed without (yet) being hurt, as when one's house has caught fire while one is away on a trip, or when one has been unfairly deprived of a promotion and never finds out about it at all. Harming is thus a broad though valuable category; we need such a term to describe damage to a wide range of human interests.

In this useful sense of the term, we must ask whether it is always possible to avoid harming others' interests. Imagine an apartment building with the usual thin walls. In one unit live a couple, both of whom get up at 5:00 A.M. to go to work. In the next unit lives a professional trombone player whose schedule necessitates his practicing late at night. Or take almost any kind of athletic contest: for one side to win necessitates that the other lose. More seriously, consider what we do when we vote in a political contest: by choosing one candidate over another, we are opting for the set of interests that this candidate represents over against the somewhat different set espoused by the opponent. And not voting does not avoid the problem; it simply confirms the choice of the majority of those who do vote.

It is a fact of our lives that conflicts of interest are always present to some degree in every human relationship. It is also true, to be sure, that some degree of harmony of interests is also present. But the degree of harmony is not such that we ordinarily have the opportunity to "do no harm." We must usually choose whose interests to harm and to what extent, and whose to affirm and to what extent.

How people *respond* to conflicts of interest is a different matter. Some people will simply be unaware that a given conflict of interests exists; some others will recognize the conflict but not be concerned about it. But frequently a conflict of interests gives rise to another type of conflict, one that is sometimes referred to as "social conflict." Lewis Coser defines social conflict as "a struggle over values and claims to scarce status, power, and resources in which the aims of the opponents are to neutralize, injure, or eliminate their rivals."[5] Social conflict, like the conflict of interests, is always present in human society, intermixed with significant elements of cooperation. Conflict, in this broad sense of strife or struggle among individuals or groups, occurs to some extent between friends as well as enemies, within close-knit communities as well as between deeply antagonistic groups, covertly as well as openly, nonviolently as well as violently. It is the type of conflict on which we are most likely to focus our attention and about which we are most likely to be disturbed, in that it has considerable potential for harm, although, as we shall see, it can be helpful as well as harmful.

However much we concentrate on it, though, social conflict is ordinarily a reflection of the conflict of interests, which is the more fundamental social phenomenon. Conflict of interests is what the strife is about. Conflict of interests does not always lead to social conflict, and certainly not always to seriously harmful social conflict, but social conflict is always in some sense an expression of conflicts of interest. If one wants to respond to social conflict effectively, then, it is necessary to look beneath the externals of the struggle to what is at stake in it, or what is thought to be at stake—the real or supposed interests involved.

If we assume that conflicts of interest are an ordinary phenomenon, so that we often do not have a choice of "doing no harm," or of "allowing no harm," that leads to a further question about harming. From the standpoint of covenant love, *ought* we always to try to avoid harming others' interests? In general we should indeed avoid doing harm insofar as we can; each need of the other is a claim upon us that we should take seriously. But in the situation in which some harm is unavoidable, it is impossible to meet all the claims, and it becomes obligatory to ask which claims to meet and which to deny. To do otherwise is not to take seriously the situation of decision in which one finds oneself. A policeman, for example, who comes upon a mugger in the act of relieving his victim of his wallet at knifepoint is in one of those situations. The policeman would be wrongheaded and irresponsible to walk away from the situation or to try to harm neither person's interests. It is his duty to restrain the mugger and thus in some sense to harm his interests—if possible, without undue risk to the victim. So it is in many situations.

When what we do may harm others, and when we believe, for whatever reason, that we should literally "do no harm," we are often tempted to either or both of two kinds of self-deception. One is to tell ourselves that what we are doing doesn't really harm anyone else's significant interests. We might convince ourselves, for example, that no one else's real interests are damaged by our enjoying an affluent life-style, or by our voting for this person who is "obviously" the best candidate for president.

The other kind of self-deception occurs when we know that what we are doing is harming some people, but we tell ourselves that these people don't really matter. They don't matter, one might maintain, because "People of that race are inferior," or "You don't understand; they are Viet Cong" (or Nazis, Japanese, Russians, Communists, etc.). The assumption is that anyone in that category has no moral claim upon us.

These are two very different kinds of self-deception. The former is a refusal to recognize the observable possible implications of one's actions; it is in effect a preference for not knowing what one is doing. The latter is a kind of pagan tribalism, under whatever religious banner; it excludes some people from our love, and by implication from God's love.

In regard to both it is better to face up to the reality of conflict of significant moral claims and to ask ourselves how to respond to it. Because we are in covenant with all other persons under God need not mean that we cannot cope morally with the conflict of moral claims. Covenant love need not be incompatible with conflicting claims or interests, nor indeed with all doing of harm. From a Christian standpoint the rule "do no harm" would better be expressed in some other way, perhaps as "do no unjustifiable harm" (though that is a truism), or more cumbrously, "do no harm to an interest that under the circumstances should have priority over conflicting interests." Better yet, we need to devise some way appropriate to covenant love whereby we can decide what interests should have priority when conflicts occur.

The fact that moral claims conflict, as represented frequently in conflicts of interest, has led to a distinction made by Sir W. D. Ross[6] between one's prima facie duty and one's actual duty. A prima facie duty is something that is one's actual duty if under the circumstances no other moral considerations happen to conflict with it—a condition which may or may not be the case. We have a prima facie duty, for example, to keep promises. If we abstract a given instance of promise-making from all possible complicating and conflicting circumstances, then in the abstract it is clear that we ought to keep that promise, because a promise is always an instance of self-obligation toward someone else. But in reality our promises are not abstracted from the circumstances, and often some conflicting prima facie duty will be present. Our actual duty refers to what we should really do in a situation in which two or more prima facie duties conflict. It may happen that keeping my promise in some situation would be immensely harmful to the person whom I promised. If so, it may very well be my actual duty not to keep the promise, for I also have a prima facie duty not to do harm.

The concept of a prima facie duty corresponds on the side of the moral agent to what I have called a moral claim on the side of the potential recipient of moral action. To have a moral claim creates a duty or obligation on someone's part, and the duty or obligation it creates is prima facie. (Although for certain purposes moral philosophers make a distinction between *duty* and *obligation,* I am using the terms interchangeably.) The concept of prima facie duty readily lends itself to thinking about conflicts of moral claims, for it reflects the recognition that in certain kinds of circumstances one has a duty in some sense of the word, while at the same time it does not presuppose that that duty must always take priority over all other conflicting duties.

Conflict is then a persisting reality of the moral life in the several senses we have distinguished: as the conflict of moral claims, as the conflict of interests, and (expressive of the latter) as social conflict or conflict as strife. Our question in this chapter is how to interpret the phenomenon of conflict within a covenantal approach to theological ethics. We must ask how we are to account theologically for the persistence of conflict, how persistent and pervasive conflict is, and what significance it has for a covenantal approach. On the way to responding to these questions, let us look briefly at the reflection of one twentieth-century theologian who took the phenomenon of conflict with great seriousness—Reinhold Niebuhr.

Reinhold Niebuhr on Conflict

The confidence that serious conflicts of interest can be overcome and a harmony of interests attained has been a persisting strain in Western culture for over two centuries. Sometimes it has found expression in the classical liberal belief in a *natural* harmony of interests—the idea that some preordained process will bring about harmony, as in Adam Smith's idea that if each of us pursues self-interest, "man is led by an invisible hand to promote an end which was no part of his intention."[7] One contemporary offshoot of this idea is the notion that if we simply eliminate governmental "interference" in the economy, things will work out to everyone's interest. At other times this confidence has appeared as the belief in an *artificial* harmony of interests—that society can create social harmony by adopting certain policies. This viewpoint sometimes leads its advocates to call for a greater and greater role for government in the belief that our coordinated efforts can ultimately eliminate conflict and produce harmony. In many different ways moralists, educators, and political figures have called for greater application of good will and human intelligence to social problems, confident that more enlightened effort can finally overcome conflicts of interest.

Reinhold Niebuhr has probably done more than any other theologian to combat this kind of optimism about conflict. He argues, contrary to the above views, that conflict is inevitable in human society, both in small, interpersonal relationships and even more among nation-states and other large groups.[8] He is at odds on this issue both with liberal capitalist social scientists and educators and also with Karl Marx, who recognized the presence of conflict in capitalist society but maintained that conflict will disappear when private property is eliminated and the period of final communism arrives. For Niebuhr, Marx's expectation is as illusory as that of the liberals.

One might ask whether Niebuhr is talking about conflict as strife, or about the conflict of interests, or both. He is clearly concerned about both and, although he does not always take care to indicate which he means, he seems to include both in his judgment of inevitability. Social conflict is always present as individuals and groups continually seek to take advantage of others and as communities attempt to govern this conflict by power.[9] But the conflict of interests is also always present, even though people do have the capacity to consider the interests of others, and even though some conflicts of interest can be moderated to some extent.[10]

Conflict is inevitable, Niebuhr maintains, because human beings are egoistic.[11] Out of our sinful pride with its denial of our limits, Niebuhr argues, we inevitably tend to assert our self-interest over against one another, and the result is social conflict. If conflict is rooted in sinful nature in this way, it is, as he repeatedly asserts, utterly unrealistic to expect that intelligence or good will can overcome it and produce a simple harmony among individuals or social groups. Nor is it reasonable to expect that nonresistance will eliminate it, as some believe; according to Niebuhr, those who do not resist will be the losers in the conflict that continues to occur. This is in general the picture Niebuhr presents of the source and place of conflict in society.

Niebuhr's normative judgments about the phenomenon of conflict are not surprising, given his judgment that it arises out of egoism. "Man knows," he writes, "both by experience and by the demand for coherence in his rational nature, that life ought not to be lived at cross purposes, that conflict within the self, and between the self and others, is an evil."[12] We might inquire as to the precise sense in which he holds it to be evil. Does he mean that conflict is nonmorally evil—that is, harmful apart from judgments about the characters of those who participate in it? Or does he mean that it is morally evil—that those who engage in conflict are morally blameworthy for doing so? It is difficult to tell, because here as with many other concepts Niebuhr does not usually make precise distinctions or identify different senses in which he uses the same term. It seems probable, though, that he judges conflict to be evil both nonmorally and morally. It is nonmorally evil in that people's interests are harmed by it and in that conflict is threatening to a relatively just social order.[13] At the same time it is morally evil in that those who engage in it are asserting themselves at the expense of others—are expressing their egoism, as Niebuhr interprets their self-assertion.

In contrast with the evil of conflict, Niebuhr sets forth the social ideal of harmony. There is some harmony in social life, to be sure, but it is constantly intermingled with conflict. The ideal kind of harmony, he believes, would be present in three relationships:

> (a) The perfect relation of the soul to God in which obedience is transcended by love, trust and confidence ("Thou shalt love the Lord thy God"); (b) the perfect internal harmony of the soul with itself in all of its desires and impulses: "With all thy heart and all thy soul and all thy mind"; and (c) the perfect harmony of life with life: "Thou shalt love thy neighbour as thyself."[14]

If the ideal is one of harmony, the highest moral norm for Niebuhr is sacrificial love: a stance that "seeketh not its own," is nonresistant (to be contrasted with any kind of resistance, including nonviolent resistance), "refuses to enter into the claims and counterclaims of historical existence," and is symbolized most fully in the Cross of Christ.[15] Sacrificial love stands in judgment over all our self-assertion and all relative attainments of justice, depending as they do upon self-assertion and participation in conflict for their attainment.

Yet having said all this, Niebuhr refuses to impose sacrificial love as a pattern to be followed in all action. For one thing it cannot be a successful strategy in the midst of competing wills;

it is likely instead to be overcome historically by the self-assertion of others. For another, even if we did act only according to sacrificial love, we would thereby fail to be responsible to others who depend upon us for the protection of their own interests. "For as soon as the life and interest of others than the agent are involved in an action or policy, the sacrifice of those interests ceases to be 'self-sacrifice.' It may actually become an unjust betrayal of their interests."[16] Therefore Niebuhr calls for us to be engaged in the conflicts of social groups, not because that is ideally right, but because if we do not, vulnerable people will be victimized by the egoism of others. We are not merely to participate in social conflict, but to do so in a way that mobilizes power in its various forms to resist the egoism of others, and most especially of those social groups that would tend to be the most harmful. The goal we are to seek in society is justice. Because "it may be taken as axiomatic that great disproportions of power lead to injustice, whatever may be the efforts to mitigate it,"[17] the desire for justice requires balancing power with power—that is, requires participation in social conflict, evil though he believes it to be.

More than any other theologian of this century, Reinhold Niebuhr has faced up to the reality of conflicting interests and the resulting social conflict in human society. He has refused to settle for "solutions" at whatever level of human conflict that gain their plausibility by the supposition that through some strategy or tactic we can cause either conflicting interests or social strife to go away. In this respect, as in many others, he provides great insight for later generations, more so than many present-day theologians and social activists recognize.

At the same time I believe that Niebuhr's discussion of conflict is deficient in his explanation of its source simply in egoism, in his judgment that conflict is simply evil, and in the norm of sacrificial love which he proposes as the ultimate standard for our response to conflict. I shall develop these criticisms in the following section in the process of setting forth an alternative theological interpretation of conflict.

Covenantal Participation in Conflict

In the interpretation that follows, I will for the most part assume Niebuhr's general position about the inevitability of conflicts of interest, as well as about the intermixture of social conflict and harmony in all our relationships. At several other points, however, I wish to present an alternative to Niebuhr's view of conflict.

1. *The source of conflict.* Niebuhr asserts that the source of conflicting interests, as well as of social struggles, is sinful egoism, and there is assuredly insight in this judgment. Egoism does indeed give rise to conflict, both within us as individuals, between individuals and between groups, and between the self and God. Yet just as surely, further reflection suggests that egoism, while *a* source of conflict, is not its only source and not even the primary one.

A theologically prior source of conflict is our created nature, a conclusion to which one should come on the basis of Niebuhr's understanding of creation. According to his discussion of created human nature, God has created us with two fundamental characteristics. One is freedom, in the sense not only of the ability to decide between alternatives, but also and especially of having the capacity for self-transcendence— standing "outside ourselves," so to speak, of needing to interpret our existence, and of having to decide upon the total direction of our lives. The other is finiteness, one's being this distinguishable individual self, embodied in this flesh in a certain time and place, and limited in every aspect of life. In Niebuhr's mature position in *The Nature and Destiny of Man*, he especially emphasizes that finiteness is good; the source of sin is not in our having a body, but in our wills, as we find ourselves caught in the ambiguity of being simultaneously free and finite.

If for purposes of this discussion we simply assume this characterization (and it is highly illuminating), it follows that conflict will be present on the basis of creation, even without introducing the further characteristic of sin. A number of free and finite selves existing in the same vicinity with limited resources will necessarily have somewhat conflicting interests and enter into struggle over those interests to some extent. Indeed, we do not even have to introduce the ingredient of freedom as self-transcendence in order to arrive at this judgment. Consider nonhuman animals. Where mountain lions and deer live in proximity, the lions tend to eat the deer, not because of human sin's effect on the situation, though that is a problem, but simply because of the lions' genetic makeup and the availability of the deer as food. If deer were not present, the lions would eat some other kind of small animal, and if the mountain lions were not present, the deer (in the absence of other predators) would tend to multiply to such an extent that they would be underfed, at least until their numbers adjusted downward. Conflict is the way things are in the animal world, with or without human beings in the picture, and we do not require the presupposition of sin to account for it. So it is also with human beings.

Sin enormously intensifies conflict, to be sure. People come to any situation with somewhat conflicting and somewhat harmonious interests, and then through unfaith toward God and untrustworthiness toward one another they bring about unnecessary harm in one relationship after another, from intrafamily conflict to war. So much is this the case that it is understandable that one would oversimplify the source of conflict by ascribing it solely to sin, especially since we have never encountered any human relationship in which created nature and its sinful distortions were not thoroughly interwoven. Logically, though, the human creation entails conflict, however much sin exacerbates it.

If created human nature entails conflict, is it still appropriate to say, with Augustine, that the creation, being God's, is therefore good? Niebuhr, considering conflict to be the result of sin, finds no difficulty in asserting that whatever is created is good, though he does not indicate clearly whether he means this as a judgment of nonmoral or moral goodness or both. We should treat these two types of goodness separately.

Regarding moral goodness, if conflict is entailed in creation, it is still the case that whatever God has created is good in the sense of not being sinful from creation. This is to say that it is not morally evil to be the kind of being whose interests are to some extent in conflict with the interests of other creatures and who participates to some extent in conflict as struggle over those interests.

2. *The nonmoral ambiguity of conflict.* Is conflict good, though, in the nonmoral sense of being beneficial? Any adequate answer to that question must be a mixed one. Conflict as struggle can be either helpful or harmful or both simultaneously in different respects. A work by the sociologist Lewis Coser, *The Functions of Social Conflict,* deals with this very question. He argues that conflict as struggle over limited values and claims has positive functions for social groups, and not only dysfunctions, that "groups require disharmony as well as harmony, dissociation as well as association; and conflicts within them are by no means altogether disruptive factors." Indeed, "a certain degree of conflict is an essential element in group formation and the persistence of group life."[18]

Coser finds, for example, that unless there is some internal conflict, a group tends to dissolve. He points to the now widely recognized fact that the expression of conflict tends to act as a safety valve, allowing strong feelings to be expressed before there is a major explosion. Conflict, he says, can actually help to bind antagonists together, as when it "revitalizes existent norms and creates a new framework of norms within which the contenders can struggle."[19]

Whether a conflict is actually helpful or harmful to a group or relationship depends, Coser asserts, upon two conditions. One is the issues over which the conflict is fought.

Internal social conflicts which concern goals, values or interests that do not contradict the basic assumptions upon which the relationship is founded tend to be positively functional for the social structure. . . . Internal conflicts in which the contending parties no longer share the basic values upon which the legitimacy of the social system rests threaten to disrupt the structure.[20]

The other condition is the type of social structure within which the conflict occurs. About this subject Coser concludes:

> Conflict tends to be dysfunctional for a social structure in which there is no or insufficient toleration and institutionalization of conflict. . . . What threatens the equilibrium of such a structure is not conflict as such, but . . . rigidity . . . which permits hostilities to accumulate and to be channeled along one major line of cleavage once they break out in conflict.[21]

These insights apply to familiar human relationships. If we consider the process of higher education, for example, it will be clear that education, at least at that level, requires some kind of conflict. As contrasted with indoctrination, education, at least at the university level, takes place when students are presented with conflicting viewpoints about how to resolve some issue. The absence of conflict of this kind leads to the absence of an issue, the disappearance of motivation to inquire into the subject, and the lack of a sense of the topic's significance. At the same time, unless the conflict of viewpoints occurs within a shared loyalty to the search for truth, unless there is mutual trustworthiness among the inquirers, and unless the group can tolerate some degree of uncertainty and lack of consensus, the conflict will tend both to destroy the relationship of the inquirers and to encourage all sides to a rigidity of viewpoint rather than a willingness to follow where the best evidence and reasoning lead.

Or consider the interpersonal dynamics of a marriage. The absence of all conflict, both conflict of interests and conflict as struggle, would not be a healthy sign. Without some degree of disagreement over something, the spouses would become utterly bored with each other. Without some degree of external struggle over inner conflicts of interest and viewpoint, the result would not be true harmony, but a pseudoharmony cloaking over actual differences. Yet if the conflicts of interest are too deep, the marriage is not likely to be good for the spouses, and if conflict as struggle does not proceed within the strong bonds of mutual loyalty, it is likely to end in destroying rather than enriching the relationship.

We are on the safest ground to conclude then that, nonmorally speaking, conflict can be either helpful or harmful or both, and to focus our attention not simply upon the general phenomenon of conflict but upon the ways it is conducted and the social framework within which it occurs.

3. *Whether it is right to participate in conflict.* In Niebuhr's view, as we have seen, self-assertion is in and of itself in conflict with the highest norm, sacrificial love. According to that norm, one ought not to enter into social conflict at all, even though the price may be the self's destruction. Nevertheless Niebuhr maintains that one is obligated to enter into social conflict for the sake of others' interests, though he judges that doing so is a moral compromise and stands under the judgment of sacrificial love.

There are several problems with this formulation of the highest ethical norm. For one, Niebuhr's sacrificial love is, as Judith Plaskow's analysis suggests, a norm developed as a judgment on those whose chief sin is egoistic, prideful self-assertion.[22] If, in contrast, one's inner distortion is the failure adequately to achieve selfhood, if it is (in Niebuhr's terms) a denial of one's freedom, the norm of self-sacrifice does not adequately state the ideal. Second, Niebuhr's characterization of love directs our attention to the wrong point—sacrificialness, including both the inner quality of being inclined to be sacrificial and the outer action of sacrificing. Christian love is better characterized in another way, as the inner quality and outer action of being faithful in one's relationships and therein being helpful to someone. An act of self-sacrifice will sometimes be the appropriate way to be faithful and helpful, but sometimes it will not. Certainly self-sacrificialness is not the most fundamental way to characterize Christian love. Still a third problem is that the norm, as Niebuhr states it, demands that one do the impossible—not enter into social conflict. How can one ever not? To withdraw from struggle is still to decide about the use of one's potential power and to have a different effect on the struggle from what one might have had. The only way not to be involved in power struggles is to be dead. And if Niebuhr replies that he indeed wishes to require the impossible of us, we must reject that requirement. Regarding what we should outwardly do, Kant's dictum, "Ought implies can," is irrefutable. It is never our duty, or at least never our *actual* duty (as contrasted with our prima facie duties), to perform an act that we cannot possibly perform, externally speaking. Our actual duty must lie somewhere within the array of possible alternatives. And among those possibilities, at least one act must be right (and not merely a moral compromise), in the sense that considering all the prima facie duties upon us, this act (and possibly some others) responds to them as well as possible under the circumstances.

We must, then, reformulate the meaning of Christian love away from Niebuhr's overly narrow concept of sacrificial love, so that it demands acts that can in fact be done. If love, as we have interpreted it as covenant love, is a concern faithfully to affirm the worth of the members of the inclusive covenant, to meet their needs insofar as possible, and to achieve true reconciliation with them insofar as possible, then it is a concern with possibles, even if they are not probables. It is a concern for what might in fact help someone, for what might actually reestablish mutual trustworthiness, and not for impossibles. This reformulation of the meaning of love meets Niebuhr's two criteria for a Christian ethic better than his own norm does.[23] On the one hand, covenant love constantly stands in judgment upon us, transcending our idolatrous values and our self-protecting (or self-rejecting) impulses. Covenant love never gives any "basis of moral complacency," for even when we do the best possible act under the circumstances, we may still be doing it from a less than loving inclination, and even though we ought to do the best possible outward act, this is not to say that we shall necessarily find the inner resources to bring ourselves to do it. On the other hand, covenant love, far more than Niebuhr's sacrificial love which requires the impossible, "remains in organic contact with the historical." Only an ethic of the possible can do that.

We must conclude that love (reconceived as covenant love) requires that we participate in the conflict of interests and in social conflict. It does not judge us for doing that, though it constantly judges *how* we do it—both our inner orientation and our outer actions.

4. *The social ideal.* Niebuhr presents an ideal of complete harmony among members of the community, accompanied by complete harmony with God and within oneself. If conflict is not necessarily evil, though, it is not necessarily to be excluded from the social ideal; to the contrary, if conflict is, as Coser argues, essential to the well-being of social groups, then in some form it is an essential part of the social ideal.

We can state the ideal kind of social relationship as a community in which the members are bound together in loyalty to one another on the basis of their shared faith in and loyalty toward God in such a way that all their conflicts of interest and all their struggles are compatible with and supportive of this faith and loyalty. It is an ideal not of pure harmony but of an underlying harmony that is able to contain within itself the necessary and unavoidable disharmonies or conflicts of life. An ideal marriage is not one in which there is no conflict at all, but one in which all the conflicts go on within the framework of a more basic mutual affirmation and contribute to that ongoing basic harmony, as well as to the couple's right relationships to others. An ideal political order, similarly, is not one devoid of conflict, but one in which the conflicts enhance the life of the whole—in which therefore the members' affirmation of one another within the wider human community is always the foundation and limit for the way they conflict with one another, as well as with those beyond their political borders. A fundamental harmony is compatible with certain kinds of conflict, and that is what we must seek.

The question then is not how to avoid all conflict; that is a wrongly conceived goal. Nor is the norm sacrificial love that refuses ever to assert oneself in any fashion and refrains from entering into conflict. Instead the question is *how* to enter into conflict in ways that contribute to a mutually affirming and faithful community, conflict that does not unjustifiably harm one another, but always seeks the enhancement of the life of each within the community of all.

The Problem of Priorities

In a world where there is always some degree of conflict of interests, there is likewise always some degree of conflict of moral claims. This is the day-to-day reality of the moral life. We do not have a simple option of moving directly from our basic moral standard to the moral ideal. On the one hand, we lack this option because we are finite: we cannot meet some legitimate moral claims because we are finite. On the other hand, we lack this option because we and everyone else are ensnared in the problem of sin, willful rebellion against God's covenant with us all; we refuse to do what we could with the resources and possibilities that we have. And we always encounter both these problems intertwined.

In this kind of imperfect world, it is not ethically sufficient simply to identify our basic moral standard, nor even to be firmly committed to it. We must go further and ask how that standard bears upon the conflicts of moral claims that we encounter. Because we cannot do all that we prima facie ought, how shall we go about deciding what we *actually* ought to do? Likewise, in this imperfect world it is not adequate ethically to identify an apparently desirable, even ideal, kind of social condition and then head straight for it or demand it loudly as everyone's policy. In the process of seeking it, we may make things worse than they would otherwise have been. In politics, for example, if we refuse to support the better of two candidates simply because that candidate does not measure up to what we would prefer, we may in effect be helping the worse of the two to get elected. In the midst of conflicts of moral claims we must always seek the best possible alternative, even if we wish, as we usually do, that a still better alternative were available.

Because we must choose among moral claims and cannot meet them all, we face the problem of priorities. To which of the conflicting claims should we ascribe the highest priority, and how should we go about deciding that question? To identify the problem of priorities is to recognize that the Christian life is not simply a matter of having "faith" and then not being concerned about what we should do. To have faith requires that we be concerned about what to do—requires that we try to get our thinking straight about moral conflicts. Moral problems are not only problems of the will: how to bring ourselves to do the right thing when we inwardly somehow do not want to do it (a severe and familiar problem). They are also problems of the intellect: how to know what we actually ought to do in the midst of conflicts of moral claims, even if we were completely committed to following the basic moral standard.

Oddly enough, at this point some ethical entreaties stop; they only state a basic standard and certain social ideals and then leave the most difficult intellectual work undone. Surely it is not enough to tell people that they should love one another, regardless of how one interprets the meaning of love. At some level of our being we know that, even if we have repressed it. Nor does it suffice to call for peace or justice or freedom or other ideals that everyone knows would be good. Beyond these important and valid ethical concerns, we need to reflect further about how to respond justifiably to the intractable and conflict-ridden world before us, how rightly to sort out the conflicts of moral claims.

The middle part of this book is about that subject.

4

Moral Conflicts I: Self and Others

In this part we must wrestle with the question of priorities when moral claims conflict. The question is not only which moral claims should have priority, though that issue repeatedly arises. It is also how the basic standard of covenant love bears upon our reasoning about priorities. At some points this standard provides a definite direction in the midst of competing claims. At others it constitutes a boundary within which any of several options might be legitimate. Decision about one's basic standard does not answer all questions of priorities, but it does decisively shape the way one approaches the problem.

We can identify several characteristic and recurring types of conflicts of moral claims. I shall discuss four types, one in each of the following four chapters. The first is conflicts between the interests of the self and those of other people—perhaps the most nagging and personally troublesome of all types of conflicts of claims. The second is conflicts among the claims of the various covenants to which any one of us simultaneously belongs: for example, claims of family versus claims of occupation or citizenship or some other, and all these claims when they conflict with the claims of the inclusive covenant. The third is conflicts among the claims of various persons to justice in the distribution of society's benefits and burdens. Finally there are conflicts between the moral claims of people insofar as they are wrongdoers, such as criminals or makers of unjustifiable war, and the claims of people insofar as they are the victims of wrongdoing. The reader will readily think of other characteristic types of conflicts of moral claims. These four will suffice, though, to illustrate how we might approach other types as they arise.

In actual life we do not have the luxury of confronting these types of conflicts one at a time. Instead we come as self-interested selves when we decide about all the other types of conflicts; we encounter conflicts of different covenants' claims in the midst of questions about justice; we quickly see in the search for justice that injustice has resulted from wrongdoing and is not a morally neutral event; and we deal with wrongdoers (ourselves as well as others) only in the midst of the other types of conflicts. It is possible, nevertheless, to focus upon each type in turn so as to gain some clarity about it. Then we can see better what is involved for our decisions in actual situations where the several types are intermingled.

The Meaning of Love for Self

The first type of conflict of moral claims I shall discuss is that between the self's interests and the interests of others. Here again I am using "interest" in an objective sense, that is, as some way in which one stands to benefit, rather than the subjective sense of that in which one is consciously "interested." A major and characteristic theme of Christian ethics, past and present, is that we should prefer others' interests to our own; and where this position has been held, it has often been accompanied by the view that we should love others more than ourselves.[1] Yet these are two separate judgments, and the second does not logically have to accompany the first. The latter judgment, about self-love, has come under criticism from several quarters, psychological as well as theological.[2] Because the question of priority among moral claims is complicated and sometimes confused by disagreements over the question of self-love, we need to consider this latter question first. My objective in this first section is to identify what we might mean by self-love and to offer a judgment about it in relation to an ethic of covenant love.

Love for Self
as Distinguished from Serving the Interests of the Self

If we are to identify the meaning of self-love, it is necessary first to distinguish two aspects of the self's relation to itself, an inner and an outer. Ordinarily when we speak of self-love, we are referring to the self's inner orientation toward itself, an orientation characterized by some sort of positive valuation. This is true even though the specific sort of self-love, that is, the nature of this positive valuation, can take many different forms, and even though self-love is the object of sharply conflicting moral judgments. The second aspect of the self's relation to itself is its external actions, which may or may not serve its interests. Once we make this inner/outer distinction explicit, it becomes clear that self-love and actions seeking to benefit the self do not always occur together. Depending upon the circumstances and upon the content of the self-love, it is conceivable that self-loving persons might on occasion either seek to benefit themselves or instead sacrifice their interests, even their lives, for the sake of others. Likewise if we consider acts done with the intention of benefiting the self, it is conceivable that a person might perform these acts either out of self-love or out of a disregard or even contempt for the self for its own sake, but only in order to preserve one's resources for the sake of serving others. Thus we must distinguish between how we value ourselves and how we treat our own interests.

It is self-love as an inner orientation that we are first considering, and whether it is an appropriate love. Only thereafter will we be in position to pursue the question of external actions benefiting the self and/or others, the question of priorities which is our chief concern in this chapter. These two issues are closely connected; our judgments and actions about the priority of interests will be shaped, though not in any simple or necessarily obvious way, by the relation of love for self and love for others.

False Self-Love and True Self-Love

Different moral judgments concerning the inner orientation of self-love often reflect different meanings ascribed to the concept of self-love. It is important to distinguish two of these meanings which call for sharply conflicting moral judgments. I shall refer to them as false self-love and true self-love. Selfishness, with which everyone is personally acquainted, is a false self-love. In the words of the *Oxford English Dictionary*, the selfish person is "devoted to or concerned with one's own advantage to the exclusion of regard for others." Lest that put the matter too neatly, we might amend the latter phrase to add: "except as regard for others is seen as a means to one's own advantage." Erich Fromm expands on the concept of selfishness as follows:

> The *selfish* person is interested only in himself, wants everything for himself, feels no pleasure in giving, but only in taking. The world outside is looked at only from the standpoint of what he can get out of it; he lacks interest in the needs of others, and respect for their dignity and integrity. He can see nothing but himself; he judges everyone and everything from its usefulness to him; he is basically unable to love.[3]

Selfishness as an inner orientation can express itself outwardly in widely different ways, from the unenlightened selfishness which crassly thrusts the self ahead of others and would not even trouble to throw a drowning person a rope, to the enlightened selfishness that moves mountains to help other persons in the hope that they will return the favor someday, or the religious selfishness that serves the neighbor in order to receive reward in heaven. Whatever the external expression, all these ways are similarly selfish in inner orientation. Ordinarily a person has both selfish and unselfish inclinations. Furthermore, few people are relentless in their selfishness; rather than exert themselves to make sure every act serves their interests, it is more usual and less demanding merely to avoid actions that clearly threaten them. Crass selfishness is less ordinary than the easygoing selfishness of anti-self-sacrifice. The selfishness that society generally disapproves is the former; it usually views the latter as "normal."

Let us not overlook the last phrase of the passage of Fromm's quoted above: the selfish person "is basically unable to love." Fromm's point is that selfishness is not really self-love at all. *"Selfishness and self-love, far from being identical, are actually opposites.* The selfish person does not love himself too much but too little; in fact he hates himself. . . . *It is true that selfish persons are incapable of loving others, but they are not capable of loving themselves either."*[4] That insight is as valid in our theological framework as in Fromm's psychology. Insofar as they are selfish, people act out of an inner unfaith, an inability to trust that they are ultimately loved and lovable, and therefore an inability to accept themselves. Not believing that their ultimate security is in God, selfish people try to establish their own security by seeking their own interests. Perhaps we should not refer to selfishness as self-love at all. Yet because the culture will continue to do so, I am speaking of it as a false self-love.

From a Christian perspective (and not only from a humanistic one like Fromm's), it is possible and desirable to identify a true self-love. From the orientation of faith in God, true self-love is self-acceptance and self-affirmation as a person. The term *self-acceptance* alone is too mild, for it may mistakenly connote mere self-toleration; I add the term *self-affirmation* to stress the positive valuing of the self that is appropriate to a belief in the creating and covenanting God. From a Christian orientation self-acceptance and self-affirmation arise from the trust that God is our source, that we thereby have worth, and that God steadfastly affirms this worth all apart from any merit of our own. What God loves, we ought not to despise—neither ourselves nor others—and we ought positively to affirm, though that does not imply selfishness.

Self-acceptance and self-affirmation are logically fully compatible, furthermore, with a recognition of a pervasive human sin, an awareness of the persistent inclination of persons to distrust God and to be untrustworthy toward God and toward one another. In the knowledge and confession of our own sin, and through acceptance of God's forgiveness, we are freed to accept and affirm ourselves as God's creatures (a point that Fromm in his rejection of the Christian doctrine of sin does not fathom). The Christian knows that sin is no more the last word about the self than it is the first, but is nevertheless a necessary word to hear.

Some theologians have pointed to a sense of self-love that is natural.[5] Interpreting the command, "You shall love your neighbor as yourself," Paul Ramsey writes that it indicates not how much love, but what sort of love one should give. "How exactly do you love yourself? Answer this question and you will know how a Christian should love his neighbor. You naturally love yourself for your own sake. You wish your own good, and you do so even when you may have a certain distaste for the kind of person you are."[6] To the extent this is the case, Ramsey has offered an illuminating test for how one should be oriented toward one's neighbor. But, as Ramsey observes in a later work,[7] it is only incompletely the case that we love ourselves for our own sakes. We are born, I suspect, with an inclination to do so, and in that sense self-love is natural; but in the developmental process many people learn to hate themselves, or, more accurately, they learn a love-hate relationship with themselves. What might be called natural is not thereby usual. Neither false self-love nor self-rejection will serve as a guide for neighbor love. Kierkegaard puts it well, even though he is as suspicious as Ramsey of human selfishness:

> If the command is properly understood, it also says the opposite: *"You shall love yourself in the right way."* If anyone, therefore, refuses to learn from Christianity how to love himself in the right way, he cannot love his neighbour either. He can perhaps cling to one or more men "through thick and thin," as it is called, but this is, by no means, loving one's neighbour. To love oneself in the

right way and to love one's neighbour correspond perfectly to one another; fundamentally they are one and the same thing.[8]

This conclusion accords well with the point Fromm seeks to express from his different perspective: "Love of others and love of ourselves are not alternatives. On the contrary, an attitude of love toward themselves will be found in all those who are capable of loving others. *Love, in principle, is indivisible as far as the connection between 'objects' and one's own self is concerned.*"[9]

True self-love, that is, self-acceptance and self-affirmation, must be nurtured, or our natural inclination will not be adequately expressed. And out of that same natural inclination comes love for others. True self-love is as rare a phenomenon as true love for others, because they are cut from the same cloth.

True self-love enables us to gain a proper perspective upon our place among the other creatures and therefore a proper regard for others' interests. In faith we know ourselves to be affirmed, and thus we are enabled to affirm ourselves simply as individual selves among a multitude of creatures and not as the center of the universe. From faith true self-love has both the freedom and the inclination to direct our resources to the needs of the other creatures. If we truly love ourselves, we are paradoxically more, not less, inclined toward the interests of others than if we do not. From true self-love flows that inner security from which arises sacrificial service to the neighbor when that is needed; self-sacrifice need not stem only from the self-rejection that must prove to ourselves by our works that we are acceptable. True self-love therefore occurs together with true love for others.

This interpretation of true self-love enables us to answer a question that logically arises from any viewpoint that affirms the worth of persons as ends and not only as means. If persons as such have worth as ends, then does not the self also have this kind of worth? Is it not wrong ever to treat oneself (and not only others) merely as a means, even a mere means to the service of others? Fromm advances the point this way:

If it is a virtue to love my neighbor as a human being, it must be a virtue—and not a vice—to love myself, since I am a human being too. There is no concept of man in which I myself am not included. A doctrine which proclaims such an exclusion proves itself to be intrinsically contradictory.[10]

Responding to this passage in his *Basic Christian Ethics*, Paul Ramsey rejects the basis of Fromm's reasoning, and therefore his conclusion.

But this is not the reason for neighbor-love. . . . Christian love does not mean discovering the essentially human underneath differences; it means detecting the neighbor underneath friendliness or hostility or any other qualities in which the agent takes special interest. The full particularity of neighborly love, finding the neighbor out by first requiring nothing of him, should not be reduced to universal brotherhood or the cosmopolitan spirit.[11]

The command is to love the neighbor, Ramsey maintains, not to love all human beings. Yet is it not also the latter? In *The Patient as Person*,[12] Ramsey speaks more often of the end-worth of human beings and of "the sanctity of human life," which he contrasts with the "ever more reducible notion" of human dignity, divorced as it is in secular thinking from any ontological ground that truly dignifies it. Then is not any human life, having sanctity as it does, appropriately to be loved, the self included? The reason for this judgment is not Kant's—that we are all rational—but that God has covenanted with us all, including oneself. To say this is not at all to advocate selfishness, nor is it some kind of concordat between self-seeking and love for others. It is not to call for that "mutual love" which, in Reinhold Niebuhr's words, "seeks to relate life to life from the standpoint of the self and for the sake of the self's own happiness,"[13] for that is a kind of enlightened selfishness and not the true self-love of which we have been speaking. It does, however, imply action which affirms the self for its own sake, as we shall see, though I shall maintain that this kind of action ought not to be selfish action. It is as wrong from Christian faith as from secular humanistic faith to treat the self as merely a means and not an end also. The theologian's quarrels with Fromm are not properly over this point, but mainly over the inadequate theological basis in his psychology for true self-love and love toward others. From Christian faith in God as fully as from Fromm's humanism, "There is no concept of man in which I myself am not included."

To come to this conclusion is not yet to discuss the question of priority as between the interests of self and others. We must remember that the true self-love of which we have been speaking is an inner orientation toward the self, fully compatible with love for others, whereas the question of priority of interests has to do with outer action.

Priority Between the Interests of Self and Others

Two Types of Relationship of the Self to Others

A decision on the question of priority between the interests of self and of others will be influenced by whether one finds there to be a morally relevant difference between two types of relationship. The first is the relationship in which the self decides between the interests of two or more other persons, as for example when an official must decide which hungry persons to give food when the agency does not have enough for all. The second is the relationship in which the self decides between its own interests and those of others, as would be the case if the food distributor were also one of the hungry persons.

Some would maintain that in both relationships the self ought to be utterly impartial, treating itself precisely the same way it should treat anyone else.[14] That is to say, the self ought to favor neither itself nor another person. The relevance of the distinction between the two types of relationships, so this argument runs, lies not in establishing priorities among interests, but only in guarding against the self's inclination to favor itself. From that point of view the distinction between the two types of relationships is not relevant to decisions about priorities of interest.

In contrast, others argue that the distinction is highly relevant. Those who do so ordinarily maintain that in a conflict between the interests of self and others, at least where nobody else is dependent upon the interests of the self that are at stake, one should favor the interests of others. W. G. Maclagan maintains that although in the first of these relationships the principle of impartiality is proper, in the second relationship it is not. To be impartial as between self and others, he says, would indeed be a great achievement in contrast to ordinary human self-centeredness, but "it would deserve to be called only quasi-moral."[15] A fully moral position, he goes on to assert, is one that places the interests of others ahead of those of the self. Unfortunately Maclagan does not explain what characteristics of the two relationships make the distinction morally significant in a way that supports his conclusion. If the distinction is morally relevant to priorities between self and others, it is necessary to identify what makes it so. Let us examine some of the possibilities.

The argument from restraint of one's own selfish inclinations. It might be argued that the relevant characteristic is each person's inclination to favor the self over others. That being the case, each should resist selfish inclinations by giving preference to the interests of others whenever there is any question whose interests have the greater claim.[16] This argument has great practical wisdom; it reflects both the Christian awareness of sin and concern for the other person. It is rather like Reinhold Niebuhr's insight about the ineffectiveness of efforts at mutual love: "The self cannot achieve relations of mutual and reciprocal affections with others if its actions are dominated by the fear that they may not be reciprocated. Mutuality is not a possible achievement if it is made the intention and goal of any action."[17] The self is, Niebuhr suggests, not likely to accept a proper balance of its interests with others unless it is willing to be sacrificial. Yet although this is a valuable insight into human nature and a valuable strategy for guarding against self-assertiveness and self-delusion, it does not suffice as an explanation of the relevant difference in the two relationships. For one thing it may be equally obligatory to seek to restrain the selfish inclinations of others. Why should it especially be the self's selfishness, rather than that of others, that ought to be restrained the most when its interests are at stake? An answer to that question would seem to call for identification of some further relevant difference in the two relationships.

The argument from one's greater right to sacrifice for oneself. The second argument is that the self has a greater right to sacrifice its own interests than to demand a similar sacrifice on the part of others. We might consider again the case offered by J. O. Urmson: "We may imagine a squad of soldiers to be practicing the throwing of live hand grenades; a grenade slips from the hand of one of them and rolls on the ground near the squad; one of them sacrifices his life by throwing himself on the grenade and protecting his comrades with his own body."[18] Urmson and others observe about this kind of case that whereas it is especially praiseworthy that the soldier sacrificed his life for his comrades, a superior officer could not decently have ordered him to do so. Urmson's main point is that this kind of action goes beyond duty. Whether that is a valid judgment we shall save for later discussion. Yet a corollary of Urmson's point does indeed appear correct: that in such cases the sacrifice ought to be left to the decision of the individual involved. In this sense every self must bear its own cross; it is a different matter entirely to lay a cross upon an unwilling party. In a passage previously cited, Reinhold Niebuhr identifies the self-delusion and injustice that are present if one fails to see this point: "For as soon as the life and interest of others than the agent are involved in an action or policy, the sacrifice of those interests ceases to be self-sacrifice. It may actually become an unjust betrayal of their interests."[19]

This reason does indeed appear to be a relevant difference between the two kinds of relationships. Yet its relevance to the question at hand is limited. Its point is only that the self has a *right* to sacrifice its own interests in behalf of those of others, not that it has any *duty* to do so, even in circumstances where much less than its life is at stake. If there is only a right, then no moral priority is yet established as between the self's interests and those of others.

The argument from "the freedom of the Christian." If the first two arguments are correct but insufficient answers to our question, further answer is available concerning the motivation of the person who has faith in God. Faith, that is, trust in the faithfulness of the covenanting God, frees a person from the kind of self-concern that would lead to defensiveness or even to worry about getting an equal share, at least where justice to others does not depend upon justice for the self. From faith one is not anxious about one's own life and possessions (Matt. 6:25).

The work of faith within the faith-er is not only negative, eliminating self-concern. It is also positive, freeing one for concern for the other. Luther as much as any theologian has caught the spirit of this freedom:

> [The Christian] ought to think: "Though I am an unworthy and condemned man, my God has given me in Christ all the riches of righteousness and salvation without any merit on my part, out of pure, free mercy, so that henceforth I need nothing whatever except faith which believes that this is true. Why should I not therefore freely, joyfully, with all my heart, and with an eager will, do all things which I know are pleasing and acceptable to such a Father, Who has overwhelmed me with His inestimable riches? I will therefore give myself as a Christ to my neighbor, just as Christ offered Himself to me; I will do nothing in this life except what I see is necessary, profitable and salutary to my neighbor, since through faith I have an abundance of all good things in Christ."[20]

Faith is thus that by which the self not only has *a right* to sacrifice its own interests for those of others, but also is *inclined* not to be anxious for the self but to give of its resources to serve others.

The argument for the duty of "second-mile" actions. If we grant all three of the preceding reasons for giving priority to the interests of others, that still leaves the question whether from a Christian perspective we *ought* to do so. It could be wise (recognizing our own selfishness), and our right, and insofar as we are persons of faith our freedom and inclination, and still not our duty. It is of course ordinarily granted that we prima facie ought to give priority to others' interests when they have a corresponding right to our doing so. But the question is whether we ought to even when to do so would be sacrificial beyond what others are entitled to expect of us. Are second-mile actions, in that sense, our duty?

Thomas Aquinas gives a negative answer to this question, with the help of the distinction between a commandment (or precept) and a counsel. "A commandment," he writes, "implies obligation, whereas a counsel is left to the option of the one to whom it is given," and he illustrates from Paul (I Cor. 9:4ff.), who went beyond what was required when he supported himself rather than be supported by those to whom he preached.[21] To follow a counsel and thus to do a good work beyond what is commanded is a work of supererogation. The question is whether there are any good works beyond what is commanded. We need not be concerned here with some further associations with the concept of supererogation, such as the idea that through such acts one can amass merit and more speedily "attain to eternal happiness."[22] That idea presupposes a very different understanding of divine grace from the one with which we are working here; nevertheless, the question remains whether the distinction between commands and counsels is an appropriate one, and whether there are good works of service to others that are not duties in the broad sense.

The Protestant Reformers vigorously reject both Aquinas's distinction and his conclusion that second-mile actions are not duties. In their view the New Testament injunctions about doing more than the law, going the second mile, and being perfect certainly appear to be commands. Calvin angrily rejects Thomas's position:

These commandments—"Do not take vengeance; love your enemies," which were once delivered to all Jews and then to all Christians in common—have been turned by the Schoolmen into "counsels," which we are free either to obey or not to obey. What pestilential ignorance or malice is this! . . . The reason they assign for not receiving them as laws is that they seem too burdensome and heavy, especially for Christians who are under the law of grace. Do they dare thus to abolish God's eternal law that we are to love our neighbor? . . . Either let them blot out these things from the law or recognize that the Lord was

Lawgiver, and let them not falsely represent him as a mere giver of counsel.[23]

Luther voices similar sentiments:

We ought first to know that there are no good works except those which God has commanded.[24]

In this faith all works become equal, and one is like the other; all distinctions between works fall away, whether they be great, small, short, long, few, or many. For the works are acceptable not for their own sake, but because of the faith which alone is, works and lives in each and every work without distinction.[25]

We should note that in the latter passage Luther lumps together two matters that should be distinguished. He asserts that when done from faith all works are equally good—that is, we would say, equally expressive of the good quality of the faithful agent. We can affirm that and still ask whether there is a legitimate function for the distinction between commands and counsels, even though Luther and Calvin both meant to reject the distinction. If we reject it, it should not be as a logical deduction from the judgment that from faith all works are equally good.

The issue is this: Do I have a duty always to give others' interests priority over my own? Am I ever entitled instead to give priority to my own interests, or even to take them into account in any way except derivatively, that is, in any way except as a means to serving the interests of others?

From the perspective of covenant love the answer to this question, I believe, is that *each of us has a strong but not an absolute duty to give priority to the interests of others*. In covenanting with all persons, God calls each one most especially to obligation to others. In addition the self in its special covenants specially obligates itself to others. The self places itself, and is placed, under the obligation of seeking to meet others' needs, either generally or in specific respects appropriate to special covenants. Persons of faith know that God has covenanted with them and steadfastly seeks their ultimate fulfillment; therefore they are not worried about that—it is in God's hands.

From that faith each one is freed for the neighbor, but from the same faith, the same perspective on life, each one is obligated to the neighbor. That is what vocation is—being called through faith to use one's various roles to be helpful to others.

Obligation to others ahead of self, including the obligation to be prepared to sacrifice for the sake of others, receives strong emphasis in the New Testament. We see it in the several passages that bid us deny ourselves and take up our cross (Mark 8:34-36; Matt. 10:38-39; 16:24-26; Luke 9:23-25; 14:27; 17:33; John 12:25); in numerous passages that point our attention toward concern for the neighbor rather than for the self (e.g., the parable of the good Samaritan, Luke 10:29-37; the parable of the last judgment, Matt. 25:31-46; and Paul's injunction, "Let no one seek his own good, but the good of his neighbor," I Cor. 10:24); and above all in the example of Jesus' crucifixion. Even in those passages that speak of reward to the self (e.g., "whoever loses his life for my sake will find it" [Matt. 16:25b and parallels] and the idea of eternal reward or punishment in the parable of the last judgment), the appeal is to lose oneself in service to Christ—Christ in the neighbor— not at all to lose one's life *in order* to find it. In the New Testament, concern for the interests of others clearly takes priority over concern for the interests of the self.

On the other hand, from the perspective of covenant love the priority of others' interests over one's own is not absolute. The reason is that the self is also one of God's creatures, thereby has worth, and is a member of God's covenant community. This point is more implicit in the New Testament than explicit, but it is nonetheless present. The people who are of more value in God's sight than the birds of the air (Matt. 6:26) obviously include the self; the body that "is a temple of the Holy Spirit" (I Cor. 6:19) is the self's body; the declaration that God loves us is an affirmation of each self, not only of others. To be in covenant is to be in a relationship in which others have obligations to the self, and not only the self to others. While that does not mean that we should be concerned first of all, or primarily, about our own interests (for our duty

117

is primarily to others), it does mean that the self, with whom God has covenanted, is not to be despised or disregarded.

Valerie Saiving has observed that women have a special problem at this point. Their experience is of often being inclined to devalue their femininity and to sacrifice their own development as selves for the sake of husband and children. "A woman can give too much of herself," Saiving writes, "so that nothing remains of her own uniqueness; she can become merely an emptiness, almost a zero, without value to herself, to her fellow men, or perhaps, even to God."[26] Saiving is right that in this situation theologians must encourage women to become individuals in their own right and not simply servants. Commenting on Saiving's insights, Barbara Hilkert Andolsen observes, "The virtues which theologians should be urging upon women as women are autonomy and self-realization," rather than a one-sided self-sacrifice.[27] Yet neither should theologians urge a one-sided autonomy and self-realization. All of us belong with, to, and for one another; none of us is ever literally autonomous—a law unto oneself—nor can we achieve true self-realization except as faithful participants in community. Yet in the framework of community, it is desirable for women and men alike to be autonomous in the sense of taking responsibility for their own decisions and for the direction of their lives, and to seek self-realization in the sense of paying attention to their own needs, feelings, and satisfactions. In a covenantal framework we can move from this kind of autonomy and self-realization to accept our various callings to responsibility toward others. For both men and women what is needed is a sense of the balance and interrelation between being a self and participating responsibly in a community.

Perhaps we can state the qualification on the absoluteness of our duty to give priority to others this way: we ought never to act toward ourselves in a way that inherently expresses lack of respect for our own being—lack of self-acceptance or self-affirmation, in the sense discussed earlier. We are persons for whom Christ died, and therefore we ought always to treat ourselves, as well as others, as ends and never merely as means.

118

That formulation does not prohibit self-sacrifice, for in the act of self-sacrifice we still can and ought to value ourselves, just as in using force against an unjust agent we still can and ought to value that agent (see chapter 7). But it calls into question actions of sacrifice for the sake of sacrifice rather than as the best way under the circumstances to serve the needs of others; actions that punish the self simply for the sake of punishing it (just as it would question such actions toward others); actions that make of the self a mere doormat in the face of others' aggressiveness; actions that waste the self and its resources (that is, spend them for no reason even plausibly sufficient); and actions that embody the judgment that whereas others' needs for the goods of this world matter in God's sight, those of the self do not. All such actions are ways of refusing to be a centered self and of rejecting the worth of the self, and that is as much prohibited by covenant love as is rejection of the worth of others.

This viewpoint can be further supported by what we might call the "infinite regress of self-denial." If one is always obligated to deny the self for some other person, then likewise that other person is obligated to self-denial for others, and so on *ad infinitum*, so that in a situation of insufficient resources an act of service would never reach a self who had any obligation, or even any right, to accept it. Gene Outka gives this illustration of the problem:

> Suppose everyone did act self-sacrificially, would the consequence not be self-frustrating? Consider a passage from the earlist Halachic Midrash, the Sifra. . . . "If two men are traveling on a journey and one has a pitcher of water, if both drink they will both die, but if only one drinks, he will reach civilization." Is it better that both should drink and die rather than that one should witness his companion's death? Or should the one holding the water drink it?[28]

If everyone should be unqualifiedly self-denying, then each should give the water to the other, and so on *ad infinitum*, or until each dies of thirst. The point is that self-sacrifice is not an end in itself, but a means to the service of others. If so, it is because others have a worth appropriate to be served, and if they do, so also does the self. One ought not to act toward oneself as though toward a nothing or a mere means.

All this is far removed from constituting any argument for selfishness or even for mere impartiality as between self and others. It is only, but crucially, an argument for the affirmation of the self as a creature of God, with worth, as others have, for the self's sake. Rather than constituting any argument for self-seeking, it amounts to an argument against giving *absolute* priority to the interests of others.

From the foregoing discussion I conclude that all four of the above arguments point to morally relevant differences between the two types of relationships, that in which the self is moral decider between the interests of two or more others, and the relationship in which the self must decide between its own interests and those of others. The relevant differences are such as to justify giving strong but not absolute priority to others in the latter relationship. This conclusion raises two issues deserving further comment.

Attention to the Self's Interests as a Means of Serving the Interests of Others

The first of these issues is whether the self has an obligation in many respects to look after its own interests for the sake of the interests of others. However much this idea may tempt the self-seeking person to rationalization, it is clear that such an obligation exists. If we are to be capable of serving the interests of other persons, we must in many ways give some concern to our own interests. That is not always the case, nor is it the case regarding all of our interests; many situations arise in which if we are to serve others' needs, we must sacrifice something— some aspect of our own interests. If a person is never externally self-sacrificial, we might justifiably presume that this person simply does not give priority to the interests of others.

But in many respects, and most of the time, there is considerable coincidence of interest between self and others. To that extent, even if the self genuinely intended as an end nothing but the service of others' interests and in no wise wished to serve its own interests for its own sake, nevertheless there would exist an obligation in many ways to look after at least some of the self's interests as a means to the service of others. We ought not, I have said, to treat ourselves, any more than others, as merely means. But we *are* means to the well-being of others and can often be more effective and responsible means by thinking of ourselves than by utterly disregarding ourselves. Thinking of ourselves for the sake of others is what Paul Ramsey has called "enlightened unselfishness," as contrasted with the carelessness-for-self of "*unen*-lightened unselfishness."[29] The difference is this, that an *un*enlightened unselfishness fails to consider that beyond the needs of persons immediately before us there will ordinarily be a host of other needy persons later whom it will also be our obligation to serve. Thus a person who is unselfish in an *un*enlightened way might, for example, take as a literal command the injunction of Jesus to the rich young man in Matthew 19:21 (unselfishly putting aside any concern thereby to "have treasure in heaven"): "Go, sell what you possess and give to the poor . . . ; and come, follow me." And having given away all material goods, that person would have severely diminished the chance of helping anyone thereafter. If we are to follow the spirit of this teaching, that is, if we are to put aside everything that stands between ourselves and utter loyalty to God, then we may indeed be obligated to keep some of our possessions, not selfishly, but insofar as doing so enables us to be better means to the good of our neighbors. So, to quote Ramsey again, one who acts from love may thereby in many situations be motivated "to stay at his post and 'sacrifice the sacrifice' "[30] rather than immediately to dispose of all one's resources or give one's body to be burned.

Certainly persons acting from faith will appropriately believe that under some circumstances their obligation would be to give away all their goods, or even their lives, for the sake of the present needs of others and to retain nothing for their needs in the future. Although one must decide that for oneself, the decision should be made with this question in mind: I can sacrifice everything only once; is this when I ought to do so? It may be that I should. There are of course other possibilities lying between the extreme of no sacrifice and that of giving all our goods or even our lives, ways of being *relatively* sacrificial, so that we might give most or much of our goods to feed the poor but retain some resources against the morrow. To do so is not necessarily to give a lower priority to others' needs in general; it may be simply to give a lower priority to another's need immediately present as compared with others' needs later on. Whatever the decision, it ought insofar as feasible to reflect a weighing of the different claims, present and likely future, upon our resources. Because the objective of covenant love is to meet others' needs rather than to satisfy an inner compulsion to be sacrificial, enlightened unselfishness is its requirement.

The outlook of enlightened unselfishness differs even more sharply, as Ramsey notes, from a third orientation, "enlightened selfishness," from which one might on occasion perform some of the same acts as the unselfish person, but for a markedly different reason. For the person of enlightened *un*selfishness, the intention of caring for the self is to be a better means to the service of others. The intention of the person of enlightened selfishness is quite the reverse: to use others merely as means to the service of the self. But the existence of the temptation to selfishness does not invalidate the obligation to be enlightened in our service of others.

Let us consider some of the different ways we can encounter the obligation to look after interests of the self as a means to serving the interests of others.

1. *The self's interests as directly representative of the interests of others.* Earlier we distinguished between two types of relationships of the self to others. The first, that in which one must decide between the interests of two or more other persons, is of particular significance in this connection. We stand in various special moral relationships to others and thereby occupy various offices, such as parent, spouse, employee, and the like. Imagine, for example, a black couple, both of whom work outside the home, with three small

122

children dependent economically upon their wages. If their employers discriminate against blacks in their wage scales, the parents owe it to their children, other things being equal, to press for fair wages, even though this requires them to advance their own interests in the process. Or King Hussein of Jordan might ask himself whether to acquiesce in the face of pressure from Israel or from Syria to sacrifice the interests of Jordanian citizens. He might conceivably decide that if he were considering only himself, he would be willing to sacrifice those interests. But it is not only his own interests that are at stake; as national leader he represents the interests of many others. That does not mean that their interests can never rightly be sacrificed, but it does mean that a national leader has a serious responsibility to the nation's citizens that sometimes can be met only by protecting his own interests along with theirs. To recall Reinhold Niebuhr's observation, the sacrifice of others' interests is something different from self-sacrifice.

To work from the perspective of covenant love is to know in advance that any moral action occurs within a network of offices and responsibilities and that we must take this network into consideration. It is to know that seldom, if ever, do we act when no one else is in any respect dependent upon us. From covenant love we seek to be faithful to the inclusive covenant and the relevant special covenants of our lives, and never merely to adhere to a standard devised with only an isolated moral agent in mind. All this is simply to draw upon the understanding of vocation—responsibility in the offices to which we have been called.

2. *Asserting one's interests as a discipline to others.* Let us imagine that a Chinese man in a midwestern United States town is being discriminated against in his wages. He has no economic dependents, the company for which he works employs no other Chinese (and there are no others in the community), and the wages, though unfairly low, are quite adequate for his present and foreseeable needs. Ought he simply to accept the unfairly low wages? Not necessarily. It can be argued that he ought to press for just wages, not primarily on his own behalf, but to discourage his employer from such

an unfair practice—to discipline, or we might say educate the employer morally. To whom does he owe this action, given these hypothetical circumstances? For one thing he owes it to the employer, were no one else adversely affected by the action. We do people no service by acquiescing before their unjust acts. They live and act within a covenant community in which they have the obligation to be just, whether or not the victims of their injustice object to the unjust treatment. We communicate an untruth to them and abet their self-delusions if we allow them to persist unchallenged in their unjust actions. Furthermore he owes it to any other Chinese who might later seek a job with that company to resist the injustice, and in this regard he indirectly represents the interests of others—others who may someday be present. But that latter consideration aside, he ought prima facie to resist as a discipline to the unjust.[31] It is of course a different and more complicated question what his *actual* duty is under these circumstances, and we ought not to leap to simple conclusions about it.

3. *Maintaining one's being as a self for others.* Over and beyond our representative and our disciplinary responsibilities, we can identify a third unselfish reason for sometimes asserting our own interests. One can contribute to the interests of other persons simply by being a self in their presence, and even more insofar as one presents oneself to them with some degree of well-being. Let us try to imagine someone who holds no office representative of others' interests: a retired widow with no children, no aged parents, no known relatives, no dependents in the ordinary sense. Our effort is in vain, I suppose, because the widow is still presumably a potential voter, but let us assume even that she has lost her vote because she has committed a felony. Virtually de-officed as she hypothetically is, she asks herself whether, given the shortage of food and other resources in the world, she ought to continue to eat and use up the energy, metals, and other resources it takes to sustain her life. Should she not, she wonders, simply leave the world's resources to others—sacrificially, because she does still enjoy her life. From the standpoint of covenant

love the answer is, I believe, quite clear, even aside from her obligation to herself for her own sake. She ought prima facie to continue to sustain her life, because her very being, her presence, can make a contribution to those she encounters day by day. They are, like her, social creatures, dependent for their psychological well-being upon their encounters with one another, over and above the identifiable material contributions or the official services they receive. Nor are any two persons alike; although the contribution to be made by the presence of any one person is replaceable in the sense that someone else could *equally* contribute, nevertheless no one else can make that *identical* contribution. No one else can enrich another in precisely that way. Our very presence can contribute to the well-being of others and ought prima facie not be denied them. This is to say that we are never really de-officed. We are always in special covenants and are continually entering into still others.

We can press this argument a step further and maintain that for the same reason we ought prima facie to be concerned for our own happiness, insofar as that is something we can intentionally affect.[32] The contribution we make to others by our presence is likely to be the greater insofar as we are happy, rather than sour, toward life. That same consideration is also reinforced by our representative responsibilities to others. We are likely to perform our offices better to the extent that we enjoy doing so and are happy in those responsibilities. Although we would still be obligated to perform most offices even though unhappy in them, still the attitude with which we go about our responsibilities is one of the contributions that we can make to those around us. But apart from our presently existing, formal offices we have an obligation to look after our own being and indeed our own well-being as a means to the well-being of others, because being ourselves before others is potentially a contribution to their lives. In this respect as well as in our representative offices we recognize our participation with one another in a covenant community, and we deny that we are first isolated individuals to whom responsibility must then be added.

Consider how much temptation I am offering to selfishness! Not only have I enjoined the proper love for ourselves and said that the priority of others' interests over those of the self is not absolute, but now I am adding to that the obligation in many respects to look after the self's interests for the sake of others. What more urging does the self need to rationalize all sorts of pursuit of selfish interests under the guise of other-regard? The experience of this very kind of rationalization is a common one. From plausible reasons for not giving *all* our goods right now to feed the poor, the common practice is to give a pittance and bask in luxury while the poor suffer. Even though there is a legitimate basis in other-regard for some degree of concern for the self's health and happiness, it is easy to become preoccupied with our own well-being and to forget the ends toward which it ought to be directed.

But, to repeat, nothing said here justifies a selfish outlook or even an impartial balance between self and others. The obligations of covenant love are strict; they call for reshaping our inner outlook to put others' interests ahead of the self's in word and deed. There is no argument that is immune to misuse, no ethical theory that cannot be twisted by the self-centered self to numb its sense of responsibility to others. What moves a person to concern for others is finally no rational argument, however cogent, but the experience of God's love, making and renewing covenant, and the awareness that fellow covenant members are in need.

Praise and Blame Concerning Self-Sacrificial Actions

The last issue I shall discuss here about the priority of others' interests concerns the appropriateness or inappropriateness of praising persons for going the second mile, or, in contrast, of blaming them for not doing so. Here we encounter conflicting moral considerations. Let us again consider Urmson's example of the soldier who falls on the grenade to save his comrades. It is sometimes observed that we would not appropriately blame a person—one of the other soldiers, for example—for not being sacrificial in that way, but that we should especially praise someone who was. In contrast we *would* appropriately blame a soldier for not performing institutional duties—for going to sleep while on guard duty, for example; and we should certainly *not* praise one, at least not under ordinary circumstances, for staying awake. There is certainly an attraction in that way of thinking. From the standpoint of covenant love, however, there is something morally lacking, something that *ought* to be done, on the part of the soldiers who do not sacrifice their lives to save their comrades. Otherwise how are we to make sense of the note of command in Jesus's injunctions to turn the other cheek, go the second mile, and love the neighbor as the self? As Calvin declared, they do indeed come to us as commands and not merely counsels. How shall we respond to these conflicting moral considerations?

The answer calls for a distinction between (1) judgments about ordinary situations where sacrificial action is needed, and (2) judgments about especially difficult conflicts of claims upon the self to be sacrificial.

1. Whether it is appropriate to blame someone for not performing a second-mile action depends upon whether that person ought to have performed it—whether it was in that broad sense a duty. I have maintained above that from the standpoint of covenant love we have a duty, and not only the freedom and the right, to give a higher priority to the interests of others than to our own. That is true precisely regarding sacrificial actions, because the very act of according another's interests priority over one's own is to a degree sacrificial. The idea that second-mile actions are not duties is a reflection of ordinary conventional morality, not of the requirements of covenant love. In a Christian context "second mile" should be understood to mean "over and beyond what is ordinarily expected," or "over and beyond what is institutionally required," and not "over and beyond what love requires." If by the strict requirements of covenant love a person ought to have gone the second mile—ought in the case of the grenade to have attempted to fall upon it—then that person is to be blamed for not having done so. That is true even if it is still the case that we remain surprised to see anyone do it and judge

that person's moral heroism to be several cuts above the ordinary. The Christian, realistic about the weakness of the will, believes that we stand under more stringent moral demands than we are likely to perform, but those demands remain our obligation nonetheless. The requirements of any adequate ethic cannot merely be expressions of a conventional morality.

If in a given situation a person ought actually to have sacrificed for the interests of others—ought actually to have fallen upon the grenade—as sometimes one ought, then that person is properly to be blamed for not doing so. Nor do we earn any special merit if we do sacrifice ourselves. However heroic our deeds, we remain in this sense unworthy servants, justified by God's grace and not by our works. Let us not misunderstand. It is quite another matter whether anyone ought to *verbalize* that blame to a soldier who did not sacrifice himself. We have no call to be self-righteous, and what we say by way of blame in such a situation, even if properly thought out, may well be misunderstood. Nor do we mean by "blame" anything like self-rejection. Blame refers here to moral disapproval of one's performance (or nonperformance) of an act, or of one's character; it does not entail rejection of the person, whether someone else or oneself.

It might be rejoined that the only person who should be blamed for not being sacrificial is one who has made a special commitment to a sacrificial way of life, someone, say, like Albert Schweitzer. We can readily grant that if anyone does make such a commitment, there is then special reason for blame in case of nonperformance, but in addition the rejoinder suggests that the blame is out of place in the absence of the special commitment. The implication is that readiness to be especially sacrificial where needed is not an obligation upon persons as such. But that implication does not fit with normative Christian ethics as interpreted here. How would there ever be a good reason to blame someone for not undertaking the initial commitment to a sacrificial way of life? Would the commitment to that way of life be merely a matter of personal preference, and one person's preferences as duty-fulfilling as another's? It is difficult to reconcile that view with the tone of the New Testament injunctions to righteousness beyond the ordinary. The early Christians believed, moreover, that they were to declare Jesus Christ to the whole world, not only among themselves. One would suppose then that they were to declare to everyone the moral outlook and way of life appropriate to followers of Jesus Christ. It follows from this belief that every person ultimately has the duty to give priority to the interests of others, whether or not one has yet made such a commitment. On this issue we must avoid a concession to conventional morality on the one hand, and on the other, a reduction of this aspect of Christian ethics to a way of life for a particular special community.

2. We need to distinguish the above type of judgment from judgments about situations where one claim upon the self to be sacrificial conflicts with another claim to do likewise. The difficulty we encounter over whether we ought to be sacrificial is often a question of whether to be sacrificial now or later. Shall we give up all our resources for the needy people immediately before us or save back something to enable us to meet the additional needy people who will appear tomorrow? We may very well be convinced we should act sacrificially, but still be unclear whether or to what extent we should do so now. The problem is compounded when we try to judge what someone else should do. Then, as Outka observes,[33] we are less likely to be in possession of the relevant information than the other person is. Furthermore, perhaps we should give the other person the benefit of the doubt, especially where the information we have does not clearly lead to one and only one assuredly right conclusion. Therefore even though persons have a duty to do second-mile actions in behalf of others, it is not always clear when and in what respects they should do so.

The upshot of this reasoning is twofold. (1) We should recognize that an ethic of covenant love is a strict and demanding ethic, to the point of self-sacrifice in behalf of others. (2) It behooves us to be continually conscious of the difficulties of judging precisely when and how one ought to be sacrificial, especially when the person in question is someone else. There is no logical contradiction between these two assertions. The distinction between commands and counsels is still useful, not in regard to the accumulation of merit, nor in distinguishing second-mile actions from basic institutional requirements, but in judgments about particular cases where it is not altogether clear what one's obligation is, and especially where the judgment is about someone else's action.

I have made two main assertions about this first question of priority in dealing with conflicting moral claims. The first is that from the standpoint of covenant love we have an obligation to love ourselves in the right way, which way is fully compatible with covenant love for others and stands in sharp contrast to selfishness. The second is that from this same perspective we have a strong and ever-present, but not absolute, duty to give priority to the interests of others above our own. This priority is less than absolute because of our obligation not to disregard or reject ourselves, not to treat ourselves as worthless in God's sight. Yet that obligation can be fulfilled in the midst of the utmost sacrifice of our own resources where the needs of others require it.

5

Moral Conflicts II: Conflicting Obligations to Different Covenants

Everyone belongs simultaneously to many covenants: to the inclusive covenant by virtue of God's covenant with all people, and to various special covenants through the special interactions into which each one of us has entered. Each of us lives in a web of multiple interrelated covenants. Because of this multiplicity conflicts arise continually in each person's life between the moral claims (real or supposed) of one covenant and those of another. The question of this chapter is how the covenant model with its standard of covenant love can provide some guidance for us in this kind of conflict. How does it help us to determine which covenant's claims should have priority?

I shall discuss this issue by a two-step process. The first will be to show that the moral claims of any valid covenant do prima facie obligate its members. The presumption is therefore always in favor of the moral claims of any existing valid covenant. The second step will be to identify ways that this presumption can be rebutted in certain kinds of conflict situations, as it necessarily must be in one way or another.

The Presumption in Favor of the Moral Claims of a Covenant

The Inclusive Covenant

The inclusive covenant is the whole of humanity created to live in covenant with God and one another.

The moral claims of the inclusive covenant include the claims to honor everyone's human rights—those rights that belong to each person because of what it means truly to be created a human being, and not because of any transaction or agreement into which people have entered. It should be self-evident that there is a strong presumption in favor of meeting each and every human right. Otherwise we could scarcely be talking about morality, which has to do with the responsibilities of human beings in their interrelationships and in which each person is obligated to be concerned for the true humanity of every other.

At the same time it is only a presumption, even though a strong one. A human right is as such not necessarily absolute, in the sense of "absolutely exceptionless" in an unlimited scope of life.[1] It is not our actual duty to meet the moral claims of every human right. If, for example, the right to free speech is a human right—if every person ought to have the moral freedom to speak her or his mind—that does not mean that this right is unlimited. There will be circumstances in which it is justifiable to limit this freedom. It is not morally permissible, for example, to shout "Fire" in a crowded theater when there is no fire. Absoluteness is not part of the meaning of human rights, but a characteristic that may or may not belong to any particular human right. When two human rights conflict, one of them has to give way, and that right cannot be absolute. Furthermore, if one person's free speech ever had to be limited for the sake of someone else's free speech, then that right could not be absolute. And so it is with nearly all rights, both human and special.

Special Covenants

Special covenants are relationships of entrusting and accepting entrustment that arise out of special historical transactions between the members and that include some but not all human beings. Their moral claims include special rights, which come to belong to their members because of these special transactions. A few of the many types of special covenants, as we have discussed earlier, are families, corporations, labor unions, churches, and nation-states.

Some human categories are not special covenants, however; they are social classifications rather than social relationships. This is true of, say, left-handedness. If we speak of all left-handed persons, we are discussing a classification, but not ordinarily an actual relationship among people. Left-handed people are not ordinarily related to one another as an entrusting and entrustment-accepting group; hence they are not a special covenant, though a covenant group of lefties could come into being. I recall an effort of some fellow students in my high school days to form a left-handed club. Their aim included affirming the interests and rights of lefties in a right-handed culture. There is much sense in the idea. The group was sufficiently inclusive to encourage my member- ship, even though I am right-handed. That suggests that what they were was not so much a group of lefties (though most of them were) as a group opposed to discrimination against lefties—an important distinction. Ordinarily lefties constitute a social classification, not a special covenant.

With that distinction in mind we need to ask whether males as such constitute a special covenant, or females, or blacks, or whites, or various other social groups. The answer depends upon the social circumstances. If there is no pattern of discrimination in a given society against some classification— women, blacks, and so forth—and if those in the classification do not band together on the basis of the commonly shared feature (femaleness, blackness, etc.), then they remain a classification but not a special covenant. But if, as in our society, there are patterns of discrimination against people because of such characteristics, and if therefore some with those characteristics band together, they have become a special covenant. When males or whites band together to discriminate against females or blacks, they also become a special covenant, though it is one whose unjust claims, like those of a robber band, come into conflict with the claims of the inclusive covenant and must be set aside. But we shall get to that subject later in this chapter.

Apart from such claims that conflict with people's human rights, there is in general a presumption in favor of the moral claims of each special covenant. The fact that we are members of a given special covenant constitutes a good and sufficient reason for honoring its moral claims, in the absence of conditions justifying the overriding of those claims.

First, this is true because we are finite. Because it is not possible for us effectively to meet everyone else's needs in all respects, special covenants are ways of identifying whose needs we should take as our special responsibilities. Through our interactions we become specially obligated to *this* spouse, *these* children, *these* fellow citizens, *these* colleagues, and the like. In some of our special covenants it is fair to speak of our having to a significant extent elected to be in them; in others we do not elect at all, but are elected, as in having these parents or initially being citizens of the country in which we were born. In most relationships the elements of choosing and of being chosen are intermingled, but however that may be, the interactions are *covenantal* in the sense in which I have been using that term. Whatever the degree of choice, we have these special relationships because we cannot have all possible persons as spouse, children, fellow citizens, or colleagues. Before the special interaction took place, those persons had no greater claim upon us than any other members of the inclusive covenant; afterward they have special claims that others do not have.

The Protestant Reformers' doctrine of vocation recognizes the limits of human capabilities as a reason for special responsibilities. Calvin expresses this idea in his discussion of callings:

> The Lord bids each one of us in all life's actions to look to his station. For he knows with what great restlessness human nature flames, with what fickleness it is borne hither and thither, how its

ambition longs to embrace various things at once. Therefore, lest through our stupidity and rashness everything be turned topsy-turvy, he has appointed duties for every man in his particular way of life. And that no one may thoughtlessly transgress his limits, he has named these various kinds of living "callings." Therefore each individual has his own kind of living assigned to him by the Lord as a sort of sentry post so that he may not heedlessly wander about throughout life.[2]

Not to recognize and affirm our finiteness through entering into some set of special covenants, "livings" as well as other special relationships, would indeed be to "wander heedlessly about throughout life." This is why we must and do enter into some set of special covenants, rather than relate to everybody simply as human-to-human in the inclusive covenant.

Second, once we do enter into a special covenant, it is binding upon us because through our special interaction with others we have obligated ourselves to them in special ways. We can obligate ourselves in special covenants either through explicit promises or through actions that obligate even in the absence of any promise.

G. Russell Grice offers an illuminating explanation of why promises specially obligate.[3] When we promise, he says, we are not simply asserting that something is or is not the case. What we are doing, instead, is "placing ourselves under an obligation." This is why we do not properly judge a promise to be correct or incorrect, but instead sincere or insincere, binding or (sometimes) not binding, and eventually kept or broken. The answer to why promises obligate, he observes, depends upon *whose* good should be served, and not only *how much* good will be done. Some utilitarians would say that a promise obligates only insofar as keeping it would produce a greater balance of good over evil in the world than not keeping it. Grice argues that this answer is inadequate because it ignores the question of who is to receive the good. We can express his idea this way: if Smith has promised Jones a job and Smith keeps the promise, Jones benefits. If instead Smith breaks the promise and gives the job to Brown, perhaps in order to produce a greater balance of good, Brown benefits. But because Smith promised Jones, Jones is specially entitled to the benefit, whereas Brown is not. Smith has created a prima facie obligation to Jones by the very act of promising.

John Rawls significantly elaborates this kind of explanation.[4] Fidelity to promises, he writes, is a special case of fairness. The principle of fairness requires us to perform our institutional obligations when two conditions are met. One condition is that "one has voluntarily accepted the benefits of the arrangement or taken advantage of the opportunities it offers to further one's interests." We do just that when we engage in promising and accepting promises. Because we accept benefits that come to us when others promise and keep their promises, we are thereby obligated to do likewise—not because promising is socially useful, but because doing otherwise would be unfair to others. The other condition is that the relevant institution within which the promise is made must be just; promises within an unjust social structure may not actually obligate because of the injustice.

Why, though, should we be concerned whether the one benefits who is entitled to do so, or whether we act fairly? In terms of the standard of covenant love, we should be concerned because each person has worth as a member of God's inclusive covenant. The one to whom we specially obligate ourselves when we promise is someone who has a worth in God's sight equal to that of every other person. That is finally why we must take our self-obligating actions with great seriousness. It is true, as Rawls says, that fidelity to promises is a special case of fairness. But fairness is in turn a case—one of the most fundamental cases, we might say—of fidelity in a broader sense than promises, fidelity among the members of God's inclusive covenant.

This explanation of why promises specially obligate applies also to many special interactions in the absence of promises. To conceive a child, to injure someone accidentally, or to gain significant power over others: interactions like these are specially obligating, whether accompanied by promises or not, for reasons similar to those just offered.

In summary, special covenants are ways of identifying those

to whom we in our finiteness have special responsibilities, or callings. In these special relationships we obligate ourselves with and without explicit promises to specific persons who are thereby entitled to our performing the obligation. Where a special covenant exists, therefore, there is a rebuttable presumption that our actual obligation is to honor its moral claims. I must emphasize, though, that the presumption is rebuttable. That is true because of the inevitable conflict among the multiplicity of covenant claims, even when the claims on both sides of the conflict are valid. It is true furthermore because some special covenant claims are unjust.

Rebutting the Presumption

The moral claims of special covenants can be justifiably overridden under some kinds of circumstances. To think otherwise would require the assumption that the claims of different special covenants can never come into conflict, whereas we frequently experience these conflicts. Also it would lead us to absolutize "the duties of one's station," to believe that whatever our special covenants require, we are always to do. Although it is impossible to live out that position consistently in practice because of the fact of conflicting legitimate claims, it sometimes receives lip service and is practiced to some degree with one or another station. It is more realistic and more expressive of a Christian recognition of the limited authority of all human groups to recognize that the claims of every special covenant must sometimes give way to other claims.

Two types of conflict of moral claims occur in which it can be justifiable to override special claims: conflicts between the claims of two or more special covenants, and conflicts between the claims of a special covenant and those of the inclusive covenant.

When the Claims of Different Special Covenants Conflict

It is a common experience that two or more special covenants can place irreconcilable claims upon us, even where either claim by itself might be legitimate. A parent is asked to choose between making a substantial monetary gift to a deserving organization to which he or she belongs and putting aside the money for the children's education. A labor union official pledges support to a political candidate only to discover during the campaign that the candidate supports certain policies that would probably be harmful to the union. When legitimate special covenant claims conflict, is there any general moral guidance to be found? How does an ethic of covenant love help to shape our response to this kind of moral conflict?

It may help us as we reflect upon this issue if we keep two cases in mind for illustrative purposes. In the first, Bill is an associate pastor of a large congregation. (If you prefer, imagine him to be a physician, attorney, company executive, professor, psychological counselor, or occupant of any other position where the working hours cannot readily be confined to forty per week and often spread into the evenings and weekends. The problems will be similar.) Bill is expected by his colleagues on the church staff and by lay members to give several evenings a week to meetings at the church. In addition denominational superiors expect him to attend frequent out-of-town meetings from which he is often unable to return before eleven or twelve at night. His wife, Martha, teaches mornings at a neighborhood kindergarten and is involved in various voluntary activities as her time allows. They have three children, ages nine, seven, and five. Bill and Martha have become increasingly aware over the past three years that Bill has little free time to be with the family except on his day off, and even then his mind is still burdened by thoughts of work he has not completed. The result is considerable tension in all the family relationships. Yet the church needs for him to carry that kind of schedule and benefits from his doing so. In this conflict between his obligations to his work and to his wife and children, which should have priority and to what extent?

The second case is an ongoing legislative issue of which we need to offer only a bare outline for present purposes. To what extent ought the government to insure that adequate health care is available for its citizens, and to what extent, in contrast, should the various private organizations of the society, and especially private health insurance organizations, the medical profession, and individual families, perform this function?

In both these cases we can distinguish two kinds of ethical questions. The first is the *substantive* question: which of Bill's obligations ought to have priority, and where should responsibility lie for the availability of adequate health care? But for our purposes a *methodological* question is more important: how should we go about determining an answer to questions like these? What criteria and reasoning should we follow? Before we discuss the methodological question, we need to clarify it somewhat further.

First, we are not directly concerned here with matters of tactics: for example, how Bill and Martha communicate with each other or what methods legislators use to try to enact (or prevent enactment of) health care legislation. Tactical questions are morally important, but here they would draw us aside from our main question, which is the issue of priorities when special covenant claims come into conflict.

Second, the conflicts posed in these cases are not merely conflicts of value, but also conflicts of prima facie obligations. The question is not only whether the good of family life or the good of pursuit of one's occupation is the higher; it is whether Bill is obligated in one relationship in a way that should have priority over the other. It is not only whether the good of private initiative and control or the good of public responsibility for equal treatment is the higher; it is also whether legislators have an obligation to relate to their citizens' health needs in the one way or the other. Weighing values is not the only, nor even the primary, way to arrive at a judgment about obligation, though it is important. We must ask what kind of moral claims people have upon one another; the possible attainment of good things is only one of several considerations that give rise to moral claims. Our need then is not merely "values clarification," but more nearly "obligations clarification."

Third, we can approach our issue of priority either in terms of the inner orientation or disposition of the moral agent or the outer shape of the acts and policies, or both. Cases like these pose both issues. They can give rise to conflicts of inner loyalties: How can Bill simultaneously be loyal both as a family member and as a member of his church staff? How can legislators inwardly accept their responsibility both to the private individuals and groups of the society and also to the political society as a community? From another standpoint, however, the focus can be upon the external actions or policies that should be adopted, apart from whether those who adopt them are fully loyal participants in their various relationships. Ordinarily, though, both issues intrude themselves and become intertwined. Our loyalties and dispositions shape the actions or policies we choose, and the actions or policies express our inner inclinations, however indirectly and implicitly. I shall focus here initially upon the question of priority in our external actions and policies. In the types of cases before us, there is no *necessary* conflict of loyalties involved. Even so, serious conflicts of priority can arise.

Some ways of answering the methodological question, how to go about determining which set of moral claims should have priority when special covenant claims conflict, are clearly inadequate. On the one extreme is the totalitarian response, which places absolute priority on the claims of the larger and more inclusive organization, most especially the nation-state, and judges that the claims of all other groups ought to give way before it. This response denies that other kinds of human relationships have their own proper place and functions. It views the state as the only social entity that matters and seeks to reduce all other human relationships to serve its purposes. In so doing it is prepared to inflict whatever harm is necessary to enforce its will.

At the other extreme is the individualistic response, which puts absolute priority upon the wishes and desires of the various individuals in society. It denies that social groups are morally any more than the sum of their individual members, any more than conveniences or obstructions to the objectives of individuals. It denies that participation in social groups inherently obligates the members. It refuses to grant that belonging to a family or economic institution or nation-state inherently carries with it moral claims upon the members.

Both totalitarianism and individualism reject a covenant interpretaton of human social life, although for opposing reasons. Both are proposed today in various quarters, but neither is able to give an adequate answer to the question of priorities. Between these extremes, however, there are several plausible answers to the question. Let us consider three possibilities.

1. *Decision in terms of the purposes of the special covenants.* One way to approach this priority question is to identify the purposes of each relevant type of social relationship—family, church, economic group, the state—and to assign priority to each type in the area of its distinctive purposes. This is an approach congenial, as far as it goes, with much of Roman Catholic as well as Protestant thought, both of which have had much to say about the purposes of the major types of human relationships.

Regarding the case of Bill and Martha, one would use this approach by identifying the purposes of marriage and of the church. We might focus upon two traditional purposes of marriage. procreation and companionship; we might identify the church's purpose as the proclamation in word and deed of the good news of God's action in Jesus Christ. Regarding the case of health care legislation, the issue would center around whether one of the state's proper purposes is to promote the general welfare (including the health care) of its people, or whether its purposes should be restricted more to the negative action of providing a secure order within which private groups can pursue welfare goals.

The contrast between the two cases is instructive. The question of purpose is directly relevant to a decision about the health care question, however unsettled the debate is between the two opposed conceptions of the state. On the other hand, identifying the purposes of family and church offers little help in the case of Bill and Martha. That conflict does not hinge so much upon determining the purposes of the two endeavors as it does upon the question of how Bill should distribute his time and other resources between the two.

This contrast suggests that identifying the proper purposes of a particular type of special covenant will be essential and directly relevant to decisions about what kinds of functions are appropriate to it. On the other hand, identifying purposes will not as readily be helpful when two covenants of different types come into conflict over the use of resources such as time, money, and other evidences of concern.

One of the weaknesses of decision in terms of purposes is that it tends to focus our attention upon *types* of special covenants—the state, the church, the economic institution, the family—rather than upon specific special covenants—Bill and Martha's marriage; the First United Methodist Church of Centerville; Blue Cross; the United States government.[5] Yet all such conflicts are between specific special covenants, not only between types. Special obligations are shaped, not only by the type of relationship, but also by the distinctive features of that specific group; for example, Martha might be blind, or the First United Methodist Church of Centerville might be in the midst of a severe crisis. We need to ask not merely how to set the priorities in general, but how to do so in a way that will take account of the specific conflict at hand. Identification of the purposes of types of special covenants is a necessary step, but it does not provide all the assistance that is needed.

2. *The principle of subsidiarity.* This principle has found expression in several papal encyclicals of the past century and in some other Roman Catholic works.[6] It presupposes attention to the purpose and nature of each major type of social relationship, but carries this concern a step further. The principle contains two parts, one negative and the other positive. The negative side declares that it is wrong to assign functions to a larger and higher organization that can be adequately performed by a smaller and lower organization. This has been called the principle of noninterference. The positive side is the principle of assistance, by which the larger and higher organization should assist the smaller and lower,

as well as individual members, when they are unable to meet their basic needs.

So understood, the principle of subsidiarity does not appear to apply to the interrelations of all human associations, at least not directly, but only to those that are hierarchical, as the relationship between a state and other associations within it, or between any hierarchical organization, such as a corporation, labor union, religious denomination, or university, and its component parts and individual members.

This application is apparent in the following expression of the principle by Father Bernard Häring:

> The state must respect the family in its precedence over the state itself. . . . [T]he family is historically and metaphysically "prior to the state and is the more original." Wherefore the state must be painfully aware of the basic rights of the family and its fundamental structure in the social order. It may not appropriate to itself anything which is within the reach of the family's power and will. What the family within the limits of its own natural capacities is able and willing to do, must be left to the family. The state must grant to the family every help and support which it requires to maintain and fulfill its duties. The principle of subsidiarity must be maintained inviolably in the relations between the family and the more comprehensive societies, especially between family and state.[7]

This is not an individualistic position. It grows out of traditional Catholic belief in the social nature of the human being and concern for the common good. On the one hand, it provides a check against the tendency of large organizations to imperialize over their subordinate groups and members. On the other, it affirms the responsibility of large organizations to assist those under them in their proper functioning. It brings Catholic teaching about the nature and purposes of family, state, church, and other institutions to bear upon judgments about what the larger and higher organization may and may not do.

Clearly there is much to be said for this position's judgments both about the major types of human associations and about subsidiarity. The properly functioning family is indeed fundamental to the well-being both of individuals and of the wider society. It needs to be guarded against the efforts of other social groups, economic and religious as well as political, to override its interests for the sake of their own. If we can picture the relation of employer (in Bill's case, the local church) to employee and employee's family as a hierarchical one, then a strong case can be made for judging that the employer should take great pains not to place destructive pressures upon the families of employees. The case might also be pressed that ordinarily Bill's prior responsibility is to his wife and children, at least to a considerable extent.

Even so, and all apart from the question of what this would mean for Bill's specific actions, the principle of subsidiarity is not an entirely satisfactory way of dealing with the conflict between special covenants. Father Häring qualifies his judgment with the phrases "within the reach of the family's power and will" and "what the family within the limits of its own natural capacities is able and willing to do." Phrases like these remind us that under contemporary social conditions the family is not fully free to pursue its traditional purposes, for example, the education of children. Too many social conditions intervene, conditions over which hierarchical organizations have only limited control. Bill's problem is not necessarily that his employers and colleagues want to dominate his time. It is the way people's needs impinge upon him, and the fact that, given his training and occupational choice and the way social institutions are organized, he must seek to meet most of these needs primarily outside his home. The conflict of claims between work and family is such that he cannot simply say either that those of his church work should always take priority, or that those of his family should. He must establish some kind of viable pattern of distribution of time and concern, and then continue to make hard decisions day by day. The principle of subsidiarity can help to set some limits, but it does not provide any simple resolution of the conflict.

We can see the same limitation upon the helpfulness of the principle in other applications. Consider this statement of Pope Pius XI:

It is indeed true, as history clearly proves, that owing to the change in social conditions, much that was formerly done by small bodies can nowadays be accomplished only by large corporations. None the less, just as it is wrong to withdraw from the individual and commit to the community at large what private enterprise and industry can accomplish, so, too, it is an injustice, a grave evil and disturbance of right order for a large and higher organization to arrogate to itself functions which can be performed efficiently by smaller and lower bodies.[8]

How are we to apply this teaching to the question of health care? Can or cannot this need any longer be met by private enterprise and industry? Yet the issue is not so much whether private efforts *can* provide health care, but whether leaders of private groups will be able and disposed to do so justly. It is not only whether public programs can provide health care with greater justice, but also whether they can provide it in proper quality and without undue waste of resources and initiative. In raising these questions I am assuming that the principle of subsidiarity has a valid point (its negative and positive sides taken together). The principle is so general, however, that it does not resolve the priority question. The debate over which level can better perform a function like providing health care is likely to be dominated by the prior political philosophical inclinations of the disputants, rather than be illuminated by the principle.

Even so, the principle of subsidiarity contains considerable wisdom. Surely where a needed social function *can* be accomplished equally well at a level of society closer to individual persons, that is a weighty reason for doing it there. Surely too, the converse is true, as the principle presupposes, that where an essential social need cannot be met as well at a lower or smaller level, it should be done at the higher level rather than be ineffectively or unjustly done, or undone, to the distress of the members of society.

3. *The activity of covenanting.* Unlike either of the first two approaches, this one focuses upon the acts by which the special covenant members entrust and accept entrustment with one another. What is central to this approach is not the

purposes of one or another type of special covenant, but the ways in which the members have come to be obligated to one another.[9] We can identify several kinds of characteristics that might be present in the activity of covenanting that would have a bearing upon priorities.

a. A particular person may be relatively irreplaceable in the functioning of one special covenant, but more easily replaceable in the functioning of another. Bill is relatively irreplaceable in his marriage, but he is relatively replaceable in his work. If he does not function effectively as husband and father, the family can ordinarily not arrange for these functions to be performed by someone else without breaking up the marriage. In regard to his work, however, it is not only possible that he might change jobs, but also that (ordinarily) the job description of associate pastor might be revised somewhat more easily and flexibly than that of husband and father. This is not always the case; he may be the only person available who can keep a large and vital organization from collapsing, or his job may inherently, and not only incidentally, be enormously demanding, like that of President or Secretary of State of the United States.

b. The effects upon the other members of nonperformance of a special covenant function can vary on a continuum from extremely harmful to mildly inconvenient. If Bill's home responsibilities are slightly inconvenienced by the expectations upon him at work, that is not sufficient justification for not meeting those expectations, even if the result of not meeting them were to be a slightly greater balance of good over evil effects for everybody concerned. As between covenants, we ought not simply to weigh total effects. Because in each special covenant we have committed ourselves to certain people and because those people therefore have a right to our honoring the commitment, the burden of proof is upon us to justify not doing so. Mild inconvenience elsewhere is not ordinarily a sufficient justification. On the other hand, an emergency or extreme harmfulness does ordinarily suffice as a justification. If there will probably be dire effects upon Bill's marriage if he does everything his church leaders expect, that

146

should be ample reason for the appropriate church authorities to reconsider their expectations, and for other institutions to do likewise regarding thousands of other "Bills."

Similarly, imagine that I have promised to meet three friends at 2:00 P.M. for a round of golf. If at 1:50 I decide that it would be useful for me to get a little more work done that day, that is hardly a sufficient reason, at that late hour, for me to break the promise, even a promise to play golf. I should have thought of that earlier. On the other hand, if at 1:50 a colleague complains of a severe pain in the lower right abdomen, I should have no hesitation about breaking the promise to play golf while I drive the colleague to the emergency room.

c. Sometimes it turns out that it would be worse for the other members of a special covenant if a commitment were kept than if it were broken in favor of a conflicting obligation. The others in the golf foursome may have discovered the truth about my golf game (how poor it is!) since I made the appointment to join them. One of them might say to me, in a gentle understatement, "Look, if you're not all that eager to play, don't feel you have to come!" Or the church staff might become aware that by having so many evening meetings they are considerably increasing the church's utility costs and might decide to restrict their evening meetings to no more than two nights a week, to the benefit of Bill's family and perhaps many other people.

d. It is sometimes relevant to priorities that one commitment has been made earlier than another. That is often the case where they are commitments of the same kind. If, for example, I sell the same car successively to two different individuals, the first buyer presumably has the valid claim to it. Where the transactions are of different kinds, this criterion is less likely to help. Whether Bill and Martha have been married longer than Bill has worked at that church, or vice versa, would not be decisive.

e. Is it a valid criterion that giving priority to one of the conflicting covenants would have serious harmful effects upon the *agent*, whereas giving it to the other would not? Perhaps, but perhaps not. It depends upon the nature of the special covenant. Marriage vows explicitly consider this possibility when they specify that each is to be loyal to the other "for better, for worse, for richer, for poorer, in sickness and in health . . . till death us do part." In the relationship of marriage—one in which those vows are appropriate to the nature of the special covenant—each member has put aside the possibility of pleading harmful personal effects, at least as long as the other person remains loyal in the marriage. But if the question is not the commitment to the relationship, but the commitment to certain external behavior in the relationship (e.g., never to have night meetings, or to be available for night work whenever needed), then the plea of serious harmful effects may be completely valid. It may justify revising the stipulations of that special covenant, though that should ordinarily be a matter for discussion among the fellow covenant members and should not be done in a way that strikes at the very nature and purpose of that type of covenant.

These are some of the ways that the activity of covenanting, in whatever type of special covenant, can help us to assign priorities when conflicts arise. This approach does not necessarily conflict with the first two; they might be combined. In fact, the third involves assumptions at many points about the nature and purposes of the types of covenants, and it reasons from these assumptions in its judgments about harmful effects.

Even if we use all these approaches together, there will be many circumstances in which they are inconclusive, or in which it will be possible for people of good will to come to opposite conclusions. When the claims of special covenants conflict, there is some moral guidance to be found, both in a covenant model of morality and in other ideas. It is not the case in such conflicts that whatever anyone decides is thereby right. Yet there is considerable room to defend different opinions on the issue. Perhaps this is one reason that conflicts of this kind are so troublesome: they often do not have clearly compelling moral solutions.

When the Claims of a Special Covenant Conflict with Those of the Inclusive Covenant

Conflicts of this kind occur when some special covenant calls upon its members to override someone's human rights—those either of its own members or of nonmembers. When this happens, that special covenant stands in conflict with the inclusive covenant of all God's children, because, as we have seen, the rights people have by virtue of membership in the inclusive covenant are human rights.

It is characteristic of conflicts of this kind that the members of a special covenant are rebelling against the inclusive covenant and are seeking to override human rights. In this sense the special covenant members express some kind of chauvinism, not only in its subconscious and unintentional manifestations, but consciously and intentionally.

One way they do this is by unjustifiably excluding some from membership or from equal concern; for example, on the basis of race or sex. Where this exclusion is consciously intended, it tends to be accompanied by an elaborate and self-righteous fabric of rationalization. So white racists have developed doctrines of the supposed inherited inferiority of blacks, and anti-Semites their theories of supposed diabolical schemes of Jews. Similarly many who seek to protect the traditional status of males have put forward biological theories of inherent female inferiority, or theological theories whereby God has ordained males to superior roles.

Exclusivists are not above defending their position with a theological doctrine of covenant. Such is the case with the Afrikaners in the Republic of South Africa. A major element in the tradition underlying their theories of *apartheid* and "separate development" is their idea that in a time of great crisis in their history God entered into a covenant with the Boer people and gave them victory over their enemies. Celebration of the Day of Covenant, December 16, has continued into present times as the most revered occasion in Afrikaner "civil religion."[10] In this imagery the idea is expressed that God has elected the Afrikaner people to special favor and wills its separation from peoples of other races. Covenant imagery is thus part of the whole web of argument by which Afrikaners seek to justify the special privileges they enjoy in their domination over black Africans, coloureds, and Asians in the Republic of South Africa.

The contrast could not be sharper between the Afrikaners' racist doctrine of covenant and the New Testament proclamation that in Jesus Christ is declared God's intention of covenant with all people. The Afrikaner covenant is a defense of domination and privilege; the inclusive covenant calls upon us to lose ourselves for the sake of others. The Afrikaner covenant calls its members especially to serve those of their own ethnic or cultural group; the inclusive covenant calls all persons to universal responsibility and sends believers to "all the world." In the Afrikaner covenant the members are biological as well as cultural descendants of the in-group; in the inclusive covenant "children of Abraham"—persons of faith—can be raised up from the stones. Nor should we suppose that the idea of special covenants explained in this chapter gives any aid and comfort to the chauvinism of the Afrikaner covenant. The Afrikaner doctrine only shows to what a degree the biblical proclamation of God's election of a people to covenant can be distorted. It is encouraging to read, however, that on 9 June 1982, a group of 123 white ministers of the Dutch Reformed Church in South Africa issued a letter declaring that *apartheid*, with the social order built on it, "is unacceptable" and "cannot be defended scripturally," and calling for "equal treatment and opportunities" for all people.[11]

Whatever the ideology it puts forward, social exclusivism of this kind is a denial of human rights. It is a denial that there is in God's intention an inclusive covenant. If its beliefs are nevertheless expressed in traditional Christian symbols, that is possible only as it twists the Christian proclamation into a tribal doctrine. Regardless of its ideology or symbolism, such social exclusivism cannot adequately express the worship of the God declared in Jesus Christ.

The other characteristic way in which special covenants conflict with the inclusive covenant is through group egoism, that is, the inordinate assertion of the claims of one special covenant over against all other claims. Group egoism may or may not be exclusivist; it is perfectly possible on the part of a group that is open to members from all walks of life, such as a nation-state. Group egoism is found in all special covenants in some degree, even when the moral claims inordinately asserted would otherwise be legitimate. We are especially familiar with it in its forms of nationalism, the self-seeking of economic organizations, the extremes to which parents sometimes go in giving priority to their own children's well-being over that of other people's children, and the self-righteousness with which religious groups sometimes seek to dominate a community's life. No social group is immune to this temptation; it is an expression of human distrust in God's grace, not merely of variable social conditions. Some special covenants find their very reason for being in the denial of the inclusive covenant and its claims, as in the case of organized crime, which exists to gain profit, prestige, and power by taking unfair advantage of the weak.

Undue loyalty to any one special covenant is necessarily accompanied by disloyalty to the inclusive covenant, by the inclination to disregard human rights for the sake of one's own group. We should distinguish here between this rebellious view and a very different kind of viewpoint that is disposed to recognize and to honor human rights but that is beset by perplexity over how to do so in especially difficult conflicts of claims. How, for example, is United States society to go about eradicating long-standing injustices against blacks in some situations without at the same time unjustly discriminating against individuals of other groups today? It can and must be done, but doing it is not simple. We must distinguish, that is, between this very real perplexity and any viewpoint that simply does not take all people's human rights seriously. It is the latter that constitutes group egoism. Inordinately to exalt a special covenant in that way is to deny, implicitly or explicitly, that the inclusive covenant is the decisive human relationship; indeed, it is to deny that there is an inclusive covenant. Behind

151

that denial stands some kind of false worship, some belief in a false god.

In contrast, from faith in the God declared in Jesus Christ, the demands of special covenants are always to be limited by the demands of loyalty to the inclusive covenant. The functions of any special covenant have their rightful place only insofar as they contribute to the true humanity of all persons—not simply to some total amount of good, but to the humanizing of persons (members and nonmembers of that special covenant) in the context of the wider human community. Where conflicts arise between the claims of special covenants and the claims of the inclusive covenant, the latter should always have priority. That is true whether or not there is full agreement about what human rights there are, and it is true even if it is often unclear what course of action this priority requires.

6

Moral Conflicts III:
Justice for Whom?

There is a sense in which if true justice is present for some in a society, it is present for all. In that sense of the term there are no conflicting claims to justice, for what would be truly just for one would be just for all. But that way of thinking starts at the end of the search for justice rather than back somewhere along the road, and we do not have that luxury. If justice is a proper distribution of the benefits and burdens of social life, or, underlying that idea, if it is a right relationship among the various members of a community, we are always in situations of more or less injustice. In any unjust situation some persons and groups are especially—unjustifiably—disadvantaged, and if we are to achieve a greater degree of justice, we must judge who they are among the many competitors for social benefits and give them special attention.

The dispute over justice is simultaneously an intellectual argument and a coercive power struggle. The protagonists disagree over the standards of what is just and over what arrangements will best express them, and they struggle and seek to bring coercive power to bear upon one another in the implementation of whatever standards the community adopts. Our intellectual formulations of the material standards

153

of justice are never utterly detached from our social loyalties and involvement in the struggle. Our beliefs may conflict with our social *position*, because our ideas are not simply determined, materially or economically, by our social position, even though social position strongly influences them. But our beliefs about justice do tend to express our social *commitments*, including commitments that sometimes go beyond merely seeking our own economic or political advantage. We are highly interested when we discuss justice, and we shape our thinking about its meaning in a way that fits what we think the social world should be like. An inquiry into the meaning of justice is clearly not an ivory tower endeavor.

In this chapter, I shall state an understanding of justice that I believe is appropriate to the interpretation of Christian ethics as the ethics of covenant love. Some who differ with this understanding of justice will find that the differences are rooted in disagreements with the basic covenantal outlook of this book. Others may differ over what such a covenantal outlook entails, either because of their own social commitments and involvements or because of questions about the moral reasoning of the argument. For them the argument may nonetheless serve to illustrate how an ethic of covenant love can be given form in the search for justice.

I shall discuss first the relation of the idea of justice to that of rights, with which it is inextricably related; second, a material standard for justice appropriate to the standard of covenant love; third, some ideas of liberation theology as they relate to the view of justice expressed here; and finally, some implications of this view of justice for action.

Justice and Rights

An ancient formula transmitted by the Roman jurist Ulpian defines justice as "a fixed and abiding disposition [or will] to give to each what is due."[1] For present purposes let us rephrase the definition somewhat: *An action or practice is just if it brings about a proper balance among the rights, along with the corresponding duties, of social life. In a parallel way a person is just who is disposed so to act.* This definition amends Ulpian's formula in three respects: (1) It recognizes that the terms *just* and *justice* are used to refer both to a quality of acts and practices and to a virtue of moral agents. (2) It makes explicit the direct relationship between justice and moral rights, a relationship that may be implicit in Ulpian's statement and that has been attributed to it by some later thinkers. It is a feature of a just action that someone has a moral right to it, so that justice as a part of morality corresponds to the realm of moral rights.[2] (3) Yet just actions and practices do not simply give all persons their rights, as Ulpian's wording might suggest. That would mistakenly presuppose that all rights are absolute and that they never conflict with one another. Moral rights often do conflict, and when they do, an act or practice is just that brings about a proper *balance* among them. What is just is not in all cases to have one's valid rights met, even though it does always involve having them adequately recognized.

When I speak of justice in this way, I am purposely *not* using the term to refer to the whole of right action and good moral character. Plato's *Republic* is about justice in that wider sense, synonymous with rightness. Similarly when Amos declares, "Let justice *[mishpat]* roll on like a river and righteousness like an ever-flowing stream" (5:24 NEB), the parallelism suggests that he is calling for justice in the sense of a righteousness like God's, rightness in an inclusive sense, and not simply justice in the more restricted sense.

This restricted use of the term is close to what Aristotle calls particular justice.[3] He identifies two aspects of particular justice: (1) distributive justice, which has to do with the way the benefits and burdens of social life ought to be apportioned, and (2) corrective or retributive justice, which seeks to remedy or correct injustice and to respond appropriately to both its victims and its perpetrators.[4] Here, then, I am concerned with particular justice—a part, though a major one, of right action and good character as a whole. In this chapter our concern is primarily (though not entirely) with distributive justice. The following chapter, which discusses a fourth problem of priority, has to do with corrective justice.

If justice is bringing about a proper balance among moral rights (along with their corresponding duties), we must anchor our idea of justice in an understanding of moral rights. It is not sufficient to understand justice simply as requiring the standard, "treat like cases alike and unlike cases differently." That standard of "formal justice"[5] is indeed a necessary characteristic of justice; it is simply the requirement of impartiality. But however necessary, it is not a sufficient test for justice. For the same reason the test of universalizing whatever norms we have is not sufficient, if applied to justice.[6] Joel Feinberg has pointed out that it would be quite possible to treat relevantly like cases alike and relevantly different cases differently and still treat them all unjustly.[7] At one time, for example, some western European legal systems imposed the death sentence upon convicted pickpockets. Even if that were done with utter impartiality, it should be deemed unjust. A convicted criminal has a right, we would argue today, not to be punished in a way vastly more severe than the seriousness of the crime. The standard of formal justice by itself would also permit us to treat like cases alike in an irrelevant or unduly superficial way. We might, for example, give all red-haired people the same income tax deduction. Under virtually any circumstances, though, color of hair is irrelevant to justice. Doing justice requires more than universalizing our norms, though it certainly requires that.

We must supplement the idea of formal justice with a theory of moral rights. This is to appeal to what Feinberg calls noncomparative justice, in which we do not merely compare the treatment of one individual with that of another, but compare the treatment of each with some objective standard.[8] A theory of moral rights appropriate to the idea of God's covenant provides the kind of standard that we need.

Justice and Human Rights

Human rights are those moral rights that belong to everyone as a member of God's inclusive covenant. We have human rights whether they are socially recognized or not. They are rooted in what it is to be human in relation to God and to one another, and are not merely conventional, not merely created by some kind of social agreement. This is why human rights are more basic than legal rights. A given legal system might refuse to grant that certain human rights exist and ought to be protected. For many years legal jurisdictions in the United States did not recognize the right of all people regardless of race or sex to equal protection of the laws, to due process, and to the vote. The United States has in part, though only in part, corrected this kind of injustice through appeals beyond existing legal conventions to claims about human rights.

Human rights are not conventional; but *judgments* about human rights are to some degree conventional, influenced by the prevailing outlook and the implicit and explicit agreements of society. Different societies and groups have vastly different and conflicting ideas about what human rights there are. But human rights themselves, rooted in what it means morally to be members of God's covenant, exist whether socially recognized or not. Each one constitutes a valid claim upon every society.

Our outlook on the ultimate nature of human existence— our faith, in the generic sense—significantly shapes our judgments about what human rights there are. The Christian community's proclamation of God's covenant love shapes how we should speak about human rights: which ones there are, and why, and which are the most fundamental. Rather than attempt a catalog of human rights, let us look at some of the major types of human rights in light of the standard of covenant love.

The equal right of each human being to respect. Covenant love's appreciation of each person's worth as a child of God leads us to view the equal right of each to respect as the most fundamental human right. It is a direct reflection of God's covenant love for each person as a human being regardless of merit. In turn it is the basis of all other moral rights, human and special. The very idea that there are any moral rights, and that they are not merely privileges granted by society for its own well-being, presupposes that there are *bearers* of rights who have worth as ends. In recognizing the equal right of each to respect, Christian ethics affirms the centrality of persons over rules, moral theories, spiritual or material "values," and tables of more specific rights.

The equal right of each to respect does not require that we treat everyone identically. People's circumstances, needs, and problems differ, and the only way to express respect alike for people who differ in these ways is to treat them in relevantly different ways. Most arguments over justice are about what kinds of different treatment are appropriate, and the task here is to answer that question in a way that expresses the standard of covenant love.

The equal right of each to respect is a positive right: that is, it is "a right to other persons' positive actions,"[9] or better here, positive dispositions. It is more fundamental than the equal right to freedom, which the legal philosopher H. L. A. Hart advances as the most basic human right.[10] From the idea of equal respect for each it does follow that people have an equal right to freedom, a negative right (that is, a right to other persons' *not* acting or being disposed in certain ways—in this case, not interfering or being disposed to interfere unequally with their freedom). But the equal right of each to respect is the more fundamental because it directly expresses the reason we should recognize any rights—that each person is worthy of respect as a member of God's inclusive covenant. It affirms our belongingness as the essential context of our right to freedom.

The equal right to respect is a right *of each* to respect. This term must be stressed because it is a necessary ingredient in any theory of justice, in that it injects the element of treating "likes alike," a kind of equality. What most significantly differentiates theories of justice is their answers to the question, "What kind of equality is called for?" Yet what is required is not only equality, not only equal respect.[11] That norm could be compatible with very little respect for anyone. Equal respect is required, but more—a deep and thoroughgoing respect appropriate to all alike as persons of worth before God.

Negative human rights. The equal right of each to respect underlies other less fundamental but still very important negative human rights besides the equal right to freedom. One group of negative rights includes, for example, the right to freedom of speech and assembly and the right to worship according to our convictions, all of these being rights to noninterference by others. This group of negative rights is sometimes spoken of collectively as "the right to liberty." They reflect the importance for our being and for our well-being of the freedom to express ourselves and to make decisions about matters central to our destiny.

Another group of negative rights includes rights such as that to immunity from physical or psychological attack, the right to privacy, and the right to enjoy our property. These are instances of "the right to security." They reflect the importance, comparable to that of the right to liberty, of the protection of persons from unjustifiable harm by others.

Positive human rights. The equal right of each to respect also underlies other positive human rights: rights to other persons' performing some act, such as providing some good or service. It is more difficult than with negative human rights, however, to say what are indeed our positive human rights, beyond the equal right to respect. Does every person have a positive human right, for example, to enough food to eat, to a certain level of health care, to an education, or to gainful employment? The Universal Declaration of Human Rights, adopted by the General Assembly of the United Nations in 1948, classifies matters like these as human rights.[12] It is plausible to do so, as long as we realize that they are not absolute rights, however fundamental they are to human well-being. All of them are things that might be in short supply. When they are, the positive, nonabsolute right to them can be translated into a negative right not to be subjected to discrimination in their distribution. To be entitled to someone else's action or forbearance, then, does not mean to be entitled to it without qualification; some human rights, such as the right of each to respect, may be absolute, but most are not.

Justice and Special Rights

Special rights, as we have seen, are those rights that arise from some special transaction or relationship in history, as from a marriage, a business contract, or a governmental relationship, and that belong only to the parties to the special transaction or relationship. Special rights constitute additional moral claims over and above human rights concerning what is just. Yet special rights are more ambiguous than human rights in determining what is just. Even though it is usually easier to determine our special rights than our human rights, it is sometimes less clear how or whether a given special right ought to count in judgments about justice, and it appears that some ordinarily ought not to count, such as the right of one burglar to another's keeping a promise to help burglarize a home.

With most special rights it is prima facie just to honor them. If a buyer, Mr. Brown, and a seller, Mr. Stone, freely contract together and agree upon a purchase at a certain price, it is prima facie just for both to keep the bargain. But suppose that Brown and Stone enter into an agreement whereby Stone sells himself into slavery to Brown. After a time Stone runs away, but is recaptured by Brown and brought to court for unlawfully making off with Brown's property (that is, Stone himself), in a jurisdiction in which slavery is legal. Regardless of these special transactions, it would be morally unjust for slavery to be legal, for Brown and Stone to enter into the enslaving transaction, and for a court to enforce it. Slavery can never be a just arrangement, because it reduces the slaves to a subhuman status, not to mention what it does to slaveholders and to others who permit the arrangement. Slavery denies an essential human quality and thus a human right,[13] and special rights are morally subordinate to human rights, as we have seen in the preceding chapter.

The point is that in contrast to human rights, it would be prima facie *unjust* to uphold some special rights and *just* to override them, because the relationship they express is essentially dehumanizing. This would be the case whenever persons transact together to deny a human right, either their own or someone else's; for example, when they agree to commit murder, to set up a system of child labor, or to set up a court system denying due process of law. Not all is just that is agreed upon.

In contrast it is prima facie just to uphold any special right that does not by its nature conflict with a human right. Most special rights are in this category and are, along with human rights, basic points of reference in the determination of justice as a proper balance among the rights and corresponding duties of social life.

This exploration into the subject of rights is a necessary prelude to asking what social arrangements are just. As Christians we do not appropriately inquire into rights primarily to assert our own. We may or may not be justified in doing that, as we discussed in chapter 4. Rather, we ask about rights primarily to identify *claims of especially high priority that others have upon us and upon one another* by virtue of their being members of God's inclusive covenant and by virtue of special transactions into which they have entered. Rights are the especially important type of moral claim on which justice is based.

Covenant Love, Justice, and the Criterion of Need

One's beliefs about justice express one's basic orientation and commitments. To reflect from the orientation of covenant love rather than some other orientation affects our concern for justice in two ways. First, *covenant love requires justice.* Against this position William Frankena has suggested that *agape* should be understood as beneficence, doing good, so that it contains no principle of justice, but must be supplemented by one.[14] In contrast, the idea of covenant love I have presented in chapter 2 contains within its meaning the requirement for justice. To have covenant love is, following God's love, to respect each person's worth individually, irreplaceably, and equally, and therefore to respect each one equally as a bearer of rights—the basis on which judgments about justice are to be made.

This understanding of the relation of love and justice contrasts also with that of Reinhold Niebuhr. For him sacrificial love is incompatible with entering into the claims and counterclaims of history—the stuff of which struggles over justice are made. To seek justice is therefore necessarily to compromise sacrificial love, even though that is what we should often do for the sake of others' interests.[15] To the contrary, covenant love as interpreted here is the most basic standard and is fully applicable to social and not only (as for Niebuhr) individual relationships. This can be so because love is viewed here in a very different way from Niebuhr's interpretation. Love can be the standard for social relations because it seeks the well-being of each within the community of all; for covenant love, sacrifice is a means the appropriateness of which is to be judged by its contribution to this well-being of each and all. Covenant love can be the standard because, not being obligated to reject the use of power, we *can* express it in the claims and counterclaims of life. It can be the standard because in social struggles it requires justice, not as a compromise of its own inner nature, but as an expression of its fundamental affirmation of all persons. To love covenantally therefore requires seeking actively the most appropriate kind of balance of people's rights. Love does indeed constantly stand in judgment over all human achievements of justice, as Niebuhr says, but for a vastly different reason—in order to identify wherein those achievements are not completely just, and not as though justice as such were a compromise of love.

Even though the relation of love and justice is much closer than Frankena and Niebuhr in their different ways view it, we cannot say with Joseph Fletcher that "love and justice are the same."[16] Love's concern is with the whole of our moral action. Justice has to do with a major part of moral action, which might be described as distribution (as Fletcher suggests, contrary to his own statement that love and justice are the same); or to put it in a way that fits more of the facets of justice, its province is the proper balance among moral rights. When Fletcher says that "justice is love coping with situations where distribution is called for,"[17] however, he means something sharply

162

different from the relation of covenant love to justice that I am presenting here. For him love requires that we seek to produce the greatest possible total of good; that is, it is apparently the principle of utility. In contrast covenant love requires us to be prepared to forgo the greatest possible production of good, if necessary, in order to recognize adequately everybody's rights. A right is an especially high priority kind of moral claim, such that simply bringing about a greater good is not ordinarily a sufficient reason to override a right. If it were, we would take our promises and commitments rather lightly, as Fletcher seems to recommend, whereas on the contrary, promises create rights in those persons to whom we promise, rights that may well take priority over our simply adding to the total of good in the world.

Covenant love requires justice, then, as essential to the affirmation of the equal, irreplaceable, and individual worth of persons. What James Childress says about justice as fairness in political life is true of justice in all human relationships:

> While love will indeed sometimes demand actions which go beyond fairness, it will rarely, if ever, require actions that are unfair or institutional structures that are unfair, primarily because fairness is tied up with the recognition of persons. . . . [T]o be oriented toward another person in love . . . means to recognize him as a person and to acknowledge various *prima facie* duties such as fairness and fair play which may not themselves be deduced from love.[18]

The second way that covenant love affects our concern for justice is that *it helps to shape judgments about the material criteria for the content of justice.* Even though we know that according to the standard of covenant love, justice is required, it is not at all easy to determine what types of actions or policies would be just. Respect for everyone and honoring people's rights require formal justice, that is, treating like cases alike and unlike cases differently. But *any* consistent ethical outlook should require formal justice. The differences in the outlooks emerge when we seek to move beyond formal justice to specify material criteria. A material criterion of justice is a way of indicating which likenesses and differences are relevant to decisions about justice, and that kind of judgment directly reflects one's basic moral standard. Our question is what criteria of justice will properly express respect for each person as a member of God's inclusive covenant.

The possible material criteria are numerous. For example:

> To each the same external action
> To each according to effort expended
> To each according to results achieved
> To each according to ability
> To each according to virtues present
> To each according to need
> To each according to rank
> To each according to legal entitlement
> To each according to promises made

The list could be expanded indefinitely, both by adding further criteria and by subdividing these; for example, kinds of abilities, virtues, and so on.

On the immediate, external level the criteria need not be the same for every type of situation. Relevant likenesses and differences for receiving medical care, for example, would be different from those for getting a promotion in one's job. Yet in all situations the external, immediate criteria should (1) express our basic moral standard, and (2) be appropriate to the morally relevant features of that situation. Furthermore, the special concern for each person that arises from covenant love implies the material criterion, *to each according to need*, to each that without which their lives as human beings are thwarted.

But what do we need? The idea of a need has a troublesome tendency to "float" in contemporary popular usage. It floats with regard to material possessions, for one thing. Many possessions now taken for granted by the middle and upper classes were once seen as luxuries available only to the few: for example, automobiles or enough money to pay for a college education. The more widely such things are available, the more we view them as indispensable. Yet they are not absolutely necessary to our lives in the sense that food, shelter, and medical care are. Still there is a truth underlying our thinking about what is a material need. In a complex urbanized society, people can be seriously disadvantaged without the means of transportation and communication and without formal education far beyond what most people ever attained a century ago. And when most people we meet have these things, it should not be surprising that those who are deprived of them feel that society holds them in low esteem.

The idea of a need also floats in that we sometimes tend to use the term interchangeably with that of a desire. The two are not utterly separable; what we need can under some circumstances be affected by what we desire. Yet a need is more than a desire; needs have an objectivity about them that desires do not have. A need is the lack, recognized or not, of whatever it is that would enable us to live faithfully in covenant with God and one another (our ultimate need) or any lack that would seriously thwart our lives (our proximate needs, as for food, shelter, or medical care). We may or may not desire what we need, but we still need it. A deep desire for something quite unnecessary may reflect a need, but a different one from what we might think. Some needs are straightforward and obvious; others are subtle, such as the need for self-acceptance or for significant communication with others. However that may be, we cannot take people seriously without taking their needs seriously and being concerned for them to be met.

Service to people's needs ordinarily requires *unequal or different* treatment in some sense, because people's needs differ. There is no paradox in saying, even so, that it also requires *impartial* treatment within the bounds of the need-criterion, in the sense that how we go about determining their needs and responding to them should be governed by a sense of the equal worth of them all and should be divorced from egoistic self-advancement, special favor, and our private preferences. In personal relationships we readily recognize the justice of doing more for those in greater need. If one family member is ill, we commonly hold (and rightly so) that it is just to offer that person special care. The need-criterion implies that we should generalize this idea further than some might want to. On the basis of need it would prima facie be just, for example, for a school district to devote greater financial resources to help students with special learning difficulties. It would be just, at least prima facie, for society to make available special financial help to those who face catastrophic medical costs. These examples suggest that both where relationships are close and personal and where they are large and impersonal, the standards of love and justice should be seen as standing together rather than in conflict.

The criterion of need leaves the way open for us to supplement it with other subordinate criteria where appropriate, such as treating people in certain ways on the basis of their effort or ability or legal entitlement or the outcome of their work. The appropriateness of each of these criteria must be tested by love's concern for people in the circumstances of the type of case at hand. To take an example from Vlastos,[19] consider whether praise is justly to be given according to merit. In university classes should professors praise excellent papers more than poor papers? Surely so, or else praise would be hollow and communication false. Even so, the basic criterion underlying the use of praise can be human need: the need of each student to learn what constitutes high-quality work and to be encouraged to it, rather than the more superficial needs or desires to pass, to get a good grade, or to be praised regardless of performance. What would be more false, Vlastos observes, than to praise all performances equally? Concern for the person whose work is being graded should operate as a control to prevent misuse of the practice of reward according to merit; the comment or grade given is not all that is important, but also the context in which it is communicated. Most importantly, from love one will remember that what is being graded is not the person, but a certain performance.

Consider another subordinate criterion, pay according to work done. This criterion is needed in order for economic resources to be distributed in the labor market. It obviously makes for inequality—because some choose not to work as much as others, because some cannot work as much or as productively as others, and because there is less demand for some kinds of skills. It is impossible to find any simple correlation between a laborer's needs and the amount or the quality of work done. If the only criterion for the distribution of goods were the work done, vast injustice would result. Yet if the work done were in no way a criterion of economic distribution, injustices at least as serious would result: freeloading would become rampant. Incentives in the form of pay for work done are needed in the economic system to restrain the inclination within us all to break covenant. Pay for work done encourages the well-intentioned to do what they ought for the wider community. Nevertheless, further criteria are needed to avoid the injustice of relying too one-sidedly on this one. The criterion of need, expressing our concern for persons, must govern this and other subordinate criteria.

Justice and the Oppressed

The more we confront cases of extreme deprivation, alienation and oppression, the more important we see the criterion of need to be. The impoverished, victims of racial or sexual or ethnic discrimination, addicts, criminals—the outcasts of all sorts—are central among those to whom a more just balance of social benefits and burdens is due. That is true even though it may be due in ways they themselves (addicts and criminals, for example) would not always prefer; in ways different from the way well-intentioned, more advantaged people might offer it; and in ways far different from the self-defensive and even vindictive treatment society often provides. *What* is due the extremely disadvantaged is not nearly as clear as *that* proportionately more is due in order to overcome the ill effects of their disadvantages.

When we are concerned about the extremely deprived today, we quickly encounter the work of that multifaceted movement known as liberation theology.[20] The work of the liberation theologians revolves around the plight of the oppressed and the obligations that this plight generates.

Although liberation theologians do not all formulate the issue in the same way, their work seems to imply an emphasis upon need as a material criterion of central importance in Christian ethics. Liberation theology arises out of the experience of oppression, whether that of Latin Americans under the economic domination of Western Europe and the United States, blacks in the white-dominated United States, women in a "man's world," or some other group. It seeks to bring people—especially the oppressed, but others as well—to self-awareness in this situation through a theological-political interpretation of the reality of oppression, and it calls for structural changes in society as a way to liberation of the oppressed into a more fully human condition.

Theology that develops out of the context of oppression is significant theology in several respects. Its theologians are able to hear the Christian proclamation with an acute sense of its bearing upon situations of injustice, and with deep awareness of the misery in which untold millions of people live throughout the world. They provide a needed balance to the work of the predominant body of professional theologians, who over the years have lived mainly among the more fortunate strata of society and some of whom have not been sufficiently sensitive to the need for social change to bring about justice. Liberation theologians can encourage a theological and ethical dialogue in which the experience and insight of the oppressed are taken with continuing seriousness.

Liberation theologians conduct their work in a posture of commitment to help the oppressed. They maintain that if theologians do not see the plight of the oppressed as a call to action, if they deal mainly in abstractions without bringing them to bear upon the needs of people and the requirements of social justice, they are necessarily doing inadequate theology. One must carry on theology as a practical and not only a theoretical endeavor: as *praxis*, whereby reflection arises out of the experience of oppression, is carried on by people dedicated to remedying injustice, and is directed continually to action and not only to intellectual conclusions. It is an issue worth discussing how *directly* theological work should lead to action—

whether reflection can be seriously weakened if it must lead too immediately to social action—but I must leave that issue to others. Here I want simply to affirm with the liberation theologians one's obligation to be in a stance of commitment and active involvement regarding justice in the process of doing theological work.

Within the framework of a deep commitment to the oppressed and disadvantaged in their needs, there is still room and need to examine various theological issues that are raised by the work of liberation theologians. Here I shall discuss three issues closely related to the question of justice for those most in need.

1. The first is the bearing of biblical views upon the concerns of liberation theology. Liberation theologians have stressed the Bible's concern for the oppressed and its demand for repentance and change on the part of oppressors. This stress is often received, understandably enough, in an unappreciative way by Christians whose circumstances are comfortable and who resist the idea that they share in the responsibility for the plight of masses of deprived people. Some among the comfortable Christians are ready to charge that the stress upon oppression and on the need for structural change has been imported into Christian thought from some alien viewpoint. Such a charge is all the more reason for us to listen with care to the way liberation theologians interpret the Bible. In all centuries people's own circumstances have influenced what they have perceived in the biblical proclamation. Liberation theologians, out of their own direct experience of oppression, have been able to see a special significance in the Old Testament account of the Exodus of the Hebrew people from bondage in Egypt, and they point to it as central to the whole Old Testament. It is on the basis of the Exodus experience that the book of Deuteronomy repeatedly commands the people to give special consideration to the alien, the orphan, and the widow in their midst (Deut. 24:16, 26:12, and elsewhere). Amos's condemnation of those who "trample upon the poor" and "turn aside the needy in the gate" (5:11, 12) is consistent with that concern, as are many other Old Testament passages.

Likewise liberation theologians have called others' attention to how the New Testament message is, like that of the Old, about deliverance from bondage—not simply a bondage and deliverance of the spirit divorced from the external bondages of social life, but in which the internal and external dimensions are inseparable. We find major passages supporting this interpretation. According to Matthew, giving food to the hungry, drink to the thirsty, clothing to the naked, and companionship to the ill and the imprisoned is identical to doing these things to Christ (Matt. 25:31-40). Again and again in Luke's gospel we hear the theme that compassion for the downtrodden is inseparably present in God's coming in Jesus Christ. In the Magnificat, for example, Mary declares:

> The arrogant of heart and mind he has put to rout,
> he has brought down monarchs from their thrones,
>> but the humble have been lifted high.
> The hungry he has satisfied with good things,
>> the rich sent empty away. (Luke 1:51b-53 NEB; cf. I Sam. 2)

Jesus' statement of his commission as given in Luke's account further expresses this focus upon the disadvantaged, citing Isaiah 61:1-2:

> The spirit of the Lord is upon me because he has anointed me;
> he has sent me to announce good news to the poor,
> to proclaim release for prisoners and recovery of sight for the blind;
> to let the broken victims go free,
> to proclaim the year of the Lord's favour. (Luke 4:18-19 NEB)

The same concern continues throughout Luke's gospel, in such passages as those about the rich man and Lazarus (16:19-31), the grateful Samaritan leper (17:11-19), and the repentant criminal crucified with Jesus (23:39-43). These are only a few of the many ways that the biblical writers declare God's special consideration for the downtrodden and call for a like concern on our part. However much interpreters may differ over the meaning of particular passages, liberation

170

theologians are surely correct in asserting that the Bible, both in the Old and New Testaments, strongly asserts God's loving concern and our obligation toward the oppressed and the needy.

2. Another topic bearing on justice for the needy is the idea of oppression. Liberation theologians specifically identify the problem they have experienced as oppression, and not simply misfortune or human error. The destitution of masses of people, the great disproportion between their power and that of the privileged, and the way social structures perpetuate these problems—these things have come about through people's exploiting other people. Misfortune is lamentable, error may or may not be our own responsibility, but oppression is especially blameworthy. To label the matter oppression is to communicate the seriousness and the responsibility that are appropriate to the situation.

At the same time that the problem calls for strong language, we must be careful to avoid overstatement or misstatement regarding oppression. This is a subject about which dedicated people have strong opposing convictions, and I shall express my own directly in the hope that it will encourage dialogue rather than polarization. Oppression is clearly present in the plight of the masses of disadvantaged. But how shall we speak of the persons involved? Liberation theologians characteristically term them the oppressors and the oppressed, and it is that dichotomy that I wish to examine. It is clear that in many instances we can justifiably use those terms to apply to a large number of persons in a particular relationship: southern slaveowners versus their slaves; those today who seek to deprive blacks of their human and political rights versus deprived blacks; the German Nazis versus the Jews (and many others) they persecuted; powerful corporations and wealthy industrialists, landowners, and right-wing governmental regimes versus the populace of rural or urban Latin American slums; men who seek to dominate women and to keep them in inferior and subservient roles versus the women they thereby exploit. Thus far the terms are appropriate.

Some liberation theologians, however, wish to apply the

terms on a global scale, and the wider the net is cast, the more questionable its applicability becomes. A major issue here is how we can best understand the fabric of society. Is it best interpreted according to a *dualist model* or some other?[21] Dualists assign everyone in society to two groups, the one oppressing and exploiting the other, with the members of each group having a significant degree of solidarity with one another. The conflict of interests between these two groups is high, and radical (as contrasted with conservative) dualists tend to advocate violent revolution as the only effective action to overcome the oppression. If the cleavage and conflict in society is as deep as this, the dualists judge, then efforts at reform by accepted social and political procedures cannot be effective. Some liberation theologians, especially in Latin America, have explicitly adopted a dualist model of society, whereas others reflect it implicitly without making all its features clear. The oppressor-oppressed dichotomy by itself suggests a dualist model, even though some who use it do not agree with all the above dualist tendencies. Such a model has obvious relevance to some types of social situations, such as the ones listed in the preceding paragraph.

There are, however, other models of society, and one or another may fit some social contexts as well as or better than the dualist model. Within the United States, Canada, Western Europe, and some countries in other regions, a *pluralist model* has much to commend it. According to this kind of model, there are many significant groups in society, not only two. These groups come into conflict over a variety of crosscutting issues; that is, the major line of division over one type of issue (e.g., economic policy) cuts across major lines of division and identification on other matters, such as religious loyalties, political parties, attitudes toward foreign policy, views on abortion, and so on. Those who are opposed on one issue may very well be allied on another.[22] In this kind of situation, there is much less of a sense of solidarity among the allies on any issue. Also it is frequently possible for social action to be effective through existing political structures, so that efforts at reform need not be discarded for violent revolution.

The question is over which model is applicable to the situation of oppression. The answer seems to depend upon the *type* of oppression situation, as reflected in the variety of recommendations of liberation theologians themselves. Black theologians in the United States today, for example, generally do not opt for revolution, recognizing as they do the pluralistic nature of United States politics and the significant possibilities for reducing injustice that are open to them through political action. This is true even though some press strongly the language of oppressor/oppressed. Many, if not most, women liberation theologians likewise tend to be skeptical of a pure dualist model. It is in Latin American liberation theology that the language and proposals of dualism are most strong, and under their circumstances one must sympathize to a major degree with the tendency.

Another way of exploring the same question is to ask about many persons whether they are oppressors or oppressed. In Hitler's Germany, contemporary South Africa, or some Latin American contexts, it is plausible to consider many persons as belonging in most respects to one or the other of these categories. In many another social setting, most people do not fit the categories. One who is oppressed in one relationship may resemble the oppressors in another: a poor white man, a wealthy white woman, or a wealthy black man or woman. Letty Russell offers us wise counsel on this subject:

> The use of the words "oppressor" and "oppressed" is not necessarily directed at particular individuals who happen by accident of birth to belong to an oppressing group. The discussion is not *ad personam* (about the person), but *ad rem* (about the thing); that is, about the fabric of society in which people are locked into various forms of oppression in a vicious circle that dehumanizes both the oppressor and the oppressed. It is an attempt to describe the world in such a way that the sickness can be confronted and changed.[23]

The more pluralistic the society, the less assignable individuals are to dichotomous categories like oppressor/oppressed. We would be wise to focus upon the term *oppression* and the existence of oppressive social systems, rather than try to assign persons.

The oppressed are seriously needy; who then are the oppressed? In some social situations they are masses of people with regard to a wide swath of their lives. Conversely many people are oppressed in some relationships but function as oppressors in others.

This reflection on the concept of oppressor and oppressed carries implications for the way we think about guilt. Insofar as we are unable rightly to assign individuals clearly to the category of oppressor, we must to that degree be guarded about judgments of guilt. The idea of guilt for injustice calls for two simultaneous kinds of judgments, as Theodore R. Weber has argued.[24] First, for purposes of assigning blame for external wrong actions, the charge of guilt must be directed toward specific individuals (even if many of them), and only insofar as one can trace a definite connection between these individuals' actions and the wrongful deeds or policies for which they are being blamed. The concept of collective guilt— the idea that simply by belonging to a particular social group (e.g., being a United States citizen) or social category (e.g., being white or male), one is guilty of the evils ascribed to that group or category—is utterly inappropriate in the realm of moral deliberation about external action. It makes no sense in this realm to blame persons for actions with which they had no traceable connection, which they did not will, and which they could not have prevented. Just as people needed to resist the "guilt by association" tactics of the right-wing witch-hunters of the 1940s and 1950s, we must resist the same tactic by other groups, including any liberation theologians who may consider people to be guilty of specific injustices simply because they participate in a given social group or have certain biological or social characteristics.

At the same time, as Weber argues, in the realm of our own self-awareness we can recognize ways in which we share *inwardly* in the guilt for oppression that we neither caused nor willed nor could have prevented. The occurrence of a heinous act (Weber's example is the assassination of Dr. Martin Luther

King, Jr.) can be the occasion in which we recognize that we have identified in the past with the supporters or doers of a moral evil, or that we have held racist or sexist or otherwise demeaning attitudes. Such inner reflection may also prompt us to see ways that we are externally supporting an injustice, thereby being to that extent guilty in the first, external sense. Even then, though, careful reflection about guilt will lead us to resist reckless charges of collective guilt for specific actions.

3. Let us consider one more aspect of liberation theology as it bears upon the criterion of need in the search for justice. We must look in two directions as we speak of liberation. One is represented by the phrase "liberation *from*," which calls our attention especially to the existence of injustices from which people need to be set free. The other is expressed in the phrase "liberation *to*," which bids us to consider what kind of relationship should come about as this setting free occurs.

It is in the vision of "liberation to" that one's religious loyalties become most clear. One might be a liberation theologian from any of a number of religious points of view. It is possible for one's vision of a "better world" to exclude those who were oppressors, for one to paint a picture of the God of Jesus Christ as only the god of oppressed groups. Yet it is utterly inappropriate for those who in the name of Jesus Christ call out for liberation to reject or be indifferent to the effort at reconciliation with all their fellow human beings, including those who have oppressed them. To reject any person or group expresses idolatry, regardless of who does so or what one's public religious identification is. It is no different inwardly from the idolatry of those who reject the disadvantaged while cynically and uncaringly exploiting them.

If we are to do liberation theology (and given such widespread misery, we must do it in some mode), it would best be covenantal liberation theology, that is, theology that aims at the liberation of all to community in God's inclusive covenant. To do liberation theology in hope for the inclusive covenant is to see life as radically social, so that however thoroughly we are liberated *from* something, we are always liberated *to* responsibility to, for, and with the whole human community. To do liberation theology in this vein is to participate in deliverance not only from external bondages, but also from the internal bondage in which we reject our fellows. It is to recognize God's forgiving grace as the reality through which the law becomes written on our hearts—through which then we are inwardly enabled to seek the community of all as the only true liberation there is. Liberation theology in a covenant mode recognizes that the needs of people are multiple—outer and inner at once, neither divorceable from the other.

To say this is not to sanction a surface harmony, as though that were reconciliation. Indeed it is to call for precisely the opposite. Reconciliation, especially between oppressors and oppressed, does not come about by refusing to face conflicts of interests or existing injustices. Reconciliation can take place only as people work through their conflicts of interest, even though some of the conflicts remain. It can happen only as changes take place that remove actual social injustices. Reconciliation in society, as between individuals, can only come after confession, repentance, and forgiveness. Repentance finds social expression in the righting of injustices. Reconciliation in this sense is our hope, our true liberation.

Action for Justice

Effective action for justice, giving priority to those most in need, requires a thoroughly social approach. Many persons in recent years have by and large opted out of social concerns to pursue their own individual fulfillment. Some of them have carried along into that private world the notion that in so doing they can still effectively seek others' good (insofar as they are interested in it) in that private framework. Justice does not come about simply through an accumulation of decent acts in individual relationships. Today's society needs a recovery not only of a sense of social responsibility, but also of realism about what is required to implement it. Here are four observations about these requirements.

First, because the most serious injustices are structured into our social lives, solutions to these injustices can be effective only as they are socially structured. The problem of injustice is not simply individual malice, however much that is present. Injustice is most serious as it comes to be structured in the policies and practices of large social institutions—national governments, political parties, corporations, unions, educational organizations, hospitals, churches. Unjust institutional policies create a context within which individuals, however well-intentioned, find their resources directed toward harmful effects they do not intend, upon people they do not know, in ways they do not see how individually to change. The problem may take the form of massive unemployment among black young people, of the widespread practice of paying women lower wages for the same work (or denying them equal access to some kinds of work), or of not seeing to it that the economically most advantaged bear an appropriately heavier share of the tax burden. These injustices come about not simply through individuals' wrongdoing in general, but through a specific kind of individual wrongdoing—action to enact or administer unjust policies in large organizations. To see injustice as structural is not a new idea, but we need repeatedly to be reminded that this is the most important form it takes.

Structural problems call for structural solutions. Overcoming structural injustices requires changing the policies and practices of large institutions as well as appealing to the hearts and minds of the individuals within them. It will take changes in institutions—governmental and private together—to overcome such injustices as the disproportionate unemployment of black youths, discrimination against women in employment, and the imbalance of the burden of taxes.

Second, in any effective program for social justice toward the most needy, government will necessarily play the key role. One definition of justice suggested at the beginning of this chapter was a proper distribution of the benefits and burdens of social life. Such a proper distribution or balance requires an overview of the society's practices, a coordinated planning

177

center. Of all the institutions of society, only government can provide that function. Harmonizing the interests of the many individuals and groups in a society does not take place "naturally," as Adam Smith thought. If left to their own uncoordinated devices, the many members of society tend to go at each other's throats, as international politics—the epitome of an uncoordinated social system—illustrates. To the extent that conflicting interests can be brought into harmony, and it is a significant though incomplete extent, that can be done only where there is active initiative for coordination on the part of government.

Precisely what government's role should be is a question that cannot be settled here. A major theme in political discussion today is "the less government the better," the idea that government is essentially a burden rather than a benefit, that government regulation should be diminished with little regard for what is being regulated, and that decisions about how people relate to one another in the economy and in other aspects of social life should largely be turned over to private groups, which in many cases means large private institutions. But private institutions and individuals are never capable of providing adequate coordination for the society as a whole. They always have built into their policy-making process the incentive to see that their own institution gains, or at least does not lose, whatever are the effects of their policies upon others. It is one proper role of government to limit the efforts of private groups to advance their own interests at others' expense, and if government does not perform that role, gross injustice is inevitable. What is at stake in the debate over the role of government is not simply technical economic questions, such as how to avoid or recover from severe recessions. What is at stake is the question of justice. It is whether as the country deals with an economic crisis the benefits and burdens of economic change will be fairly distributed. That cannot happen without active government coordination across the wide range of economic and other kinds of policy.

Whatever the proper role for government, the clichés are not the answer. Neither "the less government the better" nor "the more government the better" is true. What is true is that people must be prepared for government to play a central role that will enable the society to examine the whole array of its ways of distributing benefits and burdens, and to do so more fairly.

Third, in any effective program for social justice for the most needy, the most fundamental thing needing a just distribution is power. Power is the capacity to exercise influence upon other people to attain ends. It is the capacity to gain access to the things that are valued. Justice cannot be achieved where there are enduring great disproportions of power among the society's members. That is true for two reasons. One is that those who have the most power tend in their sinfulness to use it to promote their own ends at the expense of the weak. It does not suffice that some of the powerful have good intentions toward the weak; that will help, but inevitably the powerful tend to misread to a greater or lesser extent the effects of their actions upon the weak. Especially in large organizational life, the powerful always do less for the weak than they think they are doing. The other reason is that part of the attainment comes not simply by what people can come to control with power, but also through the sense of dignity and self-respect that develops in those who have significant power—who have the capacity to influence significantly the direction of their own lives. These are two reasons why enduring paternalism (taken either as a sexist or as a generic term) is unjust.

Efforts to distribute power more justly can take a combination of forms. Culturally, society can enable the most needy to gain educational tools essential to full participation in the society. Economically, we can strive to make sure that no persons in the society will be ruined financially by matters beyond their own control, such as unemployment or medical disaster. We can do that by seeking to provide a social-economic floor below which none of the society's members are allowed to fall. The political form of distributing power is the most important, for without it the other forms tend to be neglected. Politically we can provide every member of society with a formal and effective voice in the way the society's decisions are made. That means at the very least a significant vote—both the right to vote and the presence of elections structured so that one's vote matters.

Finally, in all these efforts toward justice for the most needy, a covenantal ethic will encourage us to seek a community in which all the members are valued participants. True justice does not come about merely through a balance of the benefits and burdens of social life. It comes only as this balance occurs within a community of mutual acceptance and affirmation. This is one reason why the structures of society are so important, for we are not simply individuals receiving a fair or unfair ration of resources, but fellow members of the same community. The role of government is crucial because we do not seek simply the right to live in isolation from one another; we seek a community in which we can go about our lives in proper relation to one another. True empowerment is more than simply giving each individual a veto power over what others do. Empowerment for community is providing the community with the means by which its members can continually renew and further their lives together. Veto power is never enough for community; enabling power, the power by which an aggregate of people can become a community, is the kind of power most needed. These are some essentials of effective action for justice from a Christian covenantal orientation.

7

Moral Conflicts IV:
Wrongdoers and the Wronged

The Problem

Paul Ramsey has written, "When choice *must* be made between the perpetrator of injustice and the many victims of it, the latter may and should be preferred."[1] As he explains, it is not the work of love to allow unjustifiable harm to continue, let alone to assist it; rather, it is love's work to deliver all God's children one can from oppression. From a Christian standpoint that judgment is, I believe, unassailable. For that reason the question that will be explored in this chapter is not *whose* interests should have priority. Rather it is *how* we are to go about preferring the interests of victims over those of wrongdoers, doers of unjustifiable harm.

The problem is how priority can be given to the wronged in a way that expresses the conviction that all people, wrongdoers and wronged alike, exist together in God's covenant. Once we view the conflict of wrongdoers and wronged from the perspective of God's inclusive covenant, we do not have the option of rejecting the wrongdoer. Both victim and wrongdoer are children of God and thereby have equal human worth. It is not as though once one person has seriously, even grievously, wronged another, we are then free to wash our hands of further respect for the wrongdoer's worth. We are not morally free to treat wrongdoers any way we please in the process of seeking justice for the wronged ones. The former matter in God's sight as much as the latter, as is reflected in the proclamation that it was sinners for whom Christ died.

Yet neither are we morally free simply to let harmful wrongdoing continue unopposed. It is not enough merely to have sympathy for the wronged. If one is responding from covenant love, it is morally necessary to seek effective expression for that sympathy. Effective expression includes at least these things: interposing an adequate defense between the oppressed and their oppressors, seeking just compensation for the wronged (whatever that might be) when the wrongful blow has already been struck, holding the wrongdoers responsible, and where feasible seeking to shape the policies of society so as to anticipate and reduce the likelihood of further such wrongful acts in the future.

An adequate response to conflicts between wrongdoers and the wronged must combine these concerns—for the wrongdoers as well as the wronged—and must seek to embody both concerns effectively in action, however deep the conflict may be.

This may be the most difficult of all the problems of priorities that we have discussed. The difficulty centers in the use of coercion, especially violent coercion. Where a wrong is serious and likely to recur, action in behalf of the wronged is ordinarily ineffective unless it is in some way coercive, and sometimes unless it is violent. Yet coercion and violence raise serious ethical questions. Are they more justifiable than the wrongs they seek to restrain, which ordinarily are coercive and violent themselves? Can we distinguish between uses of coercion and violence that are justifiable and uses that are not? Under what circumstances and by what means, from the standpoint of covenant love, might coercion and violence toward wrongdoers be justifiable? My objective in this chapter is to show how, in responding to the conflict between wrongdoers and the wronged, covenant love takes shape in a theory of justifiable and morally limited coercion.

The Idea of a General Theory of Justifiable Coercion

Power, Coercion, and Violence

Coercion and violence are emotion-laden terms, and both are used in different ways by different people—two good reasons to say what we mean by them. We can explain their meanings in terms of three concentric circles, the outer one symbolizing the concept of power, the intermediate that of coercion, and the inner one that of violence.

Power in society is the capacity to influence others, but not all social power is coercive. Coercion is the power to influence others against their wills. It is thus narrower in scope than power. There is also noncoercive power, the power to influence others by persuasion and attraction, the power to elicit a freely offered consent. Both coercion and consent are present in some way or other, in the foreground or the background, in all power relationships, though one or the other is often more prominent.

Coercion is to be distinguished on the other hand from violence, which is one kind of coercion but not the only kind. Violence is the direct infliction of physical or psychological injury upon persons or property. In recent years liberation theologians have often used the term in a wider sense than this, as what they call "structural violence." For example, Robert McAfee Brown includes this idea when he defines violence as "whatever 'violates' another, in the sense of infringing upon or disregarding or abusing or denying that other, whether physical harm is involved or not."[2] This definition seems to include not only any physical or psychological injury, but also any kind of unjustifiable harm to others' interests. It is important to protest, with Brown, any abuse and oppression of persons, whether it involves direct injury or not. Generally the term structural violence emphasizes people's suffering as a result of institutional injustices, as in cases of widespread starvation or lack of medical care, even if no one has deliberately willed or directly inflicted that suffering. In that respect the term is helpful. Yet to call all such harm "violence" risks obscuring the moral significance of violence in the narrower sense of direct and intentional injury. We can adequately express our objection to the broader kind of harm by calling it "injustice," "oppression," or as often appropriate, "structural injustice." I shall use the term *violence* in the more restricted sense.[3]

One can coerce others by directly forcing them to do something or forcibly preventing them from it. This forcing may or may not be violent—may or may not inflict injury upon them. But one can also coerce without resort to force or violence. This is ordinarily done by the *threat* of some significant deprivation. The threat would not involve violence unless it were carried out, and even then it might not. Furthermore one can coerce by the *inducement* of some great reward, in which case violence is not involved at any point, whether the reward is forthcoming or not. An inducement coerces insofar as it, like a threat, causes us to acquiesce, not because of the merits of any argument or the attractiveness of the desired course of action itself, but in spite of our preference for another course of action, simply for fear of loss. Fear of loss of a reward is not very different in its effect upon us from fear in the face of a threat. Coercion thus includes all kinds of power to influence others against their wills: by inducement as well as by threat, and by psychological and economic means short of violence as well as by violence.

The Moral Problems Raised by Coercion

Coercion raises three kinds of moral problems. First, it overrides the freedom of the coerced to act according to their own preferences. Because freedom of choice is in general a nonmoral good, even though one that can be misused, there is always a presumption in its favor, as Feinberg argues.[4] If so, all coercion requires justification.

Second, as economic coercion it can deprive the coerced of some valued possession or right or experience, such as income, food, the right to vote, or the enjoyment of their work. Economic coercion was present in the recent action of a utility company in cutting off supplies of natural gas to a whole municipality that did not pay its gas bills, and also in the temporary refusal of the municipality to pay. It is prominent in the international distribution of oil or can take the form of a complete blockade of one nation by another. These examples show that economic coercion is not necessarily less harmful than violence, even if its physical or psychological injury is indirect or delayed.

The third and most obvious problem of coercion is, of course, the physical and psychological injury that violence inflicts. Violent injury can be inflicted on the psyche as well as on the body, as when a child's ego is weakened by harsh treatment, or when prisoners are terrorized in addition to any bodily injury they may have received. Whatever the form coercion takes, the greater the harm to the coerced, the greater is the burden of proof upon anyone who seeks to justify it.

The Need for a General Theory of Justifiable Violence and Coercion

There already exists within Christian ethics a theory to test the moral justifiability of acts of war, ordinarily referred to as "just-war theory." As it has been developed and refined since the fourth century, it has become a useful instrument for the ethical appraisal of many different kinds of war.[5] Christian ethicists have also sometimes drawn upon it to assist their reflection upon other kinds of coercion, such as civil disobedience.[6] The just-war criteria can also be applied, with needed adjustments, to such instances of violence as revolution, the apprehending of criminals by police, and the punishment of convicted criminals. They can also illuminate the ethics of such nonviolently coercive actions as military strategic threats, coercive economic sanctions, and the use of coercion in small groups.

This varied usefulness of the just-war criteria suggests the possibility as well as the need for a general theory of justifiable coercion, one that would apply the criteria more broadly to the restraint of wrongdoing. A major aim of this chapter is to express such a general theory. Even though the burden of proof is upon those who wish to justify a given act of coercion, whether violent or nonviolent, nevertheless it can often be justified from a Christian moral viewpoint. Coercion, then, nonviolent as well as violent, seems to be morally ambiguous, neither always prohibited by a Christian moral viewpoint, nor simply permitted without moral restriction. Because of this moral ambiguity, what is needed is *a theory of justifiable and hence morally limited coercion.*

Yet not all Christians grant that violent coercion, at any rate, is morally ambiguous. Before discussing the details of the theory, we must consider two sharply different kinds of objections to this approach.

Alternatives to Justifiable, Morally Limited Violence

An adequate theory of justifiable coercion (including violence) would identify the conditions under which coercion can be justifiable and the restraints that should be placed upon it when it is. Two main alternatives to this idea can be found in Christian moral reflection.[7] Crusade ethics rejects the idea of moral limits upon the violent means once the objective is deemed morally justifiable, whereas pacifism rejects the idea that violence (at least in the form of war, and ordinarily any violence) can be morally justifiable.

Crusade Ethics

Some Christians (as well as some non-Christians) have taken a crusading stance toward war and often toward other forms of violent and nonviolent coercion. In all these forms crusade ethics includes the following characteristics: (1) Crusaders pursue absolute and utopian goals, such as the elimination of corruption, the destruction of some presumably evil form of government, or "war to end wars." (2) They divide the parties to the conflict into the forces of good and the forces of evil. This says more than that a greater degree of justification lies with one side than with the other. Crusaders draw an absolute moral distinction between the conflicting parties and not merely a relative distinction between the moral qualities of their efforts. These first two steps imbue the crusade ethic with an uncompromising and fanatical drive that governs its use of coercion. (3) Because of these characteristics, crusaders disavow any moral responsibility for those who are deemed to be among the forces of evil. They therefore sanction acting toward those persons without moral restraint. As Edward LeRoy Long, Jr., has described this position, "In a crusade the enemy is hated for who he is, even more than for what he does. It is natural, therefore, to seek his destruction (at least the destruction of his will) rather than his correction."[8]

James Turner Johnson, following LeRoy Walters, suggests that what we call crusades were looked upon by those who advocated them as just wars, and that they used just-war ideas to justify each.[9] The implication is that the category of "crusade ethic" is reducible to just-war doctrine. Yet insofar as a war is entered into and conducted with the above characteristics, regardless of the appeals used to try to justify it, it becomes something significantly different from war according to the just-war conditions (to be discussed later). Obviously the crusades' participants deemed them just, but that does not render them mere types of just war according to its conditions, any more than, say, Hitler's wars had just causes or reflected a just-war position because he supposed them to be just. To overlook the differences is to miss the primary moral significance of the just-war restraints.

The crusade ethic can appear in any age, in any kind of human conflict, and in widely different religious positions. In the Crusades of the Middle Ages it was present on both sides, Christians and Moslems alike. In World War I, it found expression in absolutist war aims that led the adversaries on both sides to press their causes in the face of enormous loss of life and that encouraged harsh peace terms once it ended. It found its most notable expression in World War II in the Nazis' treatment of their enemies, whether Jews or Allies, domestic or foreign opponents, military forces or civilians. Although in many ways the Allied war effort reflected just-war restraints, a crusade mentality also appeared on that side, especially in the unqualified war aim of "unconditional surrender" and in the indiscriminate destruction of German and Japanese cities. Nor is the crusade ethic restricted to war. It was present among some leaders of the Nixon administration, as expressed in its "enemies lists" and in the willingness of some officials to use any conceivable means to win electoral victory and control the apparatus of government. It has been present in the attitudes of some Christian as well as non-Christian supporters of violent revolution against oppressive governments and systems. There is a theory of justifiable and limited revolution, and that theory is not imbued with the three assumptions of the crusade ethic. But some theories of revolution judge that when resort to it is justifiable, then any successful means is permissible because it is directed toward absolutely good ends and against forces of evil. In the field of criminal justice, the crusade ethic is reflected in the view that the rights of the accused (let alone of the convicted) are not serious moral claims and that the goal of rehabilitation of the criminal is a sentimental notion of "bleeding hearts." Crusade ethics is not restricted to the political right or left alone, but can be expressed at both poles, and, somewhat less compatibly, in the middle. Its hallmark is not a certain substantive program, such as might meaningfully be called liberal or conservative, radical, progressive, moderate, or reactionary, but the morally simplistic zeal with which its advocates pursue whatever program they hold. The dominant feature is the sense of moral self-righteousness and moral indignation toward supposed wrongdoers. The sense of compassion is lacking.

Not all that masquerades under the name of morality, including Christian morality, is morally defensible. Even though crusade ethics has been the outlook in past and present of many who have identified themselves with the Christian church, it is difficult to see how this approach to war can be compatible with a Christian moral orientation. Crusade ethics retains neither the moral insight nor the compassion appropriate to Christian faith. Crusaders lose the awareness of their own sin as well as of the continued worth of the wrongdoer. They overlook that their absolute end conflicts with other real human goods. They forget that God is the God of all the world and is in covenant with all persons. Instead their God becomes a tribal god and their ethic, an ethic of exclusion. In these characteristics crusade ethics stands outside the tolerable bounds of Christian ethics, even though crusaders themselves remain persons of worth and may often identify themselves with the Christian community. Christian theology cannot include this stance as an acceptable Christian alternative without losing its essential identity. Within the church the argument between crusaders and noncrusaders is a struggle for the church's soul.

Christian Pacifism

In contrast, Christian pacifism is a plausible expression of Christian faith, even though I shall maintain that it is not a fully adequate one. My attention here is directed only to those pacifists who are Christian, even though in the twentieth century they have been influenced considerably by some non-Christian pacifists, especially Gandhi. The concern here is with Christian theological ethics and not simply with pacifist conclusions, which might be reached from a variety of possible outlooks.

What Christian pacifists usually oppose is violent rather than nonviolent coercion, and within the category of violence, war in particular, although a few pacifists have opposed all kinds of coercion.[10] In ordinary theological usage a Christian pacifist is someone who, on the basis of a Christian moral orientation, believes that it is always wrong to use violence, especially in war, but also in other types of situations. The "always" is crucial to the definition. A person is not a pacifist simply for believing that a given war is unjust and that one ought not take part in it, nor for believing that most wars are unjust, nor even that it is highly unlikely that today there could be a just war. All of those positions allow for the possibility, at least in theory, that under some circumstances it would be morally permissible to support some war. That is not a pacifist position, at least not as the term is ordinarily used by pacifist and nonpacifist theologians alike. It might very well be a just-war position, as it is of the essence of just-war theory that the application of the just-war criteria might lead one to judge that some and perhaps most wars are unjustifiable, on one or both sides. In contrast, the pacifist does not recognize conditions under which it would ever be justifiable to support a war.

This ordinary meaning of the term *pacifist* is why the term *nuclear pacifist* may be misleading. *Nuclear pacifist* usually denotes someone who either thinks all nuclear wars are inherently unjustifiable, or that it is unjustifiable to support a war under circumstances that have a significant likelihood of escalating to nuclear war. But those views admit of the possibility of judging that some wars prior to the advent of nuclear weapons were justifiable, and perhaps also that some are justifiable today in circumstances in which the likelihood of escalation to nuclear conflict is sufficiently small. The meaning of *pacifist* also makes unhelpful a term such as *selective pacifism*. Bennett and Seifert[11] seem to mean by it a position that judges wars of some types or under some kinds of circumstances to be inherently unjustifiable and other types open to the possibility of justification. But that is precisely what just-war theory judges. It is best not to becloud the deep differences between just-war theory and pacifism by a term such as *selective pacifism*. The differences are most fundamentally in *how* just-war theorists and pacifists go about arriving at their conclusions, so that a coincidence of moral judgments about certain kinds of wars does nothing to prove any "growing agreement" between pacifists and just-war theorists today. They are still as far apart in their moral outlooks as they have ever been.

Christian pacifism has long held some fundamental theological beliefs in common with just-war theory, however deeply they differ over the justifiability of wars. Christian pacifists and just-war theorists alike affirm the inclusiveness of God's covenant, and in that affirmation they stand in sharp contrast to crusaders. For both pacifism and the just war, not only the ally but also the enemy is to be valued and affirmed as a person, whatever should be the response to wrongdoing. It is consistent with both positions to hold that the doer of unjustifiable violence should be treated as an end, and not only as a means. Because the two positions hold these views in common, there is a sense in which the disagreement between them, however deep and persistent, is always "within the family" theologically to a degree to which that cannot be said about either in relation to crusade ethics.

The fundamental issue between Christian pacifists and just-war theorists is whether the use of violence against wrongdoers can ever be an expression of Christian love. For the pacifist it must seem incredible that one might affirm another person as an end, as a member of God's covenant community, and yet put that person to death. It should be recognized, of course, that for the just-war theorist it seems at least as incredible that one might recognize the frequent inability to restrain terribly harmful human wrongdoing without the use of violence and yet not ever be willing to use it to protect the weak and the oppressed.

There are two main types of arguments that are used to support the Christian pacifist position. One, "pacifism as a strategy," depends upon a particular reading of the morally relevant circumstances within which a decision is to be made about the use of violence. The other, "pacifism as obedient witness," depends upon a particular interpretation of the content of the basic moral standard of Christian ethics. Some Christian pacifists base their pacifism on the first of these arguments, some on the second, and some on both. Some who argue for pacifism as obedient witness use the pacifism-as-strategy argument to supplement their position, but others reject the pacifism-as-strategy argument altogether.

Pacifism as a strategy. This first type of pacifist argument asserts that the use only of methods of nonviolent power is a much more effective way to resist wrongdoing than is violence and does not involve the latter's cost to human life. Richard Gregg characterizes nonviolence as "moral jui-jitsu," because, he says, it puts at a disadvantage the other person who is expecting violence.[12] But its strength, several pacifists have argued, is not only the element of surprise. Because it does not aim to injure the opponent or to crush the will, it can evoke a more positive response than violence and can lead to

191

reconciliation and a better peace.[13] Furthermore, nonviolent resistance often has a strong appeal to the uncommitted bystander.

It must surely be affirmed by pacifists and nonpacifists alike that in some situations nonviolent power can be effective in checking wrongdoing. This is possible not only in face-to-face relationships, but also at the level of impersonal institutional power. Gandhi's nonviolent campaign for Indian independence was an impressive example. Martin Luther King, Jr.'s nonviolent protests against racial discrimination in the United States were far more effective than violence would have been.[14] Even if we judge that nonviolence is not always an effective strategy, it certainly can be so in some types of situations.

The most effective critic of pacifism as a strategy has been Reinhold Niebuhr. He declared that this argument optimistically underrates the persistence of human sin, that it reflects the false notion that any human conflict can eventually be resolved by negotiation, and that it sometimes leads to morally perverse judgments about the relative evils of war and of tyranny.[15] Many users of the pacifism-as-strategy argument are indeed vulnerable to some or all of these criticisms. It is depressing to see these weaknesses persist in some (not all) pacifist argumentation decades after Niebuhr so tellingly identified them.

The chief problem in the pacifism-as-strategy argument, when it purports to be valid in all situations, is that of dogmatic overstatement. Granted the effectiveness of nonviolence in some situations, in others it is not as effective in protecting people against others' wrongdoing as violence would be. Could Hitler's regime have been restrained from its persecution of the Jews by nonviolent, let alone noncoercive, means? Can the terrorists of Western Europe today be moved either by persuasion or by any available economic measures to give up their violence short of attaining their objectives? Can nonviolent means alone, of whatever kind, provide adequate security for Israel or Lebanon? Only the dogmatic give assured affirmative answers to these questions. It is as though they said, "Nonviolence is what Christian love requires, so it must be true that nonviolence will be more effective than violence." Even if the first clause is valid (and we shall shortly discuss that question), the second does not follow from it. It is the result of wishful thinking. Theological belief does not tell us whether pacifism is socially effective. We must seek to answer that question by disciplined study of society. Nonviolence is probably more effective than violence in some kinds of situations and very probably not in some other kinds of situations. But that answer undermines any position founded upon the judgment that pacifism is right because it always works. The pacifism-as-strategy argument will not serve as the justifying reason for pacifism, Christian or otherwise.

Pacifism as obedient witness. Many pacifists, including some who use the pacifism-as-strategy argument, base their pacifism instead upon a second argument. It is that whatever the external consequences of adopting only nonviolent means, the Christian is obligated in basic Christian principle, as a witness to the character and action of God, neither to use nor to sanction the use of violence. One should be a pacifist, they maintain, because to do so is to conform to God's nature and to be obedient to God's command.

Where this is offered as the fundamental argument for Christian pacifism, the pacifism-as-strategy argument only confuses the issue. If basic Christian principle prohibits the use of violence, then it prohibits it whether or not nonviolence is effective. The best statements of pacifism-as-obedient-witness are offered by those who are clear on this point, such as John Howard Yoder:

> The cross is not a recipe for resurrection. Suffering is not a tool to make people come around, nor a good in itself. . . . What is usually called "Christian pacifism" is most adequately understood not on the level of means alone, as if the pacifist were making the claim that he can achieve what war promises to achieve, but do it just as well or even better without violence. This is one kind of pacifism, which in some contexts may be clearly able to prove its point, but not necessarily always. That Christian pacifism which has a theological basis in the character

of God and the work of Jesus Christ is one in which the
calculating link between our obedience and ultimate efficacy has
been broken, since the triumph of God comes through
resurrection and not through effective sovereignty or assured
survival.[16]

In Yoder's argument the Christian should be pacifist
because that is what the Christian proclamation requires, not
because of any judgments about effectiveness. In his position
the norm for Christian ethics is present in Jesus' life and
teaching, though not in any simple way. Jesus' teaching,
Yoder repeatedly argues, is not directed only to the inner
person, nor applicable only in one-to-one relationships, but
proclaims a new human possibility in social and political
relationships as well.[17] The Christian is to love as Christ loved,
to accept suffering as Christ did, and in so doing to refuse
either to seek dominion or to use the violence of the world to
combat the world's violence. The Christian pacifist thus does
not attempt to control history. And yet this position, he
stresses, is not a withdrawal from the world; he denies that one
must, in the fashion of Ernst Troeltsch's church-sect typology,
choose between the political and the sectarian. Thus he speaks
of "revolutionary subordination"[18] to "the powers"—a con-
tinuously active and yet nonviolent approach. For him
pacifism is a way to be obedient in the world to the God who is
proclaimed in Jesus Christ, trusting in God's power to bring
resurrection.

Yoder's Christian pacifist refuses to use violence, not
because power as such is evil—it is God's power and therefore
good—but because a particular power may be so incorrigible
that we should refuse to collaborate with it. That is "a refusal to
use unworthy means even for what seems to be a worthy
end."[19] For Yoder this refusal is not an occasional matter; one
should never use violence. Presumably then any wrongdoing
that can be restrained only by violence is "incorrigible." The
refusal to use such "unworthy means" is an essential part of
his idea of what it means to proclaim and follow Jesus Christ.

Yoder's argument for pacifism as obedient witness merits

appreciation for several reasons, among them his clarity that the idea of pacifism as an effective strategy is an inadequate foundation, his refusal to reject power as such, his interesting alternative of a pacifism of obedient witness that is not a withdrawal from the social world, and his extended effort to base his position in a critical interpretation of the Bible.

Although Yoder has accurately located the fundamental issue between Christian pacifism and Christian just-war theory, it is another matter whether his position is adequate. As he assumes, the fundamental issue here is a theological question about what the Christian proclamation requires, not an empirical social scientific question about the relative effectiveness of violent and nonviolent means. Yoder's answer to the question is one that has been and should continue to be taken seriously in the Christian tradition, one that merits respect and deserves continued dialogue from those who hold other views. Yet I shall maintain that when all this has been said, there remains the question of Christian responsibility for the restraint of wrongdoing. I shall concentrate upon certain theological-ethical problems in his answer.

What does it imply for the question of the use of violence, to pattern one's love after God's as declared in Jesus Christ? That is the issue between Christian pacifists and nonpacifists. When Yoder takes Jesus' life and teaching as a model of the love that God commands, he proceeds as many others, pacifists and nonpacifists, have done in Christian history. This method in itself does not settle the issue. It is possible to differ as to the sense in which Jesus' life and teachings are to be the model. By any interpretation, though, it would appear that a major ingredient of that model should be self-denial, even to the point of cross-bearing, which Jesus both taught and exemplified. But even this point does not resolve the dispute. The nonpacifist simply maintains that self-denial and cross-bearing need not entail a refusal ever to use violence, though it does require that one never use violence (or any other means of power) simply on behalf of oneself.

In *Basic Christian Ethics* Paul Ramsey argues that Jesus' "strenuous teachings," such as the requirement to turn the other cheek, dealt only with simple moral relationships of one person to one other and did not attempt to say how we ought to act in complex cases where nonresistance would leave someone else open to injury.[20] Yoder rejects that argument, for he believes he has shown that Jesus did in fact intend his teaching, including the prohibition of violence, to apply to complex political situations as well. The argument over which is the correct interpretation would be long indeed. But let us bracket that question for the moment. Imagine, though it is debatable, that Yoder is correct, that Jesus did intend his strenuous teachings to be followed amid the complexities of politics. If so, one who takes seriously Jesus' concern for the weak and oppressed should rejoin that if Jesus had not expected an imminent end of this worldly order, he would not or should not so have intended them. This is not a rejection of the assumption that Jesus' life and teaching are in some sense a model for the Christian. Rather it is a further step in exploring *in what sense* Jesus' life and teaching are a model. Here we can see the impact of the earlier discussion of the meaning of covenant love. What is central to the biblical proclamation of God's love is God's steadfast concern and care for persons. That should likewise be central to human love. The question of violence is how that concern can best be expressed in the midst of unavoidable intense conflict.

In the New Testament proclamation, including its witness to Jesus' teaching and behavior, the concern to meet the needs of God's children is more fundamental to the meaning of love than is the prohibition of all violent means. To say that God's methods are themselves never violent is to beg the question, for it presupposes that God's will is never expressed through people's morally restrained violent resistance to unjust oppression. Because that is what the question is, that argument cannot be used as a trump card. Whether violence can ever serve God's covenant love and thereby be a worthy, even though regrettable, means depends upon the circumstances. The nonpacifist affirms that in some situations of irreconcilable conflict between the wrongdoers and the wronged, it can so serve.

196

But let us not too readily grant that Jesus did fully intend to apply his strenuous teachings, such as "turn the other cheek," to the complexities of politics. Paul Ramsey identifies the uncertainty of the matter when he asks regarding the parable of the good Samaritan, "What do you think Jesus would have made the Samaritan do if he had come upon the scene while the robbers were still at their fell work?"[21] The pacifist may think the answer to that question is clear, but part of the point of the question may be that Jesus did not tell the story that way. The fact that he did not pose the moral issue of violence in that manner, either there or elsewhere, leaves it in some doubt what he might have intended.

The issue is whether the Christian is going to take with sufficient seriousness the need of the other person. Granted that one ought to be concerned for both wrongdoer and wronged, what is to be done when one attacks the other? Yoder's pacifism does not bid one stand idly by, of course. It is active, not passive. Yet after the pacifist has used all means deemed worthy, but in vain, as Yoder recognizes will sometimes happen, then the choice becomes whether to let the wrongdoer go on with the wrongdoing. To do so, when there are morally restrained means of preventing it, is not to take the need of the oppressed with adequate seriousness. It is to consent to the wrongdoer's own lack of moral responsibility and lack of understanding of what it is to belong to the human community; it is to consent to whatever degree of destruction of God's inclusive covenant community the wrongdoers may choose to wreak, when there are available and morally restrained means to the contrary. One may speak, as Yoder does, of nonviolently siding "in favor of the men whom that power is oppressing,"[22] but this favoring finds no effective outer expression. And the oppressed find no succor in it. It is the need of the oppressed that calls one under some circumstances to the morally restrained use of violence. The need of the neighbor in the situation of oppression is what can sometimes make violence a possible worthy means. The inadequacy of pacifism as obedient witness is its failure to call for sufficiently effective action on behalf of that need.

The problem still remains for just-war theory how it can reconcile the use of violence toward wrongdoers with respect for the wrongdoer as an end. How from covenant love can the use of violence find proper moral limitation? What would that limitation look like? Let us turn now to a theory of justifiable coercion.

Toward a Christian Theory of Justifiable Coercion

Its Roots in Covenant Love

Augustine, Aquinas, and others developed Christian just-war theory as an expression of Christian love under conditions of unavoidable conflict. That must also be the case with a broader theory of justifiable violence, or an even broader theory of justifiable coercion. Whatever the conditions under which coercion and violence are morally justifiable, the argument must depend on one's basic moral standard—in this framework, covenant love. There are no justifiable exceptions to following the basic moral standard. If the justification for morally restrained coercion, including violence, cannot be found in one's basic moral standard, then it is not to be justified at all.

The meaning of covenant love contains both a positive inclination to coercion and even to violence (under certain types of conditions in which wrongdoing cannot be restrained in less destructive ways), and a negative inclination away from them. The positive inclination arises from love's respect for the equal worth of those who would wrongfully be harmed and whose moral claims would therein be seriously harmed by the wrongdoers, and from love's concern for the needs of these potential victims.

The negative element, the disinclination to violence or even to coercion, arises from the same ingredients of covenant love, though this time as these ingredients have to do with the wrongdoers. Because of its inclusiveness, covenant love does not permit unconcern for the needs of wrongdoers. Yet it appears right to say that their wrongdoing inherently justifies giving priority, at least in some respects, to the relevant needs of their victims. Even so, the wrongdoers' needs still matter.

The equal worth of the wrongdoer raises a more complicated issue. From covenant love one is obligated to have respect for the wrongdoer as an end and not a means only. Is it possible to respect someone as an end and at the same time to do that person violence, perhaps even to the point of death? An adequate answer will consider the relationship between a moral agent's inner orientation and outer action, and the bearing of this relationship upon the question of the intention of the violent act.

The inner orientation of respect for one as a human being is still due the wrongdoer, regardless of how terrible the wrong. From covenant love it cannot rightly be said that the wrongdoing inherently abrogates this obligation of respect, even though it justifies giving a higher priority to the relevant needs of the wronged. The obligation to equal respect is never abrogated, not by anything one does or any quality one possesses. Yet in some situations in which less painful alternatives are unavailable, wrongdoing may abrogate the obligation, not to equal respect, but to avoid certain kinds of injurious actions. An outer action that injures wrongdoers can reflect not an inner stance of disrepect for them but a positive concern to protect the wronged. We cannot simply equate outer acts of violence with an inner stance of disrespect. They do indeed sometimes arise from such an inner stance, but that need not be their source. We indeed might rationalize that because of the wrongdoing, that person does not matter anymore. But the other person always matters. The only condition under which violence is ever justifiable is when the other person fully matters—continues to have the same worth in our eyes as other persons. Let us put away all *rationalization* for violence and rely only upon legitimate *justification*. One is never morally justified in killing as the expression of our rejection of another person.

Much depends upon the intention of the violent act. An act's *intention* is what one seeks to accomplish by it—its objective. An intention is not the same thing as a foreknown result. This distinction is expressed in the doctrine of double effect,[23] the idea that the same action may have two effects, both anticipated, but one intended and the other not. Imagine, for example, that late one night Bill Studious is just beginning to cram for a final examination the next morning when he hears a knock at his door. There stands Art Anxious, who tells Bill he is on the verge of committing suicide. Bill puts aside his books and spends the remainder of the night with Art, trying to be of assistance. The next morning he gets Art to more professional help and goes on to the examination—and fails it, as he knew he would when he pushed aside his books. Yet his intention was to help Art, let us assume, not to fail the examination. Foreknowledge of the likely consequences of an act is not equivalent to intending all those consequences.

A similar situation can arise in the use of violence. If the police are trying to prevent a murder, their intention ought not to be to kill or otherwise harm the potential murderer, but to prevent harm to any victims. Harming the wrongdoer is beside the point of protecting the victim; it ought likewise to be "beside the intention." If the police set out intending to protect the victim, they may or may not have to harm the would-be murderer to achieve their objective. Even if that protection involves killing the murderer, that need not be their objective. Similarly in war, protecting potential war victims may require intending to incapacitate enemy combatants. That may or may not require doing them bodily harm. If one can reach the just objective of protecting the weak by taking the enemy combatants prisoner, that is what is morally required, rather than killing them.

Contrary to the position of Christian pacifism, then, the standard of covenant love does not prohibit all violence, let alone all coercion. If it did, that would mean in effect giving the wishes of the powerful wrongdoer priority over the needs of the weaker victim. It would often mean abdicating effective and constant concern for the plight of the weak, and therein rendering ineffective our special covenants with them. Because of the tragic but sometimes insoluble conflicts in human society, it is sometimes the case that covenant love with its respect for the equal worth of all persons must find expression in coercing, and at times doing violence, even to the point of taking life.

But contrary to crusade ethics, when coercion and violence are justifiable, it is only within strict limits. Those limits are necessary because the wrongdoers are of worth as God's covenant creatures, just as are the wronged and any innocent bystanders. The very reason that sometimes calls for the use of coercion and violence also calls for their moral restraint.

A theory of justifiable coercion expressing covenant love must therefore, like just-war theory, include two kinds of conditions: conditions for justifiable resort to coercion, and conditions for justifiable means of coercion. In identifying the specific conditions, I shall use the just-war conditions as a point of departure, even though some of the conditions will need modification to fit the broader subject of coercion.

Justifiable Resort to Coercion

1. *Legitimate authority.* Traditionally one reason for this condition was to prohibit private armies from conducting their own wars and enveloping the society in chaos. More recently it has required both that military authorities be kept subject to properly constituted political authority and that political leaders follow legitimate constitutional requirements.

Where justifiable means of violence other than in war are likely to reach a significant level, as in the exercise of police power, it is still morally necessary to retain the requirement of legitimate authority and not allow violence to be exercised by citizens in their private capacities. Otherwise the basic order of a society would be threatened, with private individuals and groups pursuing personal vendettas and narrow group objectives, often under the guise of serving the society. The importance of this condition can be seen from the sad example of Lebanon in recent years, with private as well as foreign armies vying for control of sections of the country.

Does *legitimate authority* mean that it is impossible for there to be a justifiable revolution? It is certainly impossible if the term means simply "legitimate *legal* authority," but it can and ought to be understood otherwise. Its more basic meaning is "legitimate *moral* authority," without which no legal authority is truly legitimate. There have clearly been governments without moral legitimacy. The cases of Nazi Germany and Idi Amin in Uganda are glaring examples. Where a regime has lost its moral legitimacy, that legitimacy might pass to some revolutionary movement within that country, if there is one seeking to act on behalf of legitimately constituted authority, as did the Twentieth of July Movement in Germany in 1944. This interpretation of legitimate authority certainly does not justify all revolutionary movements any more than it justifies all recourse to war by nation-states. In particular it does not justify romantic terrorist movements in whose eyes any government not fitting their utopian ideal is unjust and any effective means of violence against it is doable. It takes more than subjective confidence of legitimacy to constitute it. Yet in opposition to outrageously unjust regimes, there have been revolutionary groups sufficiently directed toward a just rule by constitutional means on behalf of all the people that they can rightly be said to have legitimate moral authority.

When the means of coercion are *non*violent, it is neither crucial nor practicable nor even desirable to limit its use to governmental authority. The use of economic threats and inducements, for example, is essential as a measure available to private institutions so that they can discourage wrongdoing at many points short of action in the courts. This is true even though economic coercion is easily misused. The whole range of individuals and of the relatively just institutions of society are potentially legitimate nonviolent coercers, and not government authority only, though that condition does not justify all nonviolent coercion.

2. *Justifiable cause.* This is the foremost of the conditions for resorting to war and to other kinds of coercion as well. It requires that there be a sufficient justifying reason for the resort.

This is especially true concerning war, as its costs are so great. Justifiable cause for resorting to war has traditionally been to right a grave wrong or defend a crucial right. Christian just-war theorists have maintained that such causes are ordinarily present in defensive wars, for example, in efforts to prevent an aggressor from overrunning one's country. The same types of cause—to right a grave wrong or defend a crucial right—will also sometimes justify initiating the first blows in a war, and not only engaging in defense once the enemy has struck first. This is clearest in the case of a preemptive strike in the face of an imminent enemy attack. In 1967, for example, when Israeli intelligence determined that the Arab powers were at the point of invading, the Israelis launched an air attack shortly beforehand, destroyed the Arab air arm on the ground, and thereby prevented a possible Arab victory. If it would have been justifiable for Israel to defend itself against the Arab attack after it had begun, then it was justifiable to anticipate a sure and imminent attack in order not to be put at a dire disadvantage.

The more difficult moral problem arises when an enemy attack is not imminent, and yet grave wrongs are being committed by the other country. Consider Hitler's persecution of the Jews within Germany in the 1930s, Idi Amin's more recent massacres within Uganda, and Emperor Bokassa's within the Central African Empire. These atrocities constituted grave wrongs, such that if the other criteria were met, it would have been justifiable for another country to initiate a war to bring them to a halt. Even if Idi Amin's forces had not invaded Tanzania, for example, the latter would have had justifiable cause for war in order to halt the atrocities of the Amin regime.

If it is true that under such circumstances there can be justifiable cause for initiating a war and not merely for defending against an attack, then we must reinterpret the justifiability of defensive wars. Although there is *ordinarily* just cause for defensive war, yet when the defending power is seeking to defend its right to continue committing atrocities, self-defense is no longer a justifiable cause. It is not self-defense as such that justifies, but the righting of a grave wrong or the defense of a crucial right.

This discussion of justifiable cause has proceeded thus far as though nuclear weapons did not exist. That they do raises grave questions about the just-war criteria today. Can there any longer be justifiable wars, including just causes, when conventional wars might become nuclear? This is a question of the greatest importance for just-war theory. Some today maintain that just-war theory is no longer relevant. That assertion might mean either of two things. First, it might refer to the just-war theory's theological foundations, so as to claim that those of pacifism are indisputably superior. Yet people who write off just-war theory today have not offered any especially different or more convincing case for pacifist theological foundations than were offered in earlier times, nor has the theological community arrived at any general consensus that those earlier arguments were correct and the criticisms of them (such as those expressed earlier in this chapter) mistaken. Indeed the issue between pacifism and just-war theory is seldom joined among theologians today.

Second, and more likely, those who dismiss just-war theory might be saying that according to the just-war criteria there cannot be a just war today. If this is what is meant, then the critics fail to understand their own logic. If it is by using just-war criteria that they wish to declare all wars unjust, there could scarcely be a more forceful assertion of the criteria's continuing relevance. Whether just-war standards *do* rule out all wars today needs further examination, but clearly the criteria remain highly relevant. What we need is not premature dismissal of the theory, but its continuing refinement and more careful use. Wars continue to occur, and not to use some kind of just-war criteria is to cease subjecting acts of war—perhaps the most disturbing kinds of human action today—to probing moral examination.[24]

The question raised by nuclear weapons is actually not so much about the justifiability of the cause as about another just-war criterion—proportionality. To launch a war unjustly is as much an offense today as previously, and such an atrocity is a grave wrong whether there are nuclear weapons in the world or not. The question is not whether such grave wrongs occur, but whether the evil to be prevented is as great in an age of nuclear weapons as the evil risked in preventing it. Because that is a question about proportionality, let us postpone it until we come to that criterion.

The criterion of justifiable cause is applicable to all kinds of coercion, and not to war only. What constitutes a justifiable cause for resort to coercion of any kind is a matter of continuing dispute. These disputes are too complex for me to do more here than identify some of the kinds of justifiable causes for coercion. Joel Feinberg has aptly summarized the possible grounds for coercion under six headings:[25]

1. To prevent harm to others, either
    a. injury to individual persons (*The Private Harm Principle*), or
    b. impairment of institutional practices that are in the public interest (*The Public Harm Principle*);
2. To prevent offense to others (*The Offense Principle*);
3. To prevent harm to self (*Legal Paternalism*);
4. To prevent or punish sin, i.e., to "enforce morality as such" (*Legal Moralism*);
5. To benefit the self (*Extreme Paternalism*);
6. To benefit others (*The Welfare Principle*).

By the "self" in items 3 and 5, Feinberg means the one who is to be coerced, and by "others" he means those other than the one to be coerced. As already explained,[26] a "harm" is the invasion of an interest, and harms include but are to be distinguished from hurts, which include both physical pains and forms of mental distress.

Given these meanings, it is clear that both the Private Harm and the Public Harm principles can constitute justifiable cause for some kind of coercion. Under some circumstances they are justifiable cause for violence. Both have to do directly with meeting others' needs, and more particularly with preventing infringements upon negative rights to liberty and to security. We will leave to others the debate over the conditions under which any of the other proposed grounds would constitute justifiable cause for coercion.

3. *Right intention*. This condition is closely related to justifiable cause. The latter points especially to the wrong acts to which a country should be responding if it goes to war,

whereas the former stipulates the kind of objective the country should seek. To have a right intention in restraining wrongdoing, the objective must always be to prevent, remove, or reduce the harmful effects of wrongdoing—that is, to seek a better peace.

This rules out at least two kinds of wrong intentions, whether the coercion in question is violent or nonviolent. One is coercion simply to promote personal or narrow group self-interest. That is found in wars for national self-extension—to gain territory, wealth, or prestige. It has many nonviolent parallels: for example, self-aggrandizement by a company or political party or individual, masquerading as the restraint of wrongdoing.

The other kind of wrong intention is that which seeks an objective of a sort that inherently denies the worth of the coerced, as in wars to exterminate some group, or, in private business, coercion in order to destroy someone or some group of persons. No coercion is ever justifiable that inherently expresses contempt for the coerced.

4. *Proportionality.* According to this criterion it is not justifiable to resort to war if the evil effects of doing so will likely exceed the evil to be prevented (and the good to be attained) by going to war. The same is true regarding other kinds of coercion. It is obviously not justifiable, for example, to shoot at a hostage-holder in order to free the hostages if there is a good likelihood that the hostage-holder might be talked into surrendering, and especially if the shots are likely to injure the hostages.

The principle of proportionality requires the moral agent to make a reasonable calculation, even though that may be difficult to do. However reasonable and prudent it is to calculate proportionality, we are often disinclined to be reasonable or prudent. This is especially true of anyone in a crusading mood. The crusader often uses coercion simply to harm, refusing to consider damage done to the enemy, and sometimes not even bothering over likely damage to friends, allies, self, or even the stated objective.

The just-war demand for proportionality is what might

bring us up short about war in a nuclear age. In his encyclical *Pacem in Terris*, Pope John XXIII held that in an age of nuclear weapons it can no longer be justifiable to initiate war in order to repair wrongs, though his wording may have implied that it can still be justifiable even in such an age to fight a defensive war.[27] On the one hand, Pope John's statement recognizes the immense destruction that nuclear weapons can cause, which were it to occur would probably outweigh any other evil. On the other hand, the statement distinguishes between going to war to repair a wrong to another, and doing so simply in national self-defense, which by implication might sometimes be justifiable.

Some ethicists would object that the pope's statement does not go nearly far enough, that the existence of nuclear weapons makes disproportionate any kind of war, defensive as well as offensive, because any war, anywhere, might draw in one of the nuclear powers, lead to the use of nuclear weapons, and thereby become disproportionate. This is a possible outcome, of course, but the argument fails to take account of the history of war since nuclear weapons were first devised in 1945. Of the many wars since the end of World War II, not one has involved the detonation of a single nuclear weapon. That is not a completely reassuring truth; the next war might be nuclear. Yet it should call into question the claim that wars today are likely to become nuclear. That is counter to our experience in an age of nuclear weapons. Not only have nonnuclear powers fought dozens of wars without the direct participation of nuclear powers, but the nuclear powers themselves have fought nonnuclear wars: the United States in Korea and Vietnam, China versus Vietnam, the Soviet Union in Afghanistan, and the United Kingdom against Argentina. Escalation to nuclear weapons is not automatic; it does not even seem likely under most circumstances. It is especially unlikely as long as the United States and the Soviet Union both possess an invulnerable second-strike capability, so that each would be able to retaliate even after absorbing a first strike. That is the most stable kind of nuclear balance, because both sides have the greatest possible incentive to refrain from using nuclear weapons. Even so we can easily imagine situations—with widespread nuclear proliferation and mad rulers, for example—in which the likelihood would significantly increase. Yet the existence of nuclear weapons has seemed up to now to incline nations to less extensive wars when they occur and to conduct their power struggles short of war more often than they otherwise would.

But if some *non*nuclear wars can be proportionate, it is highly unlikely that a nuclear war would ever meet this test. The recent United States Catholic Bishops' statement examines this question and concludes that once nuclear war has begun, "the danger of escalation is so great that it would be morally unjustifiable to initiate nuclear war in any form."[28] For the same reason the statement denies that nuclear retaliation would be justifiable. There is ample reason for this fear of escalation, which is shared by a number of strategic experts, who maintain that once nuclear weapons are used, the likelihood is that both sides would lose control and that the war would become unlimited.[29] Even though the statement judges that nuclear war would be disproportionate, it gives moral acceptance to some forms of nuclear *deterrence* for the time being, as a means to reduce the chances of nuclear war and to protect the independence of nations and peoples.[30]

Why take the risk of nuclear war at all? Why not simply have nuclear disarmament? But that alternative involves its own serious problems and risks. In the first place, its advocates do not tell us how to achieve it if any other nuclear power does not want it. Second, if all nations did agree to complete nuclear disarmament, how would we ensure against a nation's cheating on the agreement by producing nuclear weapons again, which if it happened would give the cheater an enormous power advantage? Third, once existing nuclear stockpiles had been reduced to a very low level on all sides, the incentive for one nation to launch a surprise nuclear attack against another's remaining stockpiles would be greatly increased. Fourth, if all nuclear arms were indeed eliminated, the chances of a general war (comparable to World Wars I and II) would be greatly increased, since a major reason no such war has occurred since 1945 has been the danger of nuclear weapons. Anyone who wants complete nuclear disarmament must be prepared, were that goal to be reached, to support major increases in nonnuclear armaments and to expect a major increase in the extensiveness of wars.

It would be far better to work for an agreement to *reduce* rather than eliminate nuclear weapons. Yet if a reduction is to decrease the chances of nuclear war, we must seek conditions under which both major nuclear powers maintain the invulnerability of their strategic nuclear weapons. Otherwise one or the other would have an incentive to launch a first strike. The best way to reduce the likelihood of nuclear war is to reduce nations' incentives to use the nuclear weapons they possess. Reducing nuclear weapons is not an automatic formula for greater safety; if done in some ways it can, by affecting incentives, increase the very risks it seeks to avoid. The focus needs to be upon nations' incentives more than on their weapons.[31]

Whatever is done with nuclear weapons, though, there will continue to be situations in which going to conventional war meets the test of proportionality. The alternative, a nation's never under any circumstances being willing to go to war, would give an enormous advantage to any nation that *is* willing and could threaten war convincingly, and this situation would not lessen the likelihood of armed violence.

When we calculate proportionality in a nuclear age, therefore, we must hold together two judgments. One is that escalation to nuclear war is possible and, were it to happen, would render the military action disproportionate beyond any ordinary calculation. The other is that under most circumstances nuclear escalation is unlikely and can be made still less likely by the way a crisis is handled. In sum, it continues to make sense to say that the criterion of proportionality can sometimes be met, though we must do so in full awareness of the dangers of nuclear war.

5. *Reasonable chance of success.* In just-war theory it is not justifiable to resort to war unless there is a "reasonable

chance" of attaining one's justifiable objectives. This requirement is simply an extension of the requirement of proportionality. It asks the agent not only to calculate the nonmoral goods and evils of resorting and of not resorting to war, but also to estimate the likelihood that the benefits of resorting to war will in fact occur. This is a way of saying that the calculation of proportionality is not a one-dimensional matter. Probability is as important for proportionality as are the weights of the values and disvalues. "Success" in war (or in other endeavors) is attaining one's justifiable objectives (not the same thing as "victory"—a war goal that is too vague and too tempting to excess). One must calculate the likelihood of success in regard to various goals at once. The Tanzanians, for example, may have thought it likely that they could prevail over Idi Amin's troops, and in that they were correct; but if they considered further, they underestimated the difficulties in bringing about a tolerable order in Uganda. The requirement of reasonable chance of success is as applicable to other means of coercion as to war.

6. *Last resort.* It is not permissible in just-war theory to resort to war unless or until all other means of resolution of the problem have been tried without success. This requirement is also an extension of the requirement of proportionality. Obviously one ought not to incur the risks to human life that war poses if a reasonable possibility exists of attaining the just objective by less destructive means.

This requirement involves two problems. The first is present in all its applications, including war. If a nation literally attempted all other imaginable avenues before going to war, or a police force before resorting to violence, or a judge before sentencing a convicted burglar to prison, it would often rule out all chance of successful defense of a just cause. But let us incorporate the idea stated in the fifth condition, "reasonable chance of success," into this one. Then "last resort" requires that all means must be tried, either actually or through a "thought-experiment," sufficiently to enable one to judge whether there is a reasonable chance that a less costly means might succeed, before resort to a more dangerous or destructive kind of coercion is justifiable. This condition does not justify an infinite postponement of resort to war or violence on the optimistic hope that eventually "something will turn up." Early resort is sometimes justifiable.

The other problem has to do with resort to coercion short of war, and especially to nonviolent coercion. The less costly the means of coercion, the less strictly obligatory it is to examine all other even less costly avenues before proceeding. Yet even with coercive means that are relatively mild—such as threats of moderate economic penalty—it is worth asking whether there is a better way to the just objective than coercion.

In the development of just-war theory, it has rightly been judged that *all six* of these conditions for resort to war must be met before the resort to war is justifiable. It is not enough simply to have justifiable grounds or any combination of conditions short of the six. That is also a valid requirement upon other forms of violence. With nonviolent coercion, however, we have judged that the requirement of legitimate authority is not always binding and that "last resort" is less obligatory the less harmful the means of coercion. Whatever the set of criteria appropriate for any form of coercion, however, that entire set must be met before the resort to coercion is justifiable.

Justifiable Means of Coercion

Justifiable resort to war—or to lesser forms of violent or nonviolent coercion—does not complete the work of moral restraint of coercion. The reason for moral restraint in resort to coercion is also the reason for restraint in *how* one uses it: respect for the worth of those to be coerced, for their victims, and for others who may be affected. Here too the conditions laid down in just-war theory apply to other kinds of coercion.

1. *Proportionality.* Not only must the condition of proportionality be met before resorting to coercion. It must also be satisfied again and again in the process of coercing. If, for example, it was justifiable and therefore among other things not disproportionate for the Allies to resort to war against

Japan after they were attacked in 1941, that did not settle the question of proportionality regarding the use of nuclear weapons. One must make a moral assessment over and over again in war. Can this particular objective be attained with less destruction? This idea is expressed in the strategic principle of *economy of force*. The British military strategist B. H. Liddell Hart expresses this idea in his statement that strategy "has for its purpose the reduction of fighting to the slenderest possible proportions" and that perfect strategy would be "to produce a decision without any serious fighting"—through such tactics as movement, surprise, and subsequent "dislocation" of the enemy.[32] This is true of all forms of coercion, in order that their harmful effects may be reduced as far as morally possible.

2. *The principle of discrimination.* This is the condition that most readily separates moral sensitivity from insensitivity, and covenant fidelity from infidelity, in the use of coercion. Here it is revealed what the coercer thinks of those coerced—whether one considers the wrongdoer as a fellow member of God's inclusive covenant or only as an evil to be stamped out or obstruction to be overcome, and whether one views bystanders as fellow human beings with their own rights or only as potential devices to be used against the enemy. Not to take this principle seriously is a sure sign one thinks that some persons stand outside the covenant, and therefore that one's *functioning* god (in this case very different from the God of Jesus Christ) is a tribal deity. Discrimination between legitimate and illegitimate targets is an essential hallmark of a Christian moral outlook.

In war the principle of discrimination *forbids direct and intentional attack upon noncombatants.* Others have explained this requirement at some length and continue to discuss its fine points.[33] Here I shall only call to mind the meaning of its basic concepts.

a. Noncombatants are those who are now (at the time the coercive means are used) not effective agents in the wrongdoing being restrained. Combatants are those who continue to be effective agents in the wrongdoing. There are, of course, matters of degree and borderline cases. Yet the spirit

212

of covenant love drives the coercer to try to target only those persons who are most obviously effective agents in wrongdoing. Given the combatant/noncombatant distinction, factory workers making tanks are in some sense borderline cases—certainly less effective agents than the tank-drivers, but more effective than their spouses and children at home. But if the just intention of a coercing love is to restrain wrongdoing, not to make people suffer, then one will aim primarily at weapons about to be used, and if ever at the factory, then at the weapons being produced rather than at the workers' families, or even, if they are avoidable, at the workers.

This distinction helps us to find who is and who is not a justifiable target in a justifiable war, revolution, law enforcement, or any other kind of violence. An enemy soldier free to act is a legitimate target; that same soldier can no longer be justifiably targeted once captured. The difference is that, once captured, he has become a noncombatant, no longer effective in the wrongdoing to be restrained. The railroad bridges in Dresden in February 1945 were legitimate targets for Allied bombers, as were the many troops streaming through the city; the local populace was not. Yet it was the populace that was intentionally attacked, and after three days and nights of continuous bombing the railroad bridges were still standing.[34] The troops, weapons, and transport facilities in Hiroshima and Nagasaki in August 1945 were properly military targets; but the general population of those cities was not, and the nuclear weapons that were dropped were indiscriminate as between the two types of targets, whether proportionate or not. The leaders and armed defenders of a tyrannically unjust government are legitimate targets in a justifiable revolution, but the many ordinary civilians are not. No matter how justifiable a revolutionary cause may be, it is wrong to terrorize the civilian populace to get at the wrongdoers. Covenant love forbids the use of noncombatants—men, women, children going about their ordinary peaceful activities in ways that would be justifiable in any context—as hostages or targets. A just cause does not make all means just. Not all is fair in war, or in other human conflicts.

b. Intentional attack is to be distinguished from *unintended side effect*. Let us assume that in a justifiable war an air attack is being carried out upon an enemy munitions dump and the forces protecting it—a justifiable target. Imagine, though, that a few civilians who live nearby are killed during the raid. If their deaths were intended, as were those of the populace of Dresden, then this is a prohibited attack upon the innocent, and it is justly labeled murder. But if the harm to them was not part of the objective, if all reasonable steps were taken to reduce such harmful effects, and if the extent of this harm is not so great as to outweigh the military significance of the target, then their deaths, while lamentable, are not murders, but unintended side effects. The case is like that of police who fire at an armed assassin and unfortunately hit a bystander. The problem is in their aim and perhaps their judgment, but not necessarily in their intention.

Intention is not, however, infinitely malleable. One cannot willfully drop fire bombs over Dresden's residential areas without intending to burn those areas. Intention has both subjective and objective aspects, and the latter are built into the shape of the act. We can rightly say that a foreseen harmful side effect of an act was not intended when, first, it was not subjectively desired by those who did the act; second, when they took what steps they could reasonably have taken under the circumstances to avoid that effect; and third, when their justifiable objective could have been as fully attained had the harmful side effect not taken place at all. Had the people living near our imagined munitions dump not lived there, it could have been quite as effectively destroyed.

Covenant love, giving priority to the needs of the wronged over those of wrongdoers, requires that we take pains in each act to intend only the restraint of the wrongdoers, that we seek to avoid harm insofar as possible.

c. The term *direct* in the principle of discrimination prohibits using noncombatants as a way of getting at wrongdoers. It is not enough that the wrongdoers are the ultimate target. Noncombatants, those who have no direct and significantly effective role in the wrongdoing in question, cannot rightly be used as mere means to coerce the wrongdoers. Although this aspect of the principle has its special problems in some types of cases of medical ethics, it continues in general to be applicable to the use of violence against wrongdoing. It prohibits taking the enemy populace as hostages; it prohibits holding a gun to the head of a criminal's child in order to influence him to surrender; it rules out torture of prisoners of war to extract information useful in tomorrow's battles. If these restrictions are "inconvenient" to military officials, police, and any others under legitimate authority, they are in the same sense that all God's children are often "inconvenient." Every serious moral claim is an "inconvenience": without it we would be morally free to act otherwise, but with it we are morally restricted. It is precisely for the weak and helpless that wrongdoing most needs to be restrained. It would contradict the very purpose of justifiable restraint of wrongdoing to use them as mere instruments to coerce unjust coercers.

In war, then, and not only on the way to war, covenant love shapes and limits what is justifiable; similarly in the midst of other means of coercion, and in resort to them. It is only with such a double set of conditions that it can be morally permissible from covenant love to use coercion, and more especially violence, to prevent wrongdoing.

It is sometimes objected that just-war theory has no effect; all think their own side is justified anyhow. But the Vietnam protest movement should have dispatched that argument once and for all. It was not only pacifists who protested that war, but for the most part people who would think some wars under other conditions justifiable, people who had their own set of criteria, however incomplete and however fuzzily used, and who used them to judge that that war was not among the justifiable ones. We hope that the criteria that people use will be adequate; we hope they will use them well. But that is an argument for better and fuller use of an adequate just-war theory, not for discarding it.

Nor is it only the nonmilitary public that can be influenced by just-war criteria. We hear of atrocities like those at My Lai in Vietnam, but accounts of moral discrimination and restraint in

215

war do not make headlines. Desmond Young relays this report told to him by General von Ravenstein of Field Marshal Rommel's desert army in World War II.[35] Rommel had sent von Ravenstein out to try to capture a British general and his staff, thought to be in an exposed position nearby:

> "I had no time to take prisoners," he [von Ravenstein] said, "In fact, when I drove through some British units and numbers of men, seeing the tanks on top of them, tried to surrender, I had to call out, 'Go away! I'm not interested in you!' What could I have done with prisoners?"

What he could have done, of course, was to shoot them as he went by, though because they were attempting to surrender it would have been an act of murder, contrary to the international laws of war and contrary to just-war theory. Following standards internalized from some source we know not, von Ravenstein, who was not a Nazi, believed that was not the right way to conduct a war, and so he could ask, "What could I have done with prisoners?" and could call out, "Go away!" The just-war criteria, however they have become known, continue to have some effect among those who fight wars and among some military commanders, including some enemy commanders, even in modern mobilized warfare. My Lai is not the only way people fight wars. Nor need it be.

Conclusion

This chapter began with the assumption that when choice is unavoidable between the interests of the wronged and those of the wrongdoers, preference should go to the former. That does not say it all. Wrongdoers are not simply that; they are in the first place persons. They themselves are in serious need, and behavior like theirs is often to be expected on the basis of their past deprivations, though these do not justify their wrongdoing. While we are restraining wrongdoing in order to serve valid moral claims of the wronged, we must also seek a more humane way of life for the wrongdoers insofar as that is possible.

The question of this chapter has been *how* rather than whether restraint of wrongdoers should be carried out, and under what sorts of circumstances. A theory of justifiable coercion, derived from the traditional theory of justifiable war, is the answer that best expresses the meaning of covenant love. It is not an answer that will appeal to those who self-righteously crusade against supposed forces of evil. Nor will it satisfy Christian pacifists, who believe that the prohibition against violence is absolute. While their moral impulse surely arises out of Christian love, I do not believe that their moral reasoning or their moral conclusions adequately express it.

The Christian, knowing the sin of the self as well as that of others, and aware of the persistence of wrongdoing on all sides, can find in the theory of justifiable coercion an expression both of the equal worth of all persons, wrongdoers and wronged alike, and of the lamentable yet valid obligation in the midst of unavoidable social conflict to use coercion, and sometimes violence, with restraint, for the sake of wrongdoers as well as the wronged.

PART III

SELECTED SPECIAL COVENANTS

8

Marriage

In the third part I shall use the concept of special covenant as a way to interpret three selected types of human relationships. I am making no effort to be comprehensive; there are many other types of human relationships, and we cannot discuss them all here. The three I have chosen—marriage, political community, and the church—differ greatly in how they are related to essential features of human nature, in the goods of life that they serve, in who the members of any particular covenant are, and in what kinds of obligations accompany each type. An examination of these three will suggest some ways to go about analyzing still other types of special covenant.

A special covenant, let us recall, is a relationship of mutual entrusting and accepting entrustment that arises out of some special historical transaction or transactions among the members. Unlike the inclusive covenant of all persons before God, any special covenant has limited membership, although the nature of the limits takes different forms with different types of special covenants. Within any special covenant each member has special rights that arise from the nature of the originating transactions and has accompanying special obligations to the other members.

About each type of special covenant it is important to ask these questions: (1) How shall we interpret this relationship as a special covenant? What goods does the relationship serve, what special obligations and rights arise out of it, and what does it mean to be faithful or unfaithful in this special context? (2) Given the standard of covenant love, what would be an appropriate kind of response to some characteristic kinds of conflicts that arise in this type of special covenant?

A Covenantal Interpretation of Marriage

Because it is not the main concern of this chapter to describe the condition of marriage today, I shall not present a picture of the crisis that marriage as an institution is facing, nor of the alternative kinds of "households" that are statistically significant, nor offer a program for rescuing marriage and the traditional nuclear family from their difficulties, if I were able to provide one. The main concern is rather with how marriage is to be interpreted and how, in light of that interpretation, marriage partners should understand their responsibilities and respond to their conflicts.

Some might suppose that given the crisis of marriage today and the rise of "alternative life-styles," one should choose a broader focus than marriage. But marriage it is, for two reasons. First and most important, from a standpoint that views human relationships covenantally and for the Christian tradition generally, marriage is the norm for intimate man-woman relationships for reasons that will become clear in the course of this chapter. Christian normative judgments about other kinds of intimate man-woman relationships— about unmarried couples, extramarital liaisons, premarital intercourse, group marriages, and all the rest—depend upon and reflect judgments about marriage, whether intentionally or unintentionally. A less important but still significant reason for this focus is that in today's society, if recent patterns remain applicable, the overwhelming proportion of adults have been, are, or will be married at one time or another. Marriage thus continues to be the center of attention in man-woman relationships for our culture, and not only for traditional Christian theology.

The first and most basic part of an ethic of marriage is our model of what the relationship is like, morally speaking. Judgments about more specific matters of moral decision, such as what role each spouse should play, whether and when divorce is justifiable, and issues of sexual practice will be heavily shaped by this model, whether it is conscious or implicit, reflective or unexamined.

One way of characterizing what the marriage relationship is like is to identify the purposes or goods that it should serve. The Christian tradition has identified several, among them (1) procreation, (2) companionship, (3) the restraint of sin, and (4) the sacrament. Of these four, the third recognizes that the institution of marriage serves to restrain the sin of concupiscence; but this purpose, while obviously important, is derivative from other goods of marriage which sin obstructs. For that reason our focus will be upon the others from which it is derived. The fourth purpose, to the extent it has to do with the enduring unity of a marriage, is a good closely related to the second, companionship. The question whether marriage should be one of the sacraments, however, raises theological controversies that, while important, we need not discuss here. It is the first two purposes that call for our special attention.

When theologians have affirmed *procreation* as a purpose and good of marriage, they have ordinarily pointed to Genesis 1:28*b*, "Be fruitful and multiply, and fill the earth and subdue it." Because the man-woman relationship in marriage not only *can* lead to procreation, but indeed inherently *tends* toward it if unrestrained, this command may look like carrying coals to Newcastle. We need not interpret the passage as commanding that we multiply without restraint, or under all circumstances. Its main point, and that of many other Old Testament passages, is that the human capacity and tendency to procreate has a proper and major place in life and is not as such an evil, though like any other human capacity it can be misused.

The term *procreation* ought not be understood too narrowly. It has been commonly interpreted to include not merely bringing children into the world, but also bringing them up to responsible maturity. Thomas Aquinas writes, "Offspring signifies not only the begetting of children, but also their education, to which as its end is directed the entire communion of works that exists between man and wife as united in marriage."[1] In a similar way the 1549 *Book of Common Prayer* speaks of "the procreacion of children to be brought up in the feare and nurture of the Lorde, and prayse of God."[2]

Likewise, the term *companionship* ought not to be understood too narrowly. It is that good whereby the husband and wife become spiritually one, that whereby each comes to provide the deepest kind of intimacy and support for the other in a sustained way. In the words of the 1549 *Book of Common Prayer*, it is "the mutuall societie, helpe and comfort, that the one ought to haue of the other, both in prosperitie and aduersitie."[3] Theologians have traditionally found this purpose expressed in Genesis 2:18: "Then the Lord God said, 'It is not good that the man should be alone; I will make him a helper fit for him.' " We might better translate the latter phrase, "a partner appropriate for him," as the Hebrew words connote, lest we distort the meaning into the notion of an assistant and lose the sense of the full mutuality of the companionship. That mutuality is nowhere better expressed than later in the same passage, when it is said that the two "become one flesh" (2:24b).

We need not dispute here which of these two purposes is more important. If we are rightly to understand marriage, we must take both with the greatest seriousness. Both are inherently related to marriage, for both are inseparably connected with the feature that distinguishes marriage from all other human relationships: it is oriented around sexual complementarity. That phrase does not mean that either spouse is superior to the other, but that each complements what the other lacks, not merely anatomically, but, some would maintain, psychologically as well.[4] As Paul Ramsey has observed, sexual intercourse inherently tends "toward the expression and strengthening of love and toward the engendering of children."[5] That is true whether or not the woman or the man consciously intends these goods. Furthermore it tends toward them for the species regardless of the degree to which a particular couple may find obstacles in the way of attaining them.

Procreation and companionship are both essentially social purposes. Companionship is a good for the other person, for the two in relationship, and for the wider community, not only for the self. Procreation is a good for the child, for the couple, and for the wider society, never merely for one of the parents. Both imply obligations toward the community, and both are attainable only in community. Marriage is then by nature profoundly social, as is recognized in the way some exegetes have taken the Genesis 2 story to witness to the essentially social nature of human life generally, and not only of marriage.

The Christian tradition has not designated individual happiness and fulfillment as purposes of marriage. It is hoped they will be by-products, but if they become the goals of the relationship, they tend to get in the way of the central purposes, procreation and companionship. Happiness and fulfillment of the self tend to arise from the right relation of the self to God, to others, and to oneself; that is, from the faithful and joyous acceptance from God of one's calling, and not from directly seeking them for their own sake.

In contrast much contemporary thinking about marriage assumes as its chief goals the happiness, freedom, and fulfillment of each individual. When someone of this persuasion reflects about questions of moral decision in marriage, such as whether marriage ought to be permanent and sexually exclusive, the arguments frequently take the form of defenses of individual freedom and affirmations of individual growth. Sexual exclusiveness in marriage is then seen as "limiting";[6] it is said to cause one to "feel less than a free man."[7] The pains and pleasures, burdens and benefits of marriage are assessed outside the context of the social purposes of the institution and the responsibilities an individual assumes upon entering into it. The outcome is at best a utilitarian calculus; at worst it is merely a calculus of goods and evils for the self. The essential sociality of the self and of marriage is thus rejected.

Christian theology further characterizes marriage, over and beyond specifying its purposes, when it speaks of how the partners are morally obligated to each other. Their obligation is best expressed in covenant terms. As a special covenant, marriage brings together a man and a woman in the most intensive relationship possible in human life. Their mutual concerns and obligations cover the whole range of life's interests, not merely a small or specific list of subjects, as might be the case in a business transaction. Once married, the two belong essentially together; they are not merely two individuals some of whose interests happen to coincide. They will be able to sustain their marriage as a growing relationship only to the extent that they commit themselves fully and steadfastly to each other and affirm each other as persons of worth, not only as individuals having convenient or useful or praiseworthy characteristics. They will find that the relationship (as contrasted with their individual goals) will grow in richness only to the extent that each is concerned about the needs of the other, dependable in accepting responsibilities, and disposed to forgive, to be forgiven, and to seek reconciliation in the face of their failings. A covenant model of marriage is one that expresses the essential characteristics of covenant love in a way appropriate for this unique kind of human relationship.

In contrast to a covenant model, much contemporary opinion views marriage as merely a limited-liability contract for the mutual advantage of each of the two spouses. Marriage is indeed a legal contract, and many legal terms have been taken over by the church into its services of matrimony. Its legal-contractual features recognize (1) that marriage is a universal human relationship, not one brought into being by the church; (2) that certain requirements must be met before a marriage legally exists, such as that each willingly consents to the marriage, that neither is already legally married to someone else, and so on; (3) that by entering into the marriage the partners receive identifiable rights and corresponding obligations, and (4) that they have obligations to the wider community, and not only to each other. Marriage is simultaneously contractual and covenantal. The covenantal, though, provides the theological framework within which the moral obligatoriness of the contract is to be understood, and not the reverse. Where marriage is viewed only or primarily as a limited-liability contract, one might argue that its obligations should be determined by what will leave each spouse with the minimum inhibition, the maximum liberty from lasting duties to the other, and the maximum opportunity for continued self-development and self-satisfaction, in spite of the marriage as much as because of it. So interpreted, the contract might be thought to be binding only insofar as it actually serves the happiness and development of the individual partner. In that image of marriage, the two spouses are considered to be essentially separate, both before and after the marriage begins, though for there to be a marriage at all there must be some coinciding interests, at least for the time being. It should not be surprising that those who hold to this model of marriage are often pessimistic about the future of marriage as an institution, and, I suspect, about the future of their own marriages as well. Theirs is likely to be a self-fulfilling prophecy. Their view of marriage has little capacity to hold the partners inwardly together; it provides little motivation and few resources for working through the inevitable conflicts and crises of a relationship as intensive as marriage.

When instead we view legal-contractual features of marriage within the framework of a covenant, we recognize that the most fundamental obligation of marriage is fully to affirm one's mate as mate—fully to respect him or her as that one human being who is one's spouse. Particular contractual matters within the marriage, however important, can then be seen in their proper light—as means to the full affirmation of the other in marriage, and not as ways of pursuing private interests in competition with the marriage.

Love means two different things in these two contrasting models of marriage. In the limited-liability model, love ordinarily means affection, an emotional feeling for the other.

If that feeling abates, and unless some deeper sense of love develops, there is little to hold the marriage together. Feelings are volatile, are not always present in both spouses to the same degree at the same time, and are easily modified with age and in the midst of conflicts. Love as affection is by itself a fragile reed upon which to try to build a marriage, though one would be rash to enter into it if affection were not present.

In a covenant framework love includes affection, but more centrally it is covenant love. It is like the love of God toward the covenant people, adapted to this special kind of human relationship. We need not accept the implied superiority of the husband in order to see the validity of Hosea's picture (chaps. 1–3) of the husband-wife relationship as a parallel to God's relation to the chosen people, or of the analogy offered by the writer of Ephesians (5:22-33) between the love of husband for wife and of Christ for the church. The analogies work in more than one way: they speak about what marital love should be like, that of wife for husband as well as the reverse; and insofar as we have experienced true marital love, they suggest something of the depth of God's love. The meaning of marital love begins with the unqualified affirmation of and respect for this person as a human being. Yet it is more; it is affirmation and respect for this person as the one human being in all the world who is one's spouse. Affection plays a major role in leading two people to decide to get married. Within the marriage its role continues to be important, but it is supplementary to love as "marriage-covenant love." Love as affection is encouraged and elicited by marriage-covenant love. The continued motivation for the marriage does not rest merely on ephemeral feelings, but on the recognition that these two persons, having covenanted together in marriage, essentially belong together. They have "become one flesh."

If someone is married, or is getting married, then from a Christian orientation he or she is obligated to accept and affirm the role of spouse as a vocation. Not everybody is called to marriage. A heterosexually oriented person may judge that she or he is called instead to a single life. Or a homosexually oriented person may recognize that given his or her orientation heterosexual marriage would be irresponsible and intolerable. These can of course be justifiable decisions, though from a covenant perspective would not the obligation still remain to adopt either a pattern of sexual restraint or one of sexual fidelity? But these topics would fill several more chapters.

When people marry and take up offices in that relationship, their appropriate chief concern is not merely to seek their own individual ends, but to carry out the responsibilities of their calling, both toward each other and toward the wider community. Each partner is called to be faithful to the other across the whole range of concerns that married persons mutually encounter. Each is to remain faithful even though things go badly—even though their initial hopes for the marriage are not met, even though the marriage is beset by conflicts, and even though the other partner is faithless. In a limited-liability contract the failure of one party to live up to its terms will often cancel the other's contractual obligation. However it may be with specific legally contracted matters in marriage, the obligation to covenant faithfulness in marriage is not canceled by the other's disloyalty. Although we sometimes must probe into what constitutes loyalty under highly adverse circumstances, within Christian faith being disloyal to one's spouse is not an acceptable option. The obligation to be faithful in marriage requires something much more basic than conformity to certain external patterns of behavior. The wedding vows are intended to convey a deep inward commitment of faithfulness between the partners for which the specific matters pledged are appropriate expressions: "Will you love her [him], comfort her, honor and keep her, in sickness and in health, and forsaking all others be faithful to her as long as you both shall live?" Similarly each pledges to take the other "for better, for worse, for richer, for poorer, in sickness and in health, to love and to cherish, till death us do part, according to God's holy ordinance; and thereto I pledge you my faith."

The wedding vows not only describe the commitments of marriage; they obligate. The very act of taking the vows in the wedding service is self-obligating on the part of each. As we have seen earlier, to promise is not only to *say* something; it is to *do* something—to obligate oneself. Yet explicit vowing is not the only way, nor even the primary way, that a man and a woman obligate themselves to each other. When other, less binding vows are taken instead, or no vows at all, the two still obligate themselves to each other by their acts in the man-woman relationship. They do this as they set up house together, wedding or no wedding. The common law recognizes this: if a man and a woman who live together hold themselves out to the public as husband and wife, then they are in legal fact married, whether there was ever a wedding service or not. In a way parallel to common-law marriage, actions can create enduring moral obligations. A man and woman living together who do not claim to be husband and wife, who in fact vigorously deny it and are (as yet) not legally married, may nonetheless be morally obligated to each other as though they were. What morally obligates in such a case is actions of each toward the other having to do with setting up house, actions that bring about mutual interdependence, the considerable power of each over the other as reflected in financial dependence, pregnancy, having children, or deep emotional interdependence. Relationships of this kind tend by their very nature to entail significant effects for the other over time. They call for each to stand responsible to the other for these effects—that is, to be faithful. Our ordinary actions in the man-woman relationship obligate us, and not only our vows. Where this is the case, it is appropriate that the vows should be spoken as well.

This conclusion would not be granted by anyone who held a limited-liability model of the man-woman relationship. To the contrary that person might see a pregnancy or the financial or emotional interdependence of the partners simply as an inconvenience, perhaps a miscalculation, that is now to be remedied either by severing the relationship or by seeking to undo the undesired effects—by abortion, for example, or by dividing up the property. But from a covenant model the intimate relationship of a man and a woman is a far more serious and binding matter than that, and its effects are not to be taken lightly. The goods of procreation and intimate companionship, and the interdependencies each entails, are properly to be pursued only within a relationship in which each partner has taken the other seriously enough to offer and to receive a vow of deep and enduring faithfulness. The wedding service aptly recognizes this seriousness in the words of the opening address, that this "holy estate" is "not to be entered into unadvisedly, but reverently, discreetly, and in the fear of God."

The Special Obligations of Marriage

Faithfulness

Whatever else the marriage partners are obligated to be and to do in the marriage, they are obligated to be faithful to each other. Other terms express some or all of the meaning of faithfulness: *fidelity, constancy, loyalty, steadfastness, dependability;* and of unfaithfulness: *infidelity, inconstancy, disloyalty, fickleness.* Although some of these terms call to mind particular ways of being faithful or unfaithful, it is important to identify the root meaning of marital faithfulness, as contrasted with particular ways of being so. Basically, faithfulness in marriage is the enduring unqualified commitment and trustworthiness of each marriage partner to the other. It is that characteristic of the relationship by which each one constantly and fully affirms the spouse for his or her own sake.

If this is the root meaning of faithfulness in marriage, then faithfulness is clearly a necessary part of the meaning of marital love. Brunner is mistaken in separating the two.[8] How would it be conceivable for a man fully to affirm a woman as his marital partner (or vice versa), to affirm her for her own sake and not merely as a means to his personal satisfaction, to affirm her for her worth and not merely her merits, to take seriously her deepest needs as a person, and not also do all this enduringly? Truly to love her would necessarily include being one on whom she can confidently depend to stand constantly responsible toward her. D. S. Bailey is right when he maintains that fidelity "must be an integral feature of love" in marriage. He writes: "The essence of fidelity may be said to consist in treating as unconditional *in its own sphere* the claim which (under God) lovers are entitled to make one upon the other, and in the ordering of their lives with constant reference to the single centre around which (under God) their individual personal lives revolve."[9]

In a parallel way unfaithfulness in its root meaning has to do with the inner orientation of the one toward the other. It is the incomplete or inconstant commitment and trustworthiness of the one to the other as spouse. It is being unwilling fully and enduringly to affirm the worth of the spouse as that one person to whom the self is now specially committed in marriage.

In marriage as in other realms of life the inner relationship of the covenanting partners is more fundamental than the external requirements that give it expression. A husband or wife might keep all the morally obligatory or expected external requirements of marriage and still be inwardly unfaithful. The husband might, for example, constantly (insofar as he knows how) serve his wife's basic emotional and material needs, might never enter into any extramarital affair, might act out a continually sympathetic and solicitous external appearance, and might do all this until the death of self or wife, all from an inner stance that does not fully and constantly affirm the wife for her own sake. The outer actions might have stemmed instead from an inner compulsiveness, from a disinclination to make an issue, or from a selfish desire to benefit from a "good deal." This *might* happen, but it is entirely unlikely. Not only do helpful external actions flow from one's inner faithful orientation, but they are unlikely to flow consistently from a contrary orientation. A spouse may dissemble for a long time, but eventually the inner orientation is likely to come out. It is the inner orientation of faithfulness that is the stable motive for outward constancy. Faithfulness in marriage is not merely great endurance. It is the constant inner love that affirms the very being of the other as spouse.

Similarly there is an inner unfaithfulness that underlies any external unfaithful acts: the failure or refusal fully to affirm the very being of the other as one's spouse. Inner faithfulness necessarily seeks appropriate outward expression, and inner unfaithfulness will also find outward expression, even if that expression does not always readily reveal the true nature of the inner orientation. The relation of the inner and outer in marriage is as Luther stated it for all of life: "Good works do not make a good person, but a good person does good works."[10]

Faithfulness in marriage is to be distinguished from three possible misinterpretations. First, it does not consist merely in keeping explicit marriage vows. If the vows were minimal, so as not to express all that is essential to a proper marriage, then keeping them would not suffice to constitute marital faithfulness. That is because the vows themselves ought to be derived from what is essential to the nature of marriage and ought to reflect the kinds of self-obligating actions that are characteristic of marriage. A morally adequate marriage covenant is more than a mere convention agreed upon by the parties.

Second, faithfulness in marriage is more than, though inclusive of, honesty. Honesty is a disposition to be "sincere, truthful, candid," so that one "will not lie, cheat, or steal" (Oxford English Dictionary). To be "honest with each other" often today refers to being completely candid, willing to say to each other what one's actual thoughts are on any subject, and not merely avoiding falsehood and deceit. Whichever way honesty is understood, faithfulness is something more, and something more fundamental. Although it is not possible to be faithful in marriage without being honest in an appropriate sense, it is possible to be honest without being faithful. One might honestly and openly seek to "do the other in." Less crassly one might with the full awareness and even the consent of the other do things in marriage that are incompatible with the other's true well-being as spouse, and incompatible with the continued mutually loyal marriage relationship. The virtue of honesty is included in the broader and more fundamental virtue of faithfulness.

Third, faithfulness in marriage has to do with more than sexual matters, though it necessarily includes sexual faithfulness. Popularly the terms *infidelity* and *fidelity* call to mind adultery and its avoidance. More appropriately, though, the terms have to do with loyalty and disloyalty in the entire relationship of the wife and husband, and not only in matters sexual, though these are included.

If we understand faithfulness in the way portrayed here, we shall make our judgments about what it means to be faithful in particular marital contexts, not simply with an eye to the unique features of the situation, but especially in terms of what is essential to a good marriage. Virtually without dissenting voice the Christian tradition has held that marital faithfulness requires both sexual exclusiveness and permanence. Only recently has the Christian tradition come to recognize adequately the significance and the validity of a third requirement: fairness in the distribution of responsibilities and benefits between the marriage partners.

Fairness Between the Spouses

Much of the Bible and the Christian tradition has a bad record on fairness in marriage, and for that matter, on fairness toward women generally. Its theologians—usually males—have made too much out of the idea in Genesis 2 that the woman was created from the rib of the man. They have made a male-serving use of the analogy in Ephesians 5 between Christ's relation to the church and the husband's relation to the wife. "As the church is subject to Christ," the author writes, "so let wives also be subject in everything to their husbands." Nor is there any shortage of other texts for those who try to "prove" that the wife should occupy a subordinate role to the husband.

It helps to explain, though not to justify, such passages as these if we remember that the biblical writers were the children of patriarchal cultures. They could scarcely have been expected to think otherwise, given the practices that were widely and usually uncritically accepted in their times. What is more surprising is the extent to which there emerges in the

234

Bible a recognition of the equal worth of women. We see it in the writers' accounts of Jesus' obvious compassion for women as for others who were downtrodden, and of his willingness both to speak with women (as with the woman at the well in John 4) and to spend time in serious discussion with them (Luke 10:38-42)—actions not viewed as appropriate in his time. We see it in Paul's repeated parallels in his references to husband and wife in I Corinthians 7:

> The husband should give to his wife her conjugal rights, and likewise the wife to her husband. For the wife does not rule over her own body, but the husband does; likewise the husband does not rule over his own body, but the wife does. . . . To the married I give charge, not I but the Lord, that the wife should not separate from her husband . . . and that the husband should not divorce his wife. (7:3-4, 10-11; cf. also verses 16, 32-34)

But we do not have to rely upon passages such as these to justify the requirement for fairness in marriage. What calls male dominance more seriously into question is the basic outlook of the New Testament proclamation of faith. In that proclamation every person stands equal before God, equally a recipient of God's grace, equally forgiven and justified through faith. In Christ, Paul writes, there is neither male nor female (Gal. 3:28); that is, that distinction has no ultimate significance.

Some theologians have claimed that this passage declares only the equality of women and men before God, and that men ought still have superior roles in marriage and other human relationships. Yet precisely because women and men stand equal before God—equal in created worth, equally recipients of God's love—it is difficult to fathom how discrimination against women (or anybody else) can be justified in human relationships. That people even seek to justify it, especially in this day, is a suspicious sign of male self-seeking, preventing them from grasping the profoundest import of the Christian gospel. Covenant love requires fairness in all human relationships.

The moral principle of fairness applies to all those situations in which "persons conduct any joint enterprise according to rules and thus restrict their liberty."[11] If one party (e.g., the wife) submits to certain restrictions, she has a right to a similar submission from any other person (e.g., the husband) who has benefited by her doing so.[12] John Rawls explains the idea of fairness this way:

> A practice will strike the parties as fair if none feels that, by participating in it, they or any of the others are taken advantage of, or forced to give in to claims which they do not regard as legitimate. . . . Usually acting unfairly is not so much the breaking of any particular rule, . . . but taking advantage of loop-holes or ambiguities in rules, . . . and more generally, acting contrary to the intention of a practice. . . . [A]cknowledging the duty of fair play is a necessary part of the criterion for recognizing another as a person with similar interests and feelings as oneself.[13]

Fairness is a requirement that follows from the recognition of the equal worth of persons. To be faithful to one's wife (or husband), it is not enough to keep the external letter of one's explicit promises; it is also necessary to keep the spirit and intention of the relationship—that is, fully to affirm the other person. Fairness is required by faithfulness.

It is not simple to state what constitutes fairness in marriage. Even though husband and wife are of equal worth before God, each other, and the world at large, the two as individuals always possess somewhat unequal abilities and attain unequal achievements. Although that does not justify the subordination of either to the rule of the other, it does often justify a division of labor that recognizes their respective strengths and weaknesses. Ordinarily the wife has more of some ability and the husband more of some other. Jessie Bernard has observed that even though in our society the husband has traditionally been expected to be dominant, it often happens that the wife is in fact the one better able and more inclined to take the lead.[14] This is only fair and ought to be as morally acceptable as the reverse. No human group resolves its internal or external problems unless on occasion someone takes the lead, though it need not always be the same person. However the talents are distributed, it is undesirable for either spouse to be dominant in a way that works unfairness upon the other, that thwarts the other, that reduces the other to a mere means to the advantage of the dominant one. Male chauvinism and female chauvinism in marriage both exist and are equally unloving.

What is fair in a marriage is in large part a matter that each couple must work out. Yet it will exclude those arrangements by which one spouse (either one) always has the last word; those in which either spouse is thought to have the right to harm the other physically; those in which one spouse only serves the sexual satisfaction of the other and is granted no reciprocal sexual concern; those in which either spouse is in effect the servant of the other, expected to do all the menial labor and to believe that she (or he) has then only done her (or his) duty; and those in which the one spouse has ample opportunity for the fulfillment of his (or her) potentialities while the other is condemned to a perpetual thwarting of her (or his) possibilities for growth and personal enrichment. However traditional that arrangement may have been, and however much the Christian churches have accepted and encouraged some aspects of it in the past, it stands in conflict with the Christian proclamation that women and men are of equal worth before God. It is incompatible with a faithful love in marriage. Fortunately, in all ages some marriages have probably been far more fair than the ideologies of marriage of their times. The quality of marital love is not always reduced to the level at which the culture talks about it.

It has been easy in the past for the churches, when speaking of the moral problems of marriage, to deal only or primarily with sexual unfaithfulness and marital breakup. They are indeed serious moral problems. But the far more widespread moral problem of marriage, perhaps the most destructive problem over the long haul, and possibly the moral problem that does as much as any other ingredient to invite sexual infidelity and marital breakup, is the belief that the marriage partners are not of equal worth and equal status and the resulting unfair roles that are structured into so many marriages. A genuine respect, each for the other, structured into fair marital practices, would go far toward reducing the inclination to marital unfaithfulness of other kinds.

Sexual Exclusiveness

Traditionally the church has taught that sexual exclusiveness should characterize marriage. The present age puts to Christian ethics the question whether this teaching is essential to the meaning of covenant love in marriage.

One traditional set of marriage vows expresses the obligation of sexual exclusiveness this way: "Forsaking all other keep you only unto her [or him]." In the most restricted sense of the term, *adultery*, which this vow prohibits, is sexual intercourse between two persons, at least one of whom is married to someone else. In a broader sense, though, the term applies to inward thoughts as well as to outward acts, as stated in Matthew 5:28: "But I say to you that every one who looks at a woman lustfully has already committed adultery with her in his heart." But even this meaning may not be sufficiently inclusive. If adultery is breaking the vow of sexual exclusiveness, it perhaps should be interpreted to include not only lustful thoughts and acts, but also other kinds of acts of inappropriate intimacy: acts of sharing with someone besides one's spouse a level of intimacy so deep as to be appropriate only to the marriage relationship. To develop this kind of intimacy with a third party in competition with or as a substitute for intimacy between the spouses is to "alienate the affections" away from the spouse.

The more fundamental aspect of this marriage vow is the positive requirement to "keep unto" the spouse, of which the prohibition of adultery is a negative implication. One keeps this positive side of the vow by orienting oneself wholly to affirm the other, sexually and otherwise, in all the ways that enhance marital intimacy and cause marital love to thrive. A good marital relationship is not something that is either present or not present; it is a matter of degree. Nor is it something static; it either grows or shrivels. The vow to "keep unto" the other, together with the vows "to love and to cherish" and to comfort, honor, and keep, express the pledge that each will constantly seek in every possible way to affirm the other person as spouse and thereby to help the marriage to be a good one. In contrast, to be cold, unfeeling, and habitually uncommunicative toward one's spouse is to break this vow by omission, even if no adulterous thought or action in the usual sense is ever present. Not to seek to sense her (his) deepest feelings, needs, and anxieties and not to seek constantly to respond sympathetically to them is not to keep the positive requirement of this vow. This positive requirement necessarily entails sexual exclusiveness in marriage.

Several critics of traditional Christian marriage argue that sexual exclusiveness ought not to be a requirement in marriage. Nena and George O'Neill write that a sexual relationship with someone outside the marriage can both assist the growth of the individuals involved and enhance the relationship of the married couple. Although they say they are not recommending an extramarital relationship, they advance the idea in a way that virtually constitutes advocacy.[15] Rustum and Della Roy offer a similar judgment, though they caution that an extramarital sexual relationship can be harmful. Whether it is appropriate, they say, depends upon "the depth of the relationship and the caring for the other," the opportunity to serve the need of the other (e.g., the third party), and the effects upon the marriage (or marriages) and upon any single party involved.[16] The chief objective toward which these authors are looking is the growth and fulfillment of the individuals involved.

These writers also discuss the meaning of fidelity in marriage. They wish to reject the idea of fidelity insofar as it is seen to require sexual exclusiveness. The O'Neills call fidelity in this sense "the false god of closed marriage," "the measure of *limited* love, *diminished* growth, and *conditional* trust," and a duty or obligation, whereas "love and sex should never be seen in terms of duty or obligation."[17] Apparently they find it difficult not to caricature their opponents: the italicized words are all misleading. *Limited:* an exclusive marital love is indeed limited in the sense of being restricted to the two spouses, but it need not therefore be limited in the sense of being constricted or stunted. *Diminished:* there is nothing inherently less open to growth in a marriage that is sexually exclusive, though there will certainly be some potentialities that each partner forgoes, as is true with any decision. *Conditional:* every trust in another human being should be conditional in the sense that we should recognize that humans are not always trustworthy, but an exclusive marriage need not and ought not to be based on conditional trust in the sense of each partner's continually worrying about the other's trustworthiness or being unwilling to commit or risk oneself with the other. Finally the O'Neills fall for that notion popular in many quarters that where there is true love there cannot also be duty, whereas something may well be our duty at the same time that we are inwardly motivated by love to do it. That is how it rightly is with marital faithfulness.

At the same time the critics of exclusiveness wish to commend faithfulness in a different sense of the word. For the O'Neills, fidelity in marriage ought to be redefined "as commitment to your own growth, equal commitment to your partner's growth, and a sharing of the self-discovery accomplished through such growth. It is loyalty and faithfulness to growth, to integrity of self and respect for the other, not to a sexual and psychological bondage to each other."[18] Similarly Ronald Mazur, distinguishing between infidelity and adultery, judges that the former is the more basic and is the problem. His understanding of a desirable fidelity is implied when he says that infidelity has to do "with constriction of love; with false security; with lack of respect for the equality of the other's personhood; with suffocating possessiveness which is life-denying. . . . Unfaithfulness in human relationships effectively means the denial of a relationship; it is a lack of trust and honesty."[19] By so reinterpreting marital faithfulness these writers wish to show that it is compatible with sexual nonexclusiveness.

But the error of that judgment is shown by a more adequate understanding of marital faithfulness. Mazur is right in saying that it has a broader reference than simply to sexual matters.

Yet he and the other critics err if they view it as no different from faithfulness in human relationships generally. It is instead a special kind of human faithfulness, one appropriate to this unique kind of relationship and its inherent rights and obligations. However broadly marital faithfulness is to be understood, sexual faithfulness, including sexual exclusiveness, is central to it. Faithfulness requires a special kind of honesty: an honest loyalty to the best interests and to the rights of the other *as spouse*; it excludes honest (and dishonest) disregard for or attack upon the rights of the spouse, whether the spouse claims those rights or not. It requires a special kind of loyalty: to the other person *as spouse*—a unique kind of relationship—and not merely loyalty to "growth," or simply to the other person as another human being.

If marital faithfulness is understood in this way, and not as loosely as these critics view it, then it is inherently in conflict with sexual nonexclusiveness. As the critics portray it, sexual nonexclusiveness implies being willing to share one's deepest intimacies with someone other than one's spouse. What this means (which they do not ordinarily recognize) is that the spouse is not as important in one's life as he or she would be if there were no third party; that one has less need for the spouse than would otherwise be the case; and that insofar as the third-party relationship is known, the security of the marriage relationship is lessened. In a later book Nena O'Neill recognizes problems like these in sexual nonexclusiveness that she had not mentioned before, even though she still stops short of ruling it out altogether:

> Sex between two people is a symbol of closeness, a gift to each other, a symbol of the love and loyalty they share. There is a deep association between sex as a physical act of closeness and our feelings of attachment and affection. . . . Given this and our internalization of traditional expectations for sex with only one person, sexual fidelity is not just a vow in marriage or a moral or religious belief, but a need associated with our deepest emotions and our quest for emotional security. This is one reason why, once we have promised and given our trust to another person in an area so closely associated with our feelings of security and

241

dependence, the breaking of the pledge of sexual fidelity seems like an abandonment and arouses feelings of jealousy and insecurity. Even when sexual nonexclusivity is agreed on between the partners, the same feelings often occur. Resentment, a feeling of rejection, anger, and insecurity follow, sometimes as strongly as they do when a clandestine affair is discovered or revealed.[20]

I suspect that these feelings of resentment and rejection are more natural and less socially conditioned than she recognizes. Where there is an extramarital sexual relationship, it means that the one spouse may well discover at any time that the other spouse has come to consider the third party to be a more appealing confidant and partner. One spouse is thereby put in the position of competitor for the affections and support of the other, unable to rely upon the constancy of the other, unfree to be fully vulnerable before the other to whom he or she is in fact only one among two or more.

It would be a rare marriage in which the couple's agreeing to sexual nonexclusiveness were not a sign of weakness in the marriage and a harbinger of its further deterioration. Why would they be interested in outside sexual relationships, unless they found the marriage boring, wanted more interest and diversity, and determined it easier to seek these things outside the marriage than to use the imagination and responsibility it would require to revive their own relationship? If they truly respected each other as spouses, they would find the difficulties of the marriage to be opportunities to affirm each other the more fully—"for better, for worse."

Sexual complementarity is naturally central to marriage. The spouses are physically and emotionally "made for each other" as man and woman, though not necessarily as these two specific individuals. The sexual relationship and the interpersonal closeness it expresses and enhances are not incidental to marriage, but central to it. Not to be exclusive in this regard is necessarily not to take the marriage relationship seriously. If a husband and wife are not exclusive sexually, it is difficult to believe that they will be faithful about much else in any way other than how we ought to be honest and reliable to every human being, and it is doubtful they will do even that much. In every special moral relationship faithfulness necessarily has to do with what is central to that kind of relationship, whatever else it may also include.

If a husband and wife are seeking to build a good marriage, and if they desire to be faithful to each other in the most fundamental marital sense, they will find that the way to do so lies in affirming each other with all possible loyalty and patience and resourcefulness in a sexually exclusive relationship. This is true not simply because it is traditional; rather, at this point the tradition has grasped the reality of the matter. In such mutual self-limitation is true marital freedom found—the freedom to be themselves with each other, confident that each is unconditionally and dependably affirmed by the other as spouse.

Permanence

In the traditional vows the obligation of permanence in marriage is expressed in the words "so long as you both shall live" and "till death us do part," as well as in the phrases "for better, for worse, for richer, for poorer, in sickness and in health." We cannot fully control the future, but we can make a binding commitment concerning how we will face that future. In these vows the commitment and obligation of the spouses is fully to intend throughout the marriage that it be permanent, and to act accordingly. Truly to intend something is not a small matter; it is to orient oneself in every respect, inward and outward, to bring that outcome about. Not to orient oneself that way is not fully to intend the outcome, but to have some other intention or conflicting intentions.

We can distinguish between two aspects of a marriage that might or might not endure. The first is its *inner spirit*, the relationship of mutual trust, loyalty, and intimacy which a woman and a man anticipate when they plan to get married. The second is the *external form* of the marriage, which includes being married in the legal sense and being considered by friends and associates to be married. Although it is not possible for a couple to have the inner spirit without *some*

243

socially recognized external form (even if that form is not legally sanctioned), it is possible for them to have the external form of a marriage without the inner spirit.

The obligation to intend a permanent marriage has to do most especially with the inner spirit. Husband and wife obligate themselves not merely to maintain the outer appearances of a marriage, but to create and maintain its inner reality. What is not to be broken "till death us do part" is first and foremost the inner unity of the partners. When the inner spirit of a marriage is destroyed beyond recovery, so that the partners are seriously destructive to each other, it can sometimes be justifiable to terminate the external form of a marriage. But it can never be justifiable to seek to destroy its inner spirit. It is primarily this spirit that the marriage partners are enjoined to nurture and seek to prolong.

The external form of the marriage—*some* stable and just form—is of great importance to its inner spirit. The form exists to help protect the marriage—from outside forces, to be sure, but also from destructive forces inside the marriage. No two people are constantly able to maintain their devotion to each other at the high level they may hope and intend. There are low points in all marriages. The external form of the marriage helps to protect it and the partners against their own weaknesses: their impatience, their whims, and their passing temptations. Amid these weaknesses the external form stands to remind them that they are still married and still obligated as a couple. The marriage is a legal fact which they would have to take active steps over some period of time to change. It would weaken all marriages if the law permitted divorce simply on the condition of one spouse's saying to the other (perhaps in the presence of witnesses), without a moment's notice, "I hereby divorce you." The "quickie divorces" that are possible in some states approach this extreme, but even with them it is necessary to take inconvenient steps over time. Some external and especially legal form of marriage is necessary to protect its inner spirit.

Even if one or both partners no longer care whether the marriage lasts, it still exists externally; and some marriages in that plight might still be restored to a spirit of inward loyalty and devotion—many more than in fact are. But other marriages, to the contrary, come to this point and are, for all anyone can tell, irreversibly broken in the inward sense. One can argue whether any marriage (like any individual) is ever past salvation, but however that may be, it is certain that many a marriage reaches a point of inward breakdown at which neither party sees how it can be saved and at which at least one party has no will to save it. The commitment to permanence in marriage is the commitment to affirm and treat each other as spouse in such a way that this point will never be reached, and better, never even approached.

A couple might come to contemplate divorce via either of two paths. (1) They might have vowed a permanent marriage together and might have renewed that vow on occasion in their words to each other, but then might have come up against a morass of problems in the face of which they found themselves unable to maintain the inner spirit of the marriage, or worse, in the face of which they wantonly destroyed it. Out of this plight one or both might seek a divorce. They would have had the mutual commitment and intention to permanence, but would have abandoned or failed in the effort to carry it out. (2) They might instead, upon entering into marriage, have agreed that they would take no vows of permanence and perhaps that it would last only a certain length of time, or else that how long it would last would be contingent upon certain conditions, such as the day-to-day desire and willingness of each partner to continue in the marriage. They would not have committed themselves to permanence at any point, nor would they have intended it, at least not as a shared intention. Even so they would have obligated themselves to a permanent marriage by their actions, marriage being the kind of relationship it is; and the law under which they were married would consider them to be married on an enduring basis, and not merely for a term.

Concerning the first path the ethical question to be raised from a covenantal interpretation of marriage is not over the initial intention to permanence, but whether the couple had maintained their commitment and how they might more successfully have carried it out. In contrast, the second path challenges the essentialness of the commitment to permanence. The second is in inner spirit a trial marriage, whether it is called that or not. One *might* say that the marriage is on trial. The partners are agreed that if the marriage does not sufficiently suit them, either can opt to terminate it without going against the demands and expectations of the other. But what this really means is that *each partner* is on trial. Neither has the assurance of being fully affirmed as spouse in the midst of all her or his weaknesses and all the couple's stresses and conflicts, because each knows that there is no commitment or shared intention of permanence "for better, for worse." Without that commitment and intention it is frequently easier to walk away from the conflicts of marriage than work to solve them. Someone might maintain that in this kind of marriage the partners are more free, but that is an illusion. Each feels morally free to terminate the marriage on demand, to be sure. But for that very reason neither is free in a more important sense, free to be utterly vulnerable before the other, free to risk oneself in all the many experiences common to marriage, such as shared confidences, conflicts of opinion and of taste, illnesses, pregnancies, financial uncertainties, or aging. Without the shared commitment to permanence, neither can be confident that the other can be depended on to stay around and stand accountable for their interdependence. Contrast a marriage viewed covenantally, one characterized by the commitment and shared intention of permanence. Both are "trying out" many things, but neither is "on trial." Both have much to learn, but each is committed to affirm the other with full constancy in the midst of all the false starts and failures of their learning together, and each knows that the other is likewise committed. The husband can then more readily relax in the confidence that, "However inept or thoughtless or self-centered I have been, she affirms me as her husband," and the wife can have the same confidence. A healthy marriage is not a relationship of indulgence, in which the sins of the one are simply overlooked by the other, but rather one of repeated falling short, repentance, forgiveness, and reconciliation. Forgiveness and reconciliation presuppose that the one who forgives is steadfastly committed to the continuation of that covenant community. Where this is not the case, forgiveness does not take place, whether in marriage or any other relationship. The commitment and intention of permanence is no invitation to irresponsibility, but it is part of the prevenient grace that each offers the other, to which the appropriate response is gratitude expressed in reciprocal love.

It might be rejoined that the above picture of marriage with the intention of permanence is more the ideal than the practice, that many marriages where permanence is intended are not characterized by any special moral sensitivity, any grasp of the meaning of forgiveness, or any special propensity to forgive. And certainly that can be the case. Many marriages that were intended to be permanent will nevertheless disintegrate. Each partner is often on trial as a matter of fact, even though both have pledged permanence. The commitment to permanence is not a sufficient condition for an enduring marriage, let alone for a happy and responsible one. But if not a sufficient condition, it is virtually a necessary one, in that marriages without it are unlikely to endure. Equally important, the commitment is *morally* necessary—essential if the spouses are to recognize and seek to carry out the inherent responsibilities of marriage, rather than looking upon themselves as individuals whose interests temporarily coincide.

Divorce

Even with the commitment and intention of permanence, many marriages come to the point where their inward spirit has been destroyed. At that point can it be justifiable to terminate the outer form of the marriage, that is, to get a divorce, even though the couple had committed themselves to a permanent marriage and were obligated to it?

To ask whether divorce can be justifiable is not to ask whether, other things being equal, it is desirable; it is not. Nor is it to ask whether the vow of permanence ought in any way to be qualified; the vow, the commitment, and the intention should be only to a lifelong marriage. The question about divorce is raised only because we know that we sometimes fail in our commitments and obligations, and because through these failures the marriage relationship can become so destructive that divorce might be the right action to take under these painful circumstances.

In no aspect of life is it justifiable to follow one basic moral standard in desirable circumstances, but to set that standard aside and to follow some conflicting standard in undesirable circumstances. It might be justifiable to follow different moral rules that express the same standard, or different tactics, but not a different basic standard. If covenant love with its obligation to faithfulness should be the guiding standard, it should govern our behavior under any conceivable circumstances. That is what it means to have a basic moral standard and to be one person rather than morally schizophrenic, to have integrity. If and when divorce is ever justifiable, it must be so on the basis of the same standard that ordinarily prohibits it.

In the previous section I distinguished between the inner spirit of a marriage and its external form. The question of divorce is not what would justify seeking to destroy the inner spirit of a marriage. Nothing would justify that. The account of Jesus' teaching in Mark 10:2-9 focuses on the inner spirit of marriage. It is a one-flesh unity, and so to understand it is incompatible with seeking to put that unity asunder. But it is not clear that Jesus spoke to the issue of what to do when the inner spirit, or one-flesh unity, of a marriage has been destroyed in marital conflict. The words attributed to Jesus in Mark 10:10-12 and the variation in Matthew 19:9 appear to be efforts by the early church to speak to that subject. The question of divorce as a serious issue lies here: what if anything would justify dissolving the outer form of a marriage? An answer offered out of covenant love must take seriously the conflict and its destructiveness.

As we seek to answer this question, help is available from a seemingly strange source—the Christian doctrine of justifiable war. The source is not as strange as it seems, though, for Christian just-war theory seeks to relate the basic Christian moral standard to another kind of undesirable and destructive human relationship. It speaks to the question of moral obligation regarding war, not by suspending the standard of love, but by asking how love can be expressed under circumstances of intense conflicts of interest among nations. Under such circumstances it is not always possible for nations to avoid highly destructive outcomes, and it is the same with intense conflict in marriage. Among the several conditions that must be met before it is justifiable to resort to war, at least three are applicable also to the question of divorce. I have in mind moral rather than legal conditions for divorce, for the legal requirements will vary from one jurisdiction to another and are likely to be less stringent than the moral conditions suggested here.

1. One condition for morally justifiable resort to divorce is that this action must be only for justifiable cause; that is, there must be *a grave wrong to be prevented or a crucial right to be protected.* The emphasis is on the graveness of the wrong and the crucialness of the right. As war is not justifiable lightly, neither is divorce. That a marriage imposes burdens—even serious ones—is not yet a justifiable cause for divorce. All responsibilities impose some burdens. Having a spouse who is an invalid would be a heavy burden, but it would not be justifiable cause for divorce. That the partners have frequent verbal conflicts, or that one spouse willingly causes the other unnecessary pain and suffering, is not in itself a sufficient cause for divorce; but that the husband regularly gets drunk and beats up the wife and children may be. The difference is the gravity of the wrong. That the spouses have difficulty communicating is insufficient cause; but that she habitually ridicules his efforts to confide in her and in many ways continually attacks his basic sense of self-respect may be sufficient. Some divorces are justifiable to protect the children from physical or psychological injury, but it is not only on behalf of the children that divorce might be justifiable. A

spouse might also justifiably seek one in her or his own defense—as an affirmation of oneself as a person in the face of behavior that if continued would likely be seriously injurious. Some argue for divorce if the marriage has not measured up to one's expectations or has seriously restricted one partner's potentialities, but on those grounds any marriage could be broken. There comes a point, though, when what is at stake is not merely the reduction of possibilities, but grave, lasting, and unjustifiable injury to that person. Then it is not unreasonable to contemplate a divorce. Perhaps the grave wrong that would most readily constitute justifiable cause is that the relationship of intimacy and mutual support between the two spouses has been destroyed beyond repair—that they are thoroughly alienated from each other—and that in this alienation one is continually attacking the other as a person.

2. The presence of this first condition alone does not suffice to justify a divorce. It must also be the case, as with war, that divorce is the *last resort* after all other possible solutions to the problem have been seen to be inadequate. Not only must there be serious destructiveness in the marriage, then, but also an apparently irreversible pattern of serious destructiveness—a pattern that continues in spite of all attempts to the contrary. Divorce is not justifiable where there is good reason to believe that the serious destructiveness can be eliminated and the inner spirit of the marriage recovered to some significant degree. Truly to affirm the other as spouse implies that in a marital conflict one will seriously attempt to resolve it within the marriage and to bring about reconciliation. Otherwise we would suspect that the one opting for divorce was looking for a way out. When has "last resort" been reached? There is no assured answer to that question. Some people give up on the marriage prematurely, while others berate themselves afterward for not trying harder, no matter how long they persisted. In some marriages, though, no matter how much one tries there is no solution, and a time comes when it is plausible to say that there is, humanly speaking, no hope for the marriage. That point must honestly be reached before a divorce is justifiable.

3. Still a third condition parallel to just-war theory is necessary for divorce to be justifiable: *a right intention*. In war a right intention is one that seeks a more just peace rather than revenge or personal or national gain, and so it is also with divorce. In the latter context "a more just peace" may mean simply a geographical and legal severing of the relationship, that is, a divorce, so that the parties are no longer at war. Divorce with that intention may be the only feasible way to affirm the alienated spouse under the circumstances of intense and irresoluble conflict. In the throes of a disintegrating marriage, each one's feelings are so intense and overpowering that it is difficult to disentangle a right intention from the almost inevitable motives of revenge and self-justification. Even so each party can aim at the objective of a more just and peaceful and less destructive life for all concerned.

However much guilt the other party may have for the breakup, some of the guilt is always one's own. For that reason a necessary (though not sufficient) ingredient of a right intention is *a sense of repentance* for the failure of the marriage. Church legislative bodies are less likely today than formerly to assume that in a marital breakup one spouse can be designated in any simple way as the guilty party and the other the offended party. One party may be more guilty than the other, though there is no exact way to measure guilt. But it is difficult to imagine a broken marriage in which one party was in no degree at fault. If his intolerable behavior was sexual infidelity, that was wrong, but she ought at least to ask herself whether in any way, subconsciously or unconsciously, she incited him to it; the phenomenon is not unknown. Or if her intolerable behavior was that she became attracted to another man and walked out on her husband, she acted wrongly, but he ought at the very least to ask himself whether somehow he encouraged her to do so. Before either party can be justified in divorcing, it is necessary to accept whatever responsibility one has for the disintegration of the inner spirit of the marriage and to accept forgiveness, if not from the alienated spouse, still from God and from the community of faith to which one belongs.

If all these three conditions are met, is it then justifiable to seek a divorce? Even then can divorce be an expression of covenant love? It would seem that divorce even under those conditions would be an act of unfaithfulness to the marriage and to the spouse. But we must stress again that faithfulness is not only or mainly an outward form, such as "always staying married regardless." It is most fundamentally an inward orientation of fully respecting and affirming the other person as spouse and seeking to embody this respect and affirmation in every circumstance. But the circumstances of the marriage may be such that the ordinary ways of affirming one's spouse are no longer available. There may be no healthy inner spirit left in the marriage. There may be no more opportunity to share intimacies and provide emotional support. There may only be occasions to diminish destructiveness. What would it mean, for example, to affirm by one's actions a husband who is a habitual wife-beater? It would not be honest with oneself or with the man to act as though that were acceptable or even tolerable behavior. It could well be far more affirmative of that husband and of the wife herself if she were to remove herself from his reach, if nothing could be done to change the pattern.

What we may have under conditions like that is a conflict between affirming the spouse as spouse and affirming him or her as human being: a conflict between that special marriage covenant and the inclusive covenant to which both of them will belong all their lives. If that is the choice, one is obligated to cut free, as painful as that will be for one or both. Under such conditions of irremediable grave destructiveness, divorce can truly be an expression rather than a denial of covenant love. One has finally been reduced to affirming the other in the only way still possible—as human being. In a justifiable divorce one is determining to continue affirming that person as human, even though no longer as spouse.

Roland Bainton has characterized just-war theory as the theory of the just *and mournful* war.[21] A similar description is appropriate for the idea of justifiable divorce. Who can ever rightly be joyous about a divorce? Even if it comes as an immense relief and perhaps as deliverance from serious danger, it is still the legal severing of a relationship for which there had once been great hope. It is possible for a divorce to express covenant love. The above criteria are offered in an effort to show how this can be. Now that the criteria are set forth, however, it appears that relatively few actual divorces would be justifiable by these tests. Yet some would, as seems appropriate when one recognizes that in some regrettable situations divorce may be the only way one spouse can continue to affirm the other in steadfast love.

From this very covenantal outlook, though, spouses will be strongly moved to seek another way. Because of people's hardness of heart we need to reflect upon divorce. Yet insofar as spouses find faith in God, they will seek first and repeatedly to contain and respond to the inevitable conflicts of marriage within a more profound mutual loyalty and commitment. As they persistently seek this route, they will often find ways to turn their conflicts toward the continued affirmation of each other and of the marriage.

9

Political Community

The Sense in Which
Political Community Is Covenantal

When we first give it any thought, we find that we are already members of political community. The contrast is sharp with marriage, into which anyone enters only through a deliberate, self-conscious choice. Can we rightly understand political community to be covenantal, then, as we did marriage, and if so, in what sense? As with marriage, how political community is to be understood is more fundamental than particular issues of moral decision within it. Offering a covenantal interpretation of political community, as I shall do, calls for considerable caution. When I assert that all the members of any particular political community are in a special covenant relationship with one another, it is necessary not only to say what I mean, but also to contrast it with some things I do not mean. In our culture it is especially needful to contrast a covenantal interpretation with various kinds of individualistic models of political community, as well as with part-whole models in which respect for individual persons is lost.

1. One way to explain the sense in which political community is covenantal is to point to the relation of politics to

society. The classical liberal tradition presupposes that a society of individuals precedes politics and is essentially nonpolitical. Classical liberal thinkers view society as a realm of people's individual activity. Politics and political institutions intrude upon that activity, perhaps unavoidably, but always in ways that infringe upon and restrict the members' freedom. There is in classical liberal thought, then, a widespread (though not unanimous) negative attitude toward political institutions as contrasted with society.[1]

The covenantal viewpoint expressed here, in contrast with classical liberal thought, holds that our lives together in society are essentially, necessarily, and thoroughly political, though not, of course, only or totally political. A community is political to the extent that it carries on the process of deliberation, decision, and action about the shape of its common life together. There is no society prior to politics and political institutions. Aristotle was right when he observed that "man is by nature a political animal."[2] Politics, the process of making decisions about the life of a community, and political institutions, the structures through which people carry on this process, are essential to social life. They are not simply added, as though a community could exist without politics. Rather, it is by political processes that communities exist at all as communities. Wherever two or three persons are in continual interaction, they find it necessary to deliberate and to devise some kinds of rules and policies, formal or informal, to regulate their relationship. Politics is a necessity in the life of families, churches, organizations in the marketplace, educational institutions, and certainly also the larger society. In the latter it expresses itself largely, though not exclusively, through "the state," the organization with the highest political authority and power in a given geographical area. Politics involves serious moral problems, but its moral evils lie in *how* it is carried on, and not in *that* it is. It does indeed restrict the freedom of a society's members, but it simultaneously enhances their freedom in other ways by enabling them to live together in ways that would otherwise not be possible. Political processes are essential to a community because political decision has to do with how the community will direct and order its life as community. Political processes, then, reflect the reality that a community is in some sense a unity, not simply an aggregate of individuals. From this perspective, politics as such is a reflection of human created nature and not simply a response to our fallen condition, however much it also participates in and responds to the fall.

2. We can further spell out the covenantal nature of political communities by speaking of their origin. Traditional social contract theorists speak of political origin simply in terms of human agency. These theorists—Hobbes and Locke as prominent examples—maintain that political communities originate purely through the voluntary agreements of individuals. The assumption is that individuals are logically, if not historically, prior to society and that political community has its foundation in the mutual agreement and consent of its individual members, that is, through a social contract. To be sure, the classical contract theorists are more interested in the political implications of the social contract than in its accuracy as a historical account,[3] but the idea of an initial contract is central to their theories. As for contemporary contract theorists, none of them to my knowledge argues that political community had its actual historical origin in a social contract. But they nevertheless start their theories from the idea of individuals' agreeing together on the conditions of political community—a logical rather than historical starting point.[4]

Although many classical contract theorists speak of moral obligation as rooted in natural law and in the natural rights belonging to each individual, and ultimately in God, they characteristically point to the idea of a contract among the individual members as the source and justification for the state. Most contemporary theorists either have little to say about the idea of natural law or avoid it altogether, and they are ordinarily neither willing nor prepared to reflect upon the idea of God in relation to political life.

In contrast, Christian covenant theory sees human agency in political community as occurring within the framework of God's action. There is no time in human history when we were not social, and furthermore, political. We are in political communities, not because we have elected to be, but because God has created us so to be and covenants with us as members of communities. People's essentially social nature finds repeated expression in the Old Testament: for example, in the Genesis 2 account of the creation and union of Adam and Eve, a programmatic statement about what it means to be human; in the accounts of God's covenanting, which is never merely with individuals, but always with a community;[5] in the way the law is directed to the plural rather than the singular "you"; and in how the prophetic indictments are expressed—usually toward groups rather than simply toward individuals. The Israelites did not initiate their covenant as a people with God; God presented them with it as a given. Even though it is described as something they could accept or reject, if they had rejected it, it would nevertheless have existed through God's action. Their choice was how to respond to this reality, not whether to constitute it as a reality. So it is with us in political communities. We are always already members of some political community. That is not an argument against calling that community covenantal, because covenants are not, like contracts, simply human contrivances. Rather, it is an indication of the kind of special covenant a political community is.

At the same time, covenant theory recognizes, as do contract theorists, the importance of human agency in giving particular political communities the characteristics they have. In political community we are not simply members of "the state," but of *this* state, with its own particular features shaped by generations of its members in interaction with the circumstances of their own history. As William F. May has observed, a covenant is rooted in a specific set of events. "It always has reference to specific historical exchange between partners leading to a promissory event."[6] The historical exchange may be publicly recognized as covenantal, as in the way that United States civil life has been consciously rooted in the covenantal events of its origin and its "new birth of freedom," so eloquently interpreted in Robert Bellah's *The Broken Covenant.*[7]

Even where a political community does not interpret its life in explicitly covenantal terms, however, it is still in fact rooted in specific events of entrusting and accepting entrustment; and it is still liable to the same kind of charge that Bellah makes against United States civil life—that the covenant has been broken.

Our political obligations are therefore never simply general, but specific obligations to identifiable persons and groups,[8] reflecting the things we and they have done—our promises, our uses of power, our accepting or not accepting one another's entrustments and thereafter responding with a mixture of trustworthiness and untrustworthiness. Therefore whereas any political community originates and exists within the framework of God's action, its policies are not simply an extension of God's will, nor is God an actor (simply more powerful than all the rest) *within* the bounds of the political drama, causing some candidates and armies to win and some to lose. Although human agency is not its own foundation in the political process and cannot substitute itself for divine agency, neither does the divine agency replace the human.

3. A third way to clarify the sense in which political community is covenantal is with regard to the bearing of consent upon membership. Contract theorists characteristically hold that voluntary consent is essential to membership in the contract. Joseph Tussman writes, "The demand for consent is the demand that membership be distinguishable from captivity. It must in some meaningful sense be voluntary."[9] It cannot be voluntary, he explains, unless the members have some actual alternative to giving consent, even if the alternative is "inconvenient, hard, or unpleasant."[10] Yet the alternatives he suggests—emigration, secession, and rebellion—are exceedingly demanding, requiring sustained effort and (with the latter two) resistance to the coercive power of the state. If a group that would prefer to emigrate, secede, or rebel decides that the costs of doing so are too great, it does not thereby give consent, at least not in the sense of a free and intentional authorization of the government as legitimate. It has merely submitted unwillingly to the government's power,

much after the fashion of a prisoner who reluctantly gives up trying to escape. As there is often no practicable alternative to continued citizenship, the consent of which Tussman speaks is not completely free.

From a covenantal standpoint the incomplete freedom of consent is no bar to full membership in the special covenant of political community. Consent and coercion are always intermingled in social life. Although a significant degree of voluntariness is present, it is always limited to a large extent by the coercive power of the state. That condition presents a serious problem for a position like Tussman's. Yet the fact that consent is always mixed with coercion is incompatible neither with membership nor with having political obligations. Some obligations, such as those of marriage, can arise only from an uncoerced consent to the relationship. But many political obligations continue to exist amidst some coercion. Even those who remain in a particular political community only because they find it difficult to do otherwise continue to have obligations toward the rights and needs of their fellow citizens, obligations which arise out of their having been members together and out of the power that they have to affect one another. This is not to deny that freedom is essential to political obligation; the question is what degree of freedom. What is essential is not an uncoerced freedom to consent to a particular state's authority, but freedom in the midst of the mixture of coercion and consent to exercise power to some degree intentionally within that community—freedom to accept others' entrustments. In a covenant framework our specific political obligations presuppose that this broad sense of freedom is widely present. That kind of freedom is indeed a prerequisite to membership, and it may be accompanied by a greater or lesser degree of consent to the state's authority.

4. Covenant theory also differs with contract theories over why we are obligated in political community. For contract theorists the most basic reason for our political obligation is that our past actions have created a duty of fair play. As H. L. A. Hart expresses it: "When a number of persons conduct any joint enterprise according to rules and thus restrict their

259

liberty, those who have submitted to these restrictions when required have a right to a similar submission from those who have benefited by their submission."[11] Following Hart, John Rawls offers a similar argument: that the principle of fairness obligates one "to do his part as defined by the rules of an institution" when, "first, the institution is just (or fair)," and "second, one has voluntarily accepted the benefits of the arrangement or taken advantage of the opportunities it offers to further one's interests."[12] Some theologians have drawn upon this idea: James Childress maintains, for example, "that political obligation in a constitutional democracy can best be understood mainly as based on the duty of fair play."[13]

Theological ethicists can find much benefit in these arguments based on fairness. Those who advance them have explained clearly how we come to stand under the duty to be fair and in general what kind of requirement fairness makes. Their emphasis upon the importance of this duty in political life is altogether fitting for theologians as well as social contract philosophers.

As a general account of political obligation, however, the argument based on fair play is deficient. It deals only with a part of our political obligation—the duty to be fair (and along with it, the duty to respect others' rights)—extremely important, to be sure, but not the whole of political obligation, as contract theorists recognize. The norm of fairness is valid only in situations in which others have generally followed the spirit of the rules—that is, only in relatively just societies. If some fellow citizens have counted the votes fraudulently, though, and have thereby stolen an election, or if the government has a persisting pattern of distributing the benefits and burdens of the economic system in a seriously unjust way, the duty of fairness no longer applies in our responses to these persons. But do we have no further political obligation toward the unfair or the political system they manipulate? For those who concentrate on the norm of fairness, that would seem to be the implication.

That is not at all the conclusion, however, in covenant theory, for it offers a broader interpretation of our basic political obligation than the argument based on fair play. We most fundamentally obligate ourselves to our fellow citizens, not simply as we benefit from their abiding by the rules, but also as we accept their entrustment through our exercise of whatever political power we have. When they participate in political community, our fellow citizens do something more radical than restrict their liberty. By entrusting themselves to the power of their fellow citizens, they seriously risk all they have, including their very lives. We imply acceptance of their entrustment when we exercise any kind of political power upon them—when we run for public office, when we seek to influence governmental officials in behalf of some policy, when we vote, and even when we seek to sway other citizens' political opinions. Through such uses of power and the acceptance of others' entrustment that it implies, we obligate ourselves even though other citizens have not conducted themselves fairly and even though the system as a whole is unjust. What we are obligated to do will depend in part upon the fairness or unfairness of the system; we have some obligation, for example, to take account of existing unfairness as we seek to protect the weak from mistreatment. But unfairness does not cancel all our obligations to those who are unfair. In much social contract theory the contract itself is the focus of attention, and one side's breaking it means that the other side is no longer bound by it. In covenant theory, in contrast, the focus is on the persons in the covenant community, not primarily on the stipulations, and being unfaithful to the covenant in no wise changes the sacredness of these persons in God's sight or their continued claims upon us as fellow covenant members. We see the spirit of covenant love in this regard in the teaching, "Love your enemies, do good to those who hate you, bless those who curse you, pray for those who abuse you" (Luke 6:27-28; cf. Matt. 5:43-44). The significance of this injunction is not as a political program to follow, but as an unambiguous affirmation of the worth and moral significance of the enemy, the abuser, and the unfair, along with everyone else. Because we are in covenant before God with our fellow citizens, we have an unchanging obligation to be trustworthy in response to their entrustment. Our acceptance of their entrustment always takes place within the framework of God's covenanting with us through Jesus Christ. In covenant theory we are to pattern our lives after the character and action of the covenanting God, and not merely after the behavior of our fellow citizens.

The concept of political communities as special covenants is thus quite different from individualistic or merely contractual models of political community. It is a concept in which our social lives are essentially political; in which human political transactions occur within the framework of God's having already placed us within covenant; in which our capacity to consent to agreements with others is always intermingled with some degree of political coercion; and in which we obligate ourselves politically, not only by accepting the benefits of others' following the rules (fair play), but by anything we do that implies acceptance of others' entrustment, including our exercise of political power.

It is also important not to confuse this covenantal view of political community with part-whole models, in which the significance of the individual members of society is lost in the oneness of the total group. Today we find this extreme most obviously in totalitarian movements, both of the right and left, when they reduce individuals to the status of mere means to their movements' utopian goals. We see the problem in any position that so emphasizes our belongingness to the social group as to lose sight of our individuality—our personal responsibility as well as our personal worth. Less obviously but still significantly, it appears to be an implication of pure forms of utilitarianism, for which the sole criterion of rightness is the tendency of an act or practice to produce the greatest possible total of experiences of satisfaction or happiness. When that alone is the criterion, then it does not matter at all which persons have those experiences, but only how great the total is. By that standard a given person can be ruthlessly sacrificed to increase the total; that is, individual persons have no worth as ends.[14]

In such holistic models the members are seen as mere parts, as a gear or wheel is a part of a machine without having any significance for its own sake. The contrast with a covenant model helps to bring out one of the latter's essential characteristics: While we are indeed essentially social and always belong to some political community, we do not lose our individuality in the process. We participate as persons rather than as parts. Each of us has rights, such as the right of free speech and the right to worship according to conscience, that are too precious to be overridden simply in order to add to the satisfaction of our fellow members. Furthermore, we are agents who not only are restrained and shaped by our society, but must also always be prepared to ask whether the society's laws and opinions are right and to take responsibility for our actions.

A covenant model seeks to avoid the dangers of part-whole models—both their destruction of individuality and their unquestioning devotion to their cause. We can avoid those dangers, though, without falling back into a one-sided individualism. To avoid them we must hold individuality and belongingness together rather than play them off against each other. Even more important, we must keep clearly before us the incommensurable, qualitative difference between any special covenant (including political community) and God's inclusive covenant, whose claims should always take priority in a conflict.

The Obligations of Political Community

The obligations of political community arise in part from characteristics that distinguish it from other kinds of special covenants and in part are formally similar to the obligations of any special covenant, though their content is shaped by the distinctive traits of political community.

Two characteristics in particular distinguish political communities from other kinds of special covenants. The first is that any given political community brings together all the people in a given geographical area under a common system of government and laws. This is true of government at any level: cities and towns, provinces and states, and countries. It is not essentially true of any other kind of human grouping, such as families, churches, or occupational organizations. If it happens on occasion that everyone in a single geographical area belongs, say, to the same religious body, it is accidental, in that the religious body could exist without that being the case.

The second essential distinguishing characteristic of political communities is that the state is the superior coercive power of the community. This is a matter of degree; and yet unless it is true to a considerable degree, the community does not endure but either splinters or succumbs to some other power. The state does not rule simply by coercion, to be sure; its citizens, as we have seen, ordinarily consent to a significant degree. But neither does it rule without superior coercive power throughout its geographical area.

Out of the interrelation of covenant love and these and other characteristics of political community, we can discern several obligations of this kind of special covenant. I shall speak of four: inclusiveness, the common good, respect for the members' rights, and loyalty. If the following discussion sounds unduly idealistic, remember that at this point we are talking about what *should* be the case, not how people necessarily behave.

1. *Inclusiveness.* One of the most serious failings of any government occurs when it rules in behalf of some but not all its citizens: when it excludes from its concern or neglects the poor, the powerless, dissenters, the unpopular, the different. We cannot ask of any government that it agree with all groups about what it should be doing; that is impossible. It is reasonable to demand, though, that it be concerned about the well-being of all, seek to include all in the common good, apply its legislative process and its resulting laws alike to all, and enable all above a reasonable age to have a significant say in the process by which they are governed.

This obligation is important in political community because of the two essential characteristics mentioned above. A government rules over everyone in a given area; and because it is difficult for its citizens to go elsewhere, rulers have an especially strong obligation to be inclusive. Likewise, a government exercises enormous power, and because each individual citizen has relatively little power, the obligation is strong to take each one's claims seriously. Any group that comes to power will be tempted, in contrast, to give special favor to its own supporters.

But does inclusiveness apply only to a community's own citizens? What obligation does a government have to aliens and to those outside its boundaries? Any government does indeed have a special responsibility toward its own citizens, because they are those who have most directly and intentionally entrusted themselves to it; they are those over whom it rules. Yet its obligations do not end with its citizens or at its own borders. As the Hebrew writers recognized, a people owes special concern to the alien in its midst. Those beyond its borders are often deeply affected by its policies and may, on occasion, be literally at its mercy—in peacetime and not only in war. High United States interest rates have contributed to unemployment both in Western Europe and in less industrialized areas, as well as to the devaluation of the peso next door in Mexico. United States economic development has an enormous effect upon both Mexico and Canada. As a Canadian leader once expressed it, living next to the United States is like trying to sleep with an elephant. To deny any responsibility for those beyond one's borders is to exalt one's country into an idol, to deny that others matter as human beings. Rulers can and should continually seek a balance between the interests of their own citizens, to whom they have special responsibility, and the interests of the citizens of the rest of the world, to whom they have an obligation even though only their own citizens have the vote. Except in serious crisis, national leaders do not find it necessary to choose starkly between the interests of their own nation and those of other nations. Usually they will find it possible to some degree to mediate between foreign and domestic claims, to moderate the demands and expectations of their own people without betraying their responsibility, and by imaginative and innovative policies to increase the area of common interest between those inside and those outside.[15]

2. *The common good.* Government, along with its citizens, is obligated to seek the common good of its people (and, to the extent possible, the common good of all people, in line with the preceding comments). Unfortunately the idea of the common good often deteriorates into a cliché; yet it is a central norm for political life.

We can contrast the common good with the individualistic idea that what society should seek is simply the sum of the good of its individual members. Jeremy Bentham stated this view simply and frankly: "The community is a fictitious *body*, composed of the individual persons who are considered as constituting as it were its *members*. The interest of the community then is what?—the sum of the interests of the several members who compose it."[16] A sum of individual interests does not constitute a *common* good, except in the minimal sense that the individual members alike seek to use the community's institutions as a means to their own individual self-interest. According to this theory there can be no social good that is anything more than an aggregate of the goods of the various individuals.

This notion can lead to sharply different political conclusions. On the one hand, it can generate the position encapsuled in the phrase, "That government is best which governs least." According to some advocates of this position, the state should at most defend against external threats and internal law-breaking, but otherwise should stand aside so that each individual and private group can freely pursue its own ends. Or the idea can lead to a radically different conclusion. If one believes that individuals' interests are largely in conflict, then one might conclude that the state should play an active internal role in society to prevent the powerful from destroying the weak. Thus from an individualistic idea of the relation of persons to society can arise support for the welfare state. Yet both positions agree that the state's chief and perhaps sole end is to enhance the interests of individuals. Their differences are over how to accomplish this end.

The idea of the common good stands in contrast with both varieties of this viewpoint. Understood covenantally, the common good is a right relationship of each member to the political community and thus to all the other members. It embodies an affirmation of the community's good that individualistic theories neglect and an affirmation of each member that part-whole theories lack.

The common good is common in the sense that it is something in which all the members share, and not merely a collection of the goods of its individual members. There is that which is common in the common good in three respects. Most fundamentally it is justice—a relationship among the members and their government, not only an attribute of individuals. No degree of enhancing the good merely of individuals as such will produce justice, because justice is a proper balance among the benefits and burdens of the community's members—a relationship. The only way justice ever comes about in a political community is through the members' coordinating their efforts to encourage it.

Second, it is conceivable (even if unlikely) that there could be a just though deeply conflict-torn society, a just though educationally and culturally undeveloped society, a just though epidemic-ridden society, or a just though economically poor society. What is common in the common good is more than justice. It includes all those conditions which not only are good for a society's individual citizens, but also enrich its common life, such as a high degree of mutual affirmation and communication among its members, of educational and cultural development, and of public health, and sufficient economic development so that its people can rise above a subsistence level to appreciate some of life's higher potentialities. All these socially shared conditions, like justice, do not come about or endure simply by individuals' seeking them; they require coordinated social endeavor.

Finally, the common good is—or can be—common in the sense that it is the shared objective of the community's members. Talcott Parsons once observed that utilitarian social theory ignores the question of how the objectives of different individuals are related. It holds that each individual will rationally seek to adopt the means that will most efficiently promote his or her desired ends, but it says nothing about whether different individuals will to any degree seek common objectives. "The failure," he writes, "to state anything positive about the relation of ends to each other can have only one meaning—that there are no significant relations, that is, that ends [of different people] are random in the statistical sense."[17] I doubt seriously that in any actual political community the objectives of the various members are related only randomly. No community could long endure that way. What it would mean if it happened is that the members would not share any common goals except accidentally. Therefore they would not intentionally or self-consciously share the goal of promoting the common good. Some societies are nearer to this condition than others. Contemporary Western industrialized societies may have a lower level of shared pursuit of the common good than some earlier nonindustrialized societies had. However that may be, the pursuit of the common good does not come about by individuals' separately pursuing their individual objectives. To the extent that it does come about, it is on the basis of community dialogue and mutual respect across whatever dividing lines of culture and outlook on life there may be. In covenant theory the objective of promoting the common good is one of the things that it is desirable to hold in common.

Part of the mission of the church is to keep before the political community the obligation to seek the common good, as well as to offer interpretations of what would contribute to the common good under various circumstances. Yet because the church is not infallible, it is presumptuous of it to relate to the civil policy process in such a way that its views cannot be adequately challenged. A covenantal interpretation of political community does not entail theocracy—rule by religious leaders. Neither state nor church can adequately perform its duties unless the different roles of the two are clearly recognized.

3. *Respect for each member's rights.* The pursuit of the common good might mistakenly be thought to conflict with the good of each member. It would be a mistake, though, because from the

standpoint of covenant love the common good includes as part of its meaning respect for the worth and therefore for the rights of each member of the community.

Ultimately the true good of the individual members is served by the common good. Yet that assertion does not presuppose a natural harmony of interests in anything like the ordinary sense. The classical liberal idea of a natural harmony was that if each individual freely pursued her or his own interests, the good of the whole would automatically be served. That idea is false, both because individuals are prone to view their interests prior to and in separation from the common good and thus to misunderstand what their true interests are, and because even if they were to understand their true interests perfectly, individuals' pursuing them apart from community coordination of their efforts would prove futile. It makes all the difference in what order of priority the objectives are arranged. The common good comes about, to the extent that we can bring it about, only through coordinated community policy and action, much of which can be done only by governments. We must aim at the common good in order to promote the true good of the members, not the reverse.

Seen from that perspective, there is ultimately in the common good a harmony of the members' true interests. At the same time many of the things in which the members *take an interest* (a different idea from their true interests)—many of the things they want and at which they aim—are in conflict with one another and with the common good. What is in harmony is the ultimate good of each—faithful participation in a faithful covenant community. So to participate is to join in the mutual respect for one another's worth as God's covenant partners and thus for one another's rights.

When Ronald Dworkin writes that it is a "postulate of political morality" that "government must treat those whom it governs . . . with equal concern and respect" as human beings,[18] that is a position compatible with the one presented here, as long as we add that it must treat all with *high* respect. Each person, Dworkin declares, has a right to be so treated. But this right, he continues, is actually two rights. One is "the right to equal treatment," which holds under some circumstances but not under others. The other, the more fundamental, is "the right to treatment as an equal," which is not a right to receive some good or opportunity being distributed, but the right to receive equal consideration with everyone else in political decisions about such distributions.[19] The secular perspective out of which Dworkin arrives at this judgment is not our concern here. That everyone has such a right clearly follows from the theological position set forth above.

To believe that every member of the political community, being also a member of God's inclusive covenant, has "the right to treatment as an equal," is to understand the common good in a way that includes the good of each member. On the one hand, it is to view the good of the community in a radically different way from part-whole theories, in which the members are merely expendable means to the ultimate social objective. Against that viewpoint we can say that it attacks the good of the whole, as well as of some members, if a government is disposed to repress, persecute, torture, or simply disregard and neglect its citizens. On the other hand, respect for each member reflects an understanding of the community's good sharply different from the way some liberal theorists view rights.[20] Contrary to extreme individualist liberal theories, most individual rights are nonabsolute; they can conflict, and some rights must at times be overridden in order to express equal high respect for all the members. Contrary to such individualistic theories, rights arise from one's socialness as a human being; they express one's membership in covenant. There is no general human right to freedom, but only rights to certain kinds of freedoms compatible with our social nature and with recognition of the worth of other persons.

4. *Loyalty.* As in any special covenant, political community has its own appropriate kind of faithfulness. Loyalty is an obligation in political community in two senses: the loyalty of the community's officials to the community and its members, and that of the members to the community and to one another.

The first of these loyalties is expressed in public officials' faithfulness to their responsibility. This faithfulness includes as a major dimension the affirmation of the worth of all the members and therefore of each one's rights. It is unfortunate that the obligation to be loyal is ordinarily approached only as a matter of the members' loyalty as citizens. Why not also recognize that officials are loyal or disloyal regarding their official responsibilities? Public officials are disloyal—unfaithful to their political covenant—when they accept kickbacks, use their office to become wealthy at the public's expense, seek to fix elections, knowingly bring false accusations against their citizens, deprive them of due process, subject them to terror, or simply through neglect allow them to become destitute. Political loyalty is a topic not rightly confined to reciting the Pledge of Allegiance and waving the flag. Genuine love for one's country on the part of a public official takes the form of faithfulness in regard to the responsibility of one's office on behalf of the citizenry.

The second sense of loyalty, that of the members toward the community and one another, is equally important and incumbent upon all persons in their capacities as citizens. In recent years it has fallen into disrepute in some quarters, as though it were not obligatory to accept responsibility toward one's political community and thus also toward the state through which it determines and administers policy. Loyalty does not require agreement with current governmental orthodoxy at any given time, nor with popular political opinions. The highest loyalty is the kind that looks beyond official views and actions to the common good which the state is obligated to promote; this loyalty attempts through constructive criticism to redirect opinion and policy in the direction of the common good. Loyalty can be compatible with civil disobedience when the disobedient person is seeking conscientiously to affirm the system of law by public and nonviolent refusal to obey a particular law deemed unjust.[21] But civil disobedience is an unusual kind of action. One has an obligation, generally speaking, to obey the law, because insofar as a society is seeking to be just, the law is an effort to express the community's conception of justice and its efforts to move toward the common good. Loyalty requires acceptance of personal burdens for the sake of the community—burdens often embodied in law-abidingness, and not primarily in protest: burdens such as the duty to seek to be informed about issues before voting, or to accept the pluralism of loyal political viewpoints that is essential in guarding against some of the errors and misuses of power in a political community, or to pay one's taxes honestly according to the laws, even though the tax laws could be more nearly just. For those of the appropriate age, political faithfulness requires acceptance of the burden on occasion of helping to defend the country against outside threats—unless one is a conscientious objector to all war. Those who protest the requirement to register for the draft seldom express their reasons in terms of conscientious objection to all war. From a nonpacifist viewpoint, that a country might pursue a war unjustly, which indeed it might, is no justification for refusing to accept some burden for its defense. Participation in the benefits of political community entails, out of fairness, if for no further reason, a corresponding willingness to share in its burdens. Accepting, by our participation in political life, the entrustment of fellow citizens obligates us to do our part for their protection when the lot fairly falls our way.

Citizens' loyalty is then a matter of accepting the responsibilities that follow from being members of a political community, sharing in its power, its deeds and misdeeds, and its opportunities to assist people, both within and beyond its borders, in response to their entrusting. As with the loyalty of officials, that of members is not primarily a matter of patriotic words and symbols, though these have their place. It is embodying in one's civic behavior the faithfulness appropriate to those who have received much from their community, and in whom others have placed their trust.

Conflict and Covenant in Political Community

To whatever extent we fulfill our obligation in political community, we must do so in the midst of conflict—the conflict of moral claims, the conflict of interests, and conflict as struggle or strife. There is no direct or simple route in political life from the identification of a moral obligation to its fulfillment. Conflict is unavoidably present to some degree in social life, and political communities must deal with it in order to work out community policy.

Political conflict is neither a harmless game nor a dire evil; it is ambiguous, involving both opportunities and risks. How it is conducted depends to a considerable extent upon the structure of each political community, and especially upon the degree to which a community is made up of a single, or dualistic, or pluralistic centers of power and interest. It is my judgment that a number of Western political communities, including the United States, are more accurately characterized as pluralistic in their organizations of power than as monolithic or dualistic, though all three tendencies can be present in different respects. Some other countries would be better described as power-monolithic or power-dualistic. It is a matter to be determined by observation, not by deduction from theological presuppositions. Those who have made a special study of political conflict in a pluralistic society can help us see the particular shape that conflict tends to take under those conditions. I shall draw upon such studies[22] to offer the following theses as applicable at least to most of the Western, industrialized, democratic political communities:

1. People have multiple interests: for example, interests in the economic well-being of one's family, in the unhampered practice of one's religious faith, in the protection of all one's basic rights, in seeing justice done, in the security of one's nation.

2. A person's own multiple interests partially conflict with one another. Perhaps we want to increase our savings as security against the future, and yet we also want to pursue graduate study or travel abroad or live in a larger house. We may have to choose between these desires. Similarly one person's interests conflict to some extent with those of other persons.

3. Social conflict as strife tends to arise over the pursuit of

273

people's conflicting interests. This is especially true in a democracy, which for present purposes we can understand as "a competitive political system in which competing leaders and organizations define the alternatives of public policy in such a way that the public can participate in the decision-making process."[23] Strife is especially visible in a democracy because the political system permits it to be. Yet conflict and consensus both occur, closely interwoven and not simply mutually opposed. Seymour Martin Lipset writes, "Consensus on the norms of tolerance which a society or organization accepts has often developed only as a result of basic conflict, and requires the continuation of conflict to sustain it."[24]

4. In a democracy people tend to band together in parties and pressure groups to promote their shared interests against conflicting groups. Lines of cleavage form between the opposing sides over some issue: for example, over the government's role in the economy. Conflict over this issue divides the two sides, but it simultaneously tends to unite those on the same side.

5. There are countless possible conflicts of this kind, just as there are countless interests and possible issues, but only a few become the basis for political organization. Most potential conflicts in society do not come to the surface, which is just as well, as otherwise society would be torn asunder with conflict.

6. Those conflicts that do come to the fore often tend to organize people along different lines of cleavage; that is, the dividing lines overlap or "crosscut." Those who roughly agree about the role of government in the economy, for example, are not all likely to agree on federal aid to parochial schools, or on United States foreign policy toward Israel, or on some other issue. At other times cleavages reinforce one another, so that one encounters the same opponents in issue after issue.

7. Which lines of cleavage become the dominant ones in the political conflict is highly important. Those who can define the issues for the public can usually gain an advantage in a political contest. Which conflicts become dominant will depend at one level upon the skills and resources of the contestants. At a

deeper level, though, it will in a complicated way reflect what people want most—their priorities, which issues should be contested in politics and which should be kept out of the contest for one reason or another. In recent decades, for example, the United States public has tended to place the issue of the government's role in the economy near the center of political conflict; at the same time, it has continued to keep issues of conflict between religious bodies away from the center of conflict, not necessarily because these are thought unimportant, but often because of the feared consequences of making them central and the availability of an acceptable partial solution in the First Amendment. The question of which conflicts become dominant and how a conflict is conducted is of such importance that one way to understand political activity in a democracy is as *the management of conflict*.

8. Conflict can reach various levels of moderation or severity. Robert A. Dahl has identified several conditions that affect the intensity or severity of a political conflict:[25] (a) The distribution of attitudes toward the conflict among citizens and leaders. The more extreme the attitudes and the more people who hold extreme and opposing views, the more severe the conflict tends to become. (b) The patterns of cleavage. When lines of cleavage reinforce each other, conflicts tend to become severe; when cleavages crosscut, conflicts tend to be less severe. (c) How much is at stake and what the possible solutions are. The more people stand to gain or lose in the conflict, the more intense it tends to become. Conflicts that are zero-sum games, in which one side can gain only by the other side's losing, tend to be more severe than conflicts in which solutions exist in which both sides can become better off. (d) The political institutions. Institutions tend to make for less severe conflict if they require opposing leaders to negotiate with each other, provide acceptable ways to end negotiations and come to a decision, and reflect widespread agreement on procedures for negotiation and decision.

Political conflict presents a serious dilemma for a covenant ethic. Conflict as strife is ambiguous. On the one hand, it performs valuable functions in political life. It can enable human needs and convictions to find expression, call into question existing injustices, and press political leaders to move beyond established policies that no longer promote the common good as they once did. As discussed in chapter 3, it can act as a safety valve, help to bind a group together, and revitalize existing norms or give rise to new and more appropriate norms.

On the other hand, political conflict can be seriously harmful, both to a community and to its individual members. It can produce effects opposite some of those cited above: drown out cries for help in the community, evoke reactions against relatively just policies, and stifle dissent so as to support an insensitive political orthodoxy. Too intense a level of conflict in the community can undermine its shared interpretations, symbols, and norms; can erode the fabric of mutual trust; can atomize its people so that each group or even each member comes to suspect and fear every other; and at the extreme, can physically tear it to shreds. Without dwelling on the extremes of Spain of the late 1930s or Lebanon or El Salvador more recently, we can see some of the destructive effects of serious domestic political conflict in the case of Belgium, torn by two national groups, each with its own language and traditions; in Canada, with its quarrel over the status of Quebec; in many a city or town divided by a bitter labor-management dispute; in some African countries where different tribes vie for dominance (or simply for survival); in national United States policies of the Joe McCarthy era; in Northern Ireland for more than a decade of religious-social-political strife; in Argentina, with its recent pattern of violent attack upon individuals and their human rights by governmental and nongovernmental groups; and the list could be much expanded.

The dilemma is how a political community can achieve the benefits of conflict without enduring its serious harms. Conflict is not incompatible with covenant; indeed, some kinds of conflict help people express what is implied in living faithfully with one another in the same political community. But some kinds of conflict are incompatible with the well-being of a community, and some objectives and means of pursuing a conflict are incompatible with covenant loyalty to one another.

We must resist overly simple moral judgments about the subject. There are always some persons who condemn as a trouble-maker or subversive anyone who dissents or who leads opposition. This is a well-known tactic to divert the public's attention away from the cause of the problem and to transfer the blame to others. We have seen it used recently in Poland, Argentina, Iran, and South Africa, and it appears now and then in the United States. Inciting conflict is not wrong as such; it depends upon the circumstances and the means and objectives of the conflict.

At the other extreme a few people, romantic about conflict, think that we should never repress or sublimate any conflict but should face every human issue "openly and honestly." But it is impossible to deal with every human conflict, and it would be undesirable if it were possible. There are endless conflicts and potential conflicts among people, and we cannot give our attention to more than a few. To focus on one conflict enough to come to grips with it entails putting other issues aside for the time being. Furthermore, if we did bring up every potential conflict, we would make life unbearably contentious, rouse people's feelings to the boiling point, and quickly convert political community into a condition of chaos where every person is enemy to every other.

Are there some generalizations we can make about how to deal with conflict within the special covenant of political community? Can we identify some objectives and limits that are usually appropriate, even if there are exceptions? The following suggestions may encourage others to probe further into the question:

1. As in marriage and other special covenants, conflict within political community should always be conducted as within covenant. In God's sight and given our mutual entrustments, what binds us to one another in political community is more fundamental than what divides us. True, what binds is often less conspicuous than the issue at conflict;

it is easy to lose sight of mutual obligations and to be caught up in party spirit and indignation. In some relationships of life, in contrast, we ordinarily find ourselves inclined to recognize the covenantal framework of any conflict—relationships with our children, for example, and often with sisters and brothers. Can we so believe in the inclusiveness of God's covenant that we see all our fellow citizens as our brothers and sisters—in our affections and commitments, and not merely rhetorically?

2. What binds us politically in God's sight also generally finds concrete, observable embodiment in common interests within the community. In the midst of intense conflict, we would usually be wise to recognize that our opponents and we still have much in common in terms of economic and political and social interests, that the game is rarely zero-sum, that with political imagination and courage we could shift the terms of the conflict from "how to defeat them" to "how to resolve this quarrel within the family to the healing and benefit of as many as possible." That was the spirit with which Lincoln approached the aftermath of the Civil War that he never lived to see. It is equally appropriate to any less severe conflict.

3. We sometimes have the option of turning the intensity of a social conflict up or down, perhaps by our words or where we invest our resources. In responding to that choice, it is desirable to keep in mind that usually the common good might be served or harmed either way. The option is a genuine dilemma; it does not ordinarily admit of only one right response. Sometimes the intensification of peaceful conflict may be the only way to achieve a greater degree of justice, as Martin Luther King, Jr., perceived in his campaigns in Birmingham and elsewhere for the rights of black people. That very intensification could conceivably have polarized the wider political community so sharply that the chance of constructive policy would have been diminished, or if carefully conducted it could instead have evoked public support that would make possible gains for justice—which is what happened in that instance. Yet we cannot be sure how the consequences will work out. When the injustice is

sufficiently great, as it was in that instance, we must assign a higher priority to overcoming it than to the maintenance of community harmony, which in such a case could be no more than a superficial harmony purchased at the price of deceiving our consciences. When the issue at conflict is less one of justice and more a matter of the relative advantages of competing, privileged groups, we would do well to consider the possible harmful effects of the struggle on the community and give priority to the common good above the gains for either group. The problem is that in many instances we do not know which kind of case is at hand; it is too easy to convince ourselves that if *our* interests are in question it is a matter of justice, but if others' are, it is a matter of privilege.

4. The *means* we use can intensify a conflict beyond what we might have intended, and certainly beyond justification. Because we are covenant members with our adversaries in politics, whoever they are, it is necessary to avoid and combat attitudes, rhetoric, and overt behavior that portray community opponents as enemies. Within covenant the ultimate objective is one in which there is a place for both sides within the community. The rhetoric of enmity invites the participants to seek to eliminate and not only to gain an advantage over the opposition. With this attitude, dissent or difference of opinion can become tantamount to disloyalty. If instead the objective is cooperation after the conflict, as is appropriate in an election campaign, then the attitudes, language, and tactics of enmity and rejection have no place.

5. In the conflict between competing parties in a democracy, the existence of a freely competing loyal opposition is a higher priority than the victory of "our side," even if ours is (as anyone tends to believe) the "right side." Nikita Khrushchev's question to President Dwight Eisenhower when the Soviet premier was visiting in the United States reveals the outlook of many who do not understand the rationale for democracy: "Why do you need two parties when only one can be right?" From a Christian understanding of human nature, democracy is seen not as a means to the election of the "right people," nor even as a means for the people to express their wisdom.

Christians should be beyond illusion about how wrongheaded any group of people can be—majority or minority. Democracy as a system of freely competing parties is desirable for other reasons: (a) It enables every citizen to express his or her own political needs and perceptions. However inadequate our proposed solutions to problems may be, our perception of our own problems and needs is usually more accurate than what some other unknown person would say in speaking for us. (b) It tends to restrain the capacity of governmental officials to misuse their power. Those leaders who overreach themselves—and anyone, of whatever political persuasion, might do that, given enough power—can more easily be replaced than if there were no competing parties. (c) It stimulates the parties through their competition for power to find more adequate solutions to political problems. Obviously democracy does not always adequately serve these purposes, but the likelihood is that a nondemocratic system would serve them even less well. Given these reasons for a system of freely competing parties, one of the highest priorities of political morality is to avoid tactics that place the loyal opposition at an unfair disadvantage.

Thus it is morally wrong to misrepresent the viewpoint of one's opponents, or to seek to intimidate them in their exercise of free speech in political campaigns, or to interfere with the opposing party's choice of its nominees, or to slice up electoral districts so that the opposition vote counts for less than its actual strength, or to play the demagogue by appealing to the group hatreds of the voters. That some of the above tactics are standard practice among many in politics indicates the degree to which success at the polls often replaces the common good as a political objective, or the degree to which some political figures, worshiping their own image, define the common good in terms of their own success.

Yet political conflict is not inherently unscrupulous. Many a candidate or elected official has expressed moral standards without which our political life would be much the poorer. For a few illustrations one might refer to John F. Kennedy's *Profiles in Courage*.[26] Kennedy describes the behavior under severe pressure of persons like Sam Houston, who as governor of Texas sought in 1860 and 1861 to keep his state from seceding from the Union, and Senator Edmund G. Ross of Kansas, who in 1868, though threatened by his constituents, refused to go against his conscience and vote for the impeachment conviction of President Andrew Johnson, whom he considered to be innocent of the charges. Nor is political courage restricted to a past century. In our own time we have seen the example of a southern governor who, after witnessing the spectacle of a successful race-baiting campaign for senator in his state, thereafter traveled around the state calling the voters to account for succumbing to such an appeal. And when Edward Brooke of Massachusetts, a black, having won election to the United States Senate in 1966, congratulated his opponent Endicott Peabody for keeping the issue of race out of the campaign, Peabody is said to have replied that he would prefer to lose rather than to campaign with racist appeals. By such standards, expressed in the midst of many who show less moral stature, men and women in politics help to preserve something of the covenantal fabric of political community.

6. It should be a high priority not only to conduct politics within the political community as we find it, but also to seek to promote a greater sense of community among its members. The United States is becoming more pluralistic as a political community. This development is to be welcomed insofar as it represents acceptance of diversity of tradition or lineage or opinion within a wide spectrum compatible with an open society. But some other kinds of pluralism can undercut the fabric of community, such as development of political attitudes and practices that set the members at one another's throats. Are there ways we can strengthen our sense of respect for and fairness toward one another? If so, we would do well to discover and use them. Can we provide more opportunity for meaningful communication among groups of different ethnic or religious or economic backgrounds? Can we demonstrate by the policies of government and private organizations that all such groups are legitimate members of the community? Can we work to encourage crosscutting rather than polarizing

conflicts? A community does not embody a covenantal outlook simply by speaking and hearing about the idea; the concept must find expression in political behavior.

7. The work of a political leader is a high calling—a vocation. Those who have pursued it with few moral scruples have given the name "politician" an insulting connotation. But a political community cannot thrive without good leadership, and its leaders are by definition politicians—managers of political conflict. In our covenant with one another under God, we are always in need of politicians who see their work as the service of the common good. Those who accept this calling enter an arena of intense conflict and mixed morality. But they do not become immoral for being active in that arena. Where conflict is intense, the stakes are higher and the risks are greater, but the human needs are also correspondingly great. The calling of a politician is to seek to help the members of the community to express their covenant with one another and with the world beyond their borders.

10

The Church

The Church as Covenantal

In *The Structure of the Divine Society*, F. W. Dillistone examines two concepts of the church, organic and covenantal, and concludes that both are needed because neither alone can "unlock all the mysteries of the Church's life."[1] Expressed that way, his conclusion is unassailable. Even so, the concept of covenant is a richer concept than Dillistone realizes, even if it is not a key that fits all locks.

Dillistone's characterization of covenant ideas in the Bible and in Christian history is nevertheless extremely helpful. He recognizes that what is central to a covenant is the relationship between the covenanting parties, and that whenever that relationship takes second place to any set of stipulations, a covenant is distorted into a legalistic contract.[2] He also rejects the mistaken notion that in biblical theology grace and law are in conflict. Instead he writes, "The covenant-community lives ever under the dialectic of Grace and Law and any relationship in which either of these elements fails to find a proper place is not worthy to be called a covenant."[3] He highlights the covenantal emphasis upon the personal and the freedom of the parties as a balance to the danger in organic theories of losing sight of the individuality of a society's members.

Even so, Dillistone's concept of covenant is unnecessarily restricted. Consider the following ways he speaks of the idea:

> In the main the covenant implies a purposive rather than a natural social-group, an eschatological rather than an ontological society. . . . The normal pattern of covenant is thus clear: two principals, each representing wider social groups, commit themselves to the realization of a common purpose and unite their common resources within a single relationship in order that the desired end may be achieved.[4]

> The sign which constitutes the form of the Church, like the sign which determines the nature of a human covenant, is directed primarily to the future rather than to the past.[5]

> The Church's Covenant, like a human covenant, is based upon man's freedom of self-determination. Nothing is more characteristic of human covenants than their absolute dependence upon the voluntary principle. If there is coercion, it is meaningless to speak of covenant. This does not mean that either party to the covenant can act in a completely uncontrolled and unconditioned way. A man who enters into a covenant carries his past with him even if he solemnly repudiates his past. . . . Each party is influenced by unseen forces.[6]

One problem with this characterization is that the past plays a more important role in covenants than Dillistone recognizes, in human-to-human as well as God-to-human covenants. The past not only limits our possibilities, as the last quotation above suggests. At least as significantly the past enables us to understand what we are doing as we act in the present and look to the future. Yahweh initiates the Sinai covenant by first putting it in proper historical perspective: "I am the Lord your God, who brought you out of the land of Egypt, out of the house of bondage" (Exod. 20:2). Only by reference to this past do the children of Israel know with whom they are covenanting. The past carries a similar significance in Paul's declaration of how the church is to understand itself.

> And he died for all, that those who live might live no longer for themselves but for him who for their sake died and was

284

raised. . . . Therefore, if any one is in Christ, he is a new creation; the old has passed away, behold, the new has come. All this is from God, who through Christ reconciled us to himself and gave us the ministry of reconciliation; that is, God was in Christ reconciling the world to himself, not counting their trespasses against them, and entrusting to us the message of reconciliation. (II Cor. 5:15, 17-19)

Here the reference is simultaneously to the past and to the future. The church's task does indeed lie in the future—proclaiming the message of reconciliation. But the church knows of this task, and of God's love out of which it arises, only because of its memory of Jesus Christ's death and resurrection. The past provides the decisive event out of which the new covenant has meaning and from which its special responsibility arises. Covenants are always simultaneously past- and future-oriented, and neither can rightly be deemed more important than the other. The future is meaningless, and our commitment regarding it is purely arbitrary, unless we approach it from a past that provides decisive meaning. The past is deadening unless it points us to the better understanding of the present and to responsibility in the future. It is true that covenants, including the church, are eschatological, but they can be that only because they are rooted in a significant past.

The other problem in Dillistone's conception of covenant lies in his one-sided emphasis upon the voluntary. Covenants indeed provide a major role for acts of the will, without which no covenant group would exist. It is not enough qualification of this emphasis, however, to remind us, as Dillistone does, that our wills are limited. Our willing to covenant as church is shaped from the start by God's willing, God's entrustment of a calling to the church. Human willing is always the second action, never the first; it is always a response to God's action. In the case of the church, as with the children of Israel, we *find* ourselves chosen for covenant. We do not will in absolute freedom to be in this covenant; rather, we will to accept or not accept God's entrustment. If we do not accept it, we are deciding not to be in the church or not to understand the church as God's chosen special covenant with its own God-designated special responsibility. While we are not forced to accept the covenant of the church, we do face a *forced choice:* either to accept God's entrustment to us as church or to reject the understanding of existence that God's election of the church signifies. Likewise the responsibility that belongs to the church as a special covenant chosen by God is not one about which we bargain. We do not determine it by our wills; rather, we seek to understand it with our intellects, and in the process we accept or reject it.

God initiates and determines the task of the church. However much our wills are involved in our participating in the church, nevertheless the existence of the church expresses the intention of God and not merely our own willing. One implication of the Christian proclamation of Jesus Christ is that it is God's intention from creation that there should be a church—a community responsible to proclaim God's disposition and action. The covenant that is the church depends absolutely upon God's initiative, not upon "the voluntary principle." In this covenant the human parties voluntarily respond to limited options. In some important senses the church is a voluntary organization. In at least as important a sense, though, it is a chosen community responding to a Given, or a Giving.

With these modifications, though, I wish to affirm Dillistone's relational conception of covenant and his resistance to legalistic or defensive interpretations of it. Some earlier theologians whom Dillistone discusses have not been as careful or insightful in their covenantal theory as he has been. In particular it is important to avoid some problems in the covenant theory of the seventeenth-century "federal theologians," those in Europe as well as the New England Puritans. I wish to deny that there was, as some federal theologians asserted, a "covenant of works" between God and Adam through which the children of Adam are condemned by their inability to keep it, a covenant which these theologians contrasted with a "covenant of grace"[7] through Jesus Christ. God's covenants have a single intention—human salvation;

and all God's covenanting is the expression of grace toward sinful creatures incapable of working their own salvation.

Furthermore, when I shortly distinguish between the church as a special covenant and the inclusive covenant, I do not mean to say, as did some of the federal theologians, that the church covenant is with those who are elected to salvation, whereas those outside it are elected to damnation.[8] Such an interpretation of the church distorts the Christian proclamation. Nor do I want to argue, as did many of that school, that God's action in history can be divided into periods represented by different covenants.[9] This is an earlier form of modern Dispensationalism that imposes upon history arbitrary differences in God's intention and thereby loses sight of the unchanging nature of God's love. Finally we must keep in mind that God's covenant with us is never a bargain, never a quid pro quo; unfortunately some federal theologians encouraged precisely this notion by the way they conceived of covenant.[10]

What I do wish to say is summed up in this thesis: *The church is the special covenant that exists, through God's grace, in response to God's action in Jesus Christ and that has as its special calling the proclamation in word and deed of God's inclusive covenant with its declaration of God's love and its demand for faith in God and love with justice toward all persons.* Various facets of this thesis call for explanation.

The church is a covenant community. This is not to exclude other images of the church; far from it. Paul Minear[11] has identified eighty or more in the New Testament in addition to those closely related to the concept of covenant. Nevertheless, several New Testament writers use covenant language regarding the church, even when they do not use the Greek term for covenant, *diathēkē.* They use covenant terms for various theological purposes, sometimes with a direct but more often an indirect bearing upon the church.

a. In a few instances they contrast the "old covenant" with the "new covenant." When Paul writes that through Christ, God has "made us sufficient as ministers of a new covenant, not of letter, but of spirit, for the letter puts to death but the spirit gives life" (II Cor. 3:6, Plummer's translation, ICC), "covenant" refers not primarily to the church, but to that new (literally, "fresh") covenant relationship through Christ out of which the church arises. The author of the Letter to the Hebrews similarly contrasts the "first covenant" with the "new covenant" (especially in chaps. 8–9). Here again the "new covenant" appears to refer to the relationship that constitutes the church, not to the community that results from it.

b. Some other New Testament contexts express the relationship of old to new as one of promise and fulfillment, as we have seen,[12] an idea that presupposes the Old Testament assertion of God's self-binding in covenant with the chosen people. The bearing of this covenant imagery upon the church is indirect; the writers by implication portray the church as arising out of God's action in fulfilling the promises of the covenant.

c. Another use of covenant language speaks directly of the church. In various passages New Testament writers present the church as "the people of God." Minear has identified various usages of this idea, all presupposing Old Testament traditions of God's covenant with Israel.[13] First Peter, for example, speaks of the church in a passage rich with covenant allusions: "But you are a chosen race, a royal priesthood, a holy nation, God's own people, that you may declare the wonderful deeds of him who called you out of darkness into his marvelous light. Once you were no people but now you are God's people; once you had not received mercy, but now you have received mercy" (2:9-10). In Galatians, Paul speaks of Christians as Abraham's descendants (3:29; cf. Rom. 4:16), to which he adds, "heirs according to promise." Thereafter, to reinforce the point, he calls the church "the Israel of God" (6:16). Other allusions to the church as the people of God appear in Ephesians 2:12, in Hebrews' use of the Jeremiah 31 "new covenant" passage, and perhaps in Revelation 2:14.

These are a few of the ways that New Testament writers give evidence of a covenant framework in their thinking about the church. These passages tend to support the judgment, suggested more generally by the content of the Christian gospel, that the church can be understood theologically as a covenant community.

To speak this way of the church is to refer to the acts of entrusting and accepting entrustment, explicitly and implicitly, that characterize the church, as similar kinds of acts would be present in other communities. This language does not imply a judgment about whether any particular Christian group came into being through some explicit, intentional act of covenanting among the members, nor about the form of polity churches have or should have.

In the life of the church, entrusting and accepting entrustment occur in two relationships at once: the relationship between God and the believers, and the relationship among the believers. In the first, God as well as the believers entrusts, and each in turn accepts the entrustment of the other. It is obvious that the believers are risking themselves, expressing trust in God and entrusting themselves to God, insofar as the Christian proclamation actually shapes their self-understanding and action as a church and as its members. Correspondingly God steadfastly accepts the believers' entrustment; that is the significance of the message that God is faithful to the promise.

It is not so obvious, though still true, that God also risks—entrusts something to the church. God entrusts a mission, the work of declaring in word and deed God's inclusive covenant as revealed in Jesus Christ. In this respect God is dependent upon the church—not necessarily upon one specific identifiable set of people but upon *some* set—to carry out this special responsibility. Although some resist the idea that God is in any way dependent upon any creatures, much of our theological language implies some kind of divine dependence, an idea that process theology has helpfully analyzed. To say, for example, that God delights in the repentance of a sinner is to imply that God's delight would be to some degree frustrated in the absence of this repentance. To say that God loves us is to imply that God finds satisfaction in our well-being and is dissatisfied when our lives are thwarted.

The alternative to this idea is the notion that it does not matter to God what we do or what happens to us. To the contrary, the Christian proclamation is that God cares greatly. This is suggested in the idea of God's covenanting. To covenant is to risk. By entrusting responsibility to the church, God risks the responsibility's not being carried out. True, the responsibility might be removed and given to others, but the same situation would still exist. God's dependence in this regard is quite compatible with the assertion that the church is utterly dependent upon God's grace and with the belief that any creature is dependent upon God in a thoroughgoing way in which God is not dependent upon it. Even so, God entrusts, and correspondingly those who belong to the church are in the position of accepting God's entrustment, either explicitly or implicitly, with the responsibility to God and their fellows that accompanies membership in this covenant. The language of covenant is the language of mutual risk and dependence.

Entrusting and accepting entrustment also occur in the relationship among the believers. Although the most fundamental relationship is between God and the believers, anyone who joins the church also entrusts to the other believers, as they in turn do toward the new member. As new members of the church, we are risking that our fellow believers might mislead us about the meaning of the message that Jesus Christ is Lord, that they might not take seriously our need for spiritual support, that they might not hold us accountable for our responsibilities as believers in God when we fail to take them with sufficient seriousness. Any believer is a weak reed; without the support of a community of believers, past and present, we cannot find or maintain any steadfastness in faith and love.

And consider what those existing members are risking when they receive us into membership: that we may not mean what we say but may be joining for ulterior motives, and that we may, intentionally or not, corrupt the message and work of the church. Both sides of this relationship are vulnerable. To say that the church is a covenant community is to speak of our mutual interdependence and correspondingly of our mutual responsibilities.

The church is a special covenant. This implies that, like other kinds of special covenants, some people belong to it and others do not. Although we find it difficult to say exactly who does and who does not belong, some people are certainly outside the church. Yet that does not imply that they are outside God's covenant love, because the church is not to be understood as the body of all those whom God loves. Those outside the church are nonetheless members of God's inclusive covenant, as are those inside. The inclusive covenant is not some "covenant of works," nor merely the remainder of the human race besides the elect. It is the whole body of God's children, all of whom God loves, with all of whom God intends covenant from the beginning, and for all of whom God is seeking and working salvation. All matter alike in God's sight, not only those who confess faith through Jesus Christ.

One implication of this distinction between the inclusive covenant and the church as one type of special covenant is that the church need not fear having standards that must be met in order for one to be a member. When we fear requiring much of church members because that might tend to exclude them from the church (which it might), there may be lurking in the back of our minds the notion that we would then be excluding them from God's love or from salvation—which we would not. This notion is pernicious: in the first place it is a symptom of presumption on the part of those who hold it, suggesting that they think that being in the church is a privilege and a sign of God's special favor. Too often the formula that Cyprian stated in the third century after Christ, "Outside the church no salvation," has been used to express that outlook. Second, it leads church people to misunderstand their mission—what they are to do with the gospel entrusted to them. The church need not fear high standards, though they should be standards essential to its mission, not eccentric notions or ways of seeming superior. The standard underlying all valid standards for church membership is that one confess faith in Jesus Christ as Lord and intend to orient one's life in its entirety around this lordship. Not to require this standard would be to deny the church's calling. Yet to hold up this standard before new and old members alike is in effect to restrict membership to those who seriously resolve to accept God's entrustment and who seriously intend to accept the church's mission as their own.

The idea that the church is a special covenant should not be confused with the notion that it is merely a contract. Although those two terms can be used variously and even synonymously, I have in mind here again two very different concepts. By a contract I mean here a kind of relationship arrived at by a process of bargaining and in which the continuation of the relationship depends upon each party's performing certain stipulated actions. There is a proper place for this concept within the life of the church, as well as elsewhere. In addition to other ways in which we characterize the church, it is a legal entity. Its place in the legal system of any society is continually being worked out by a process of explicit and implicit bargaining. Its enjoyment of its legal rights as an institution depends in part upon its performance of certain stipulated obligations, such as its conforming to legal regulations about the acquisition and sale of property, and its respect for the system of civil law within which it exists. In these respects the church is emphatically a contractual organization.

Yet the church is not only, nor primarily, contractual in the above sense. It is contractual only within a more basic framework that is covenantal. The church came into being not by a process of bargaining, any more than did the relationship between God and the children of Israel, but by God's gracious and unilateral initiative. It endures as the church of Jesus Christ only because in the midst of our failures God steadfastly seeks after us and reentrusts to us the church's mission. Failure to perform what is stipulated does not entail dissolution of the covenant, as is the case in a legal contract. The same is true of the relations of member to member. The church could not endure except as the members repeatedly find themselves enabled through Jesus Christ to forgive and accept one another in the midst of their insufficient faithfulness. The relationship is first and foremost covenantal, and the contractual elements in its life are subordinate to the covenantal basis.

The Church's Mission

As a special covenant the church has a responsibility to those beyond its boundaries that is different from other types of special covenants: *the proclamation of God's inclusive covenant both in word and in deed.*

The church's mission is to proclaim God's inclusive covenant. God wills to unite with the whole of humanity in one covenant community. In Karl Barth's words, "By its whole nature the creature is destined and disposed for" covenant with God.[14] The Christian witness is that this covenant has been decisively declared in Jesus Christ. To say that every person belongs to the inclusive covenant is not to assert anything at all about people's awareness or will, but to speak of God's will. All people are members whether they know it or not and whether they agree to it or not. As members they have responsibilities to and for one another, and corresponding needs and human rights, apart from their understanding or commitment, or the absence thereof.

Yet in another sense, as we have seen, the inclusive covenant awaits human belief, trust, and loyalty before it is fully present. In this sense it is an eschatological hope, awaiting completion. Because of human alienation from God, one another, and self, the inclusive covenant is not fully realized. It is truly present but not fully present. The witness to our mutual belongingness is always present in various ways, even in the midst of our dividedness, but it awaits full expression in word and deed.

The church's special calling and responsibility is to declare the reality of the inclusive covenant as God has made it known through Jesus Christ. This idea can be expressed in other terminology. A leading thesis of Vatican II's *Dogmatic*

Constitution on the Church, for example, is closely akin to this idea: "By her relationship with Christ, the Church is a kind of sacrament or sign of intimate union with God, and of the unity of all mankind. She is also an instrument for the achievement of such union and unity."[15] Karl Rahner has stated the meaning of this passage more succinctly: "The Church is the sacrament of the salvation of the *world.*"[16]

This characterization of the church's mission reflects the conviction that it has to do with the most fundamental human need, one that underlies and is present in the midst of the more readily visible needs for food, clothing, shelter, health, and the like. We need to be made whole; we need health of the spirit; in the traditional language of the church, we need salvation. That wholeness is a matter simultaneously of faith in God and community with one another. Gutiérrez has expressed it this way: "We do not have two histories, . . . one by which we become children of God and the other by which we become each other's brothers."[17] Our history is one, in relation at once to God and to one another; and our healing will be one, expressed in both relationships together, the one the foundation of the other.

To these two dimensions of our one fundamental need there correspond two inseparable dimensions of the church's mission. One dimension corresponds to our need to have faith in God. Here the church has the task of proclaiming in the face of human unbelief in God the truth of our lives—that God has elected us to covenant and seeks our recognition of this reality. Its task is to proclaim in the face of human distrust of God that the power that undergirds our lives can be relied upon in all our relationships. It must witness in the face of human disloyalty to God and practical loyalty to false gods that the unalterably loyal God forgives us in the midst of our inconstancy and seeks our reconciliation with God, with one another, and with ourselves.

The other dimension of the church's mission corresponds to our need to be fully participating members of the human community, living in covenant love and justice with one another. Here the church is called to express in deed and in word what it would mean for people to be rightly related to one another in the inclusive human community. How the church appropriately pursues this dimension of its calling can be expressed in several ways. First, it is called to teach and work for justice in society. In its teaching office the church has the responsibility to help shape the conscience of the society concerning people's obligations to one another and the implications of this obligation for social life. In its action as a part of the wider society, the church has the responsibility to join in efforts to bring about greater justice in social policies and practices.

Second, the church is called to work for right relationships within its own community as well as in the wider society. Within its walls the church has a duty to express love and justice in the relations of its members to one another and to the Christian community: in its unqualified devotion to God, its continuing theological ethical reflection on its responsibilities, its respect and affirmation of its members regardless of their rank or talents, its openness for all to join as members who confess its faith, its honesty in the use of its own material possessions, its dependability in the pursuit of its calling, and its efforts at reconciliation in the midst of ever-present conflict within the church as within any human group. This inward work of the church is not mere institutional maintenance, but rather a continuing institutional renewal. But the church's primary duty lies outward rather than inward, and inward renewal is largely for the sake of outward work. Within the society at large the church is called to seek patterns of mutual affirmation, social practices by which people can better attack the immense injustices that beset them on every side.

Third, the church's calling in the world belongs both to individual Christians and to the church as a body. Obviously individual Christians in their roles as citizens have a duty to bring their faith to bear upon social issues through the various groups to which they belong. But to stop at that would leave them with insufficient support in the midst of society's conflicts. The church as a body is called to help its members find effective means of action, to keep before them the awareness of their Christian orientation in the midst of the secular society, and to assist them to bring their judgments carefully to bear upon complex social issues. The church is not the state, but that does not prohibit it from joining in deliberations about what the state should be doing. The church does not have simple or infallible answers to complex social problems, but that does not disallow it from participating actively in the search for better responses.

In these many ways the church's mission is the proclamation of the inclusive covenant. Yet that proclamation in word and deed must be done in the midst of continuing conflict within the church over its role in society and over what social policies would be most just.

Conflict and Dialogue over the Church's Action in Society

The idea of the church as a special covenant should help us deal with the problem of conflict within the church. Church conflict has been present from the earliest times, as the New Testament amply testifies. We see instances of it in the division over whether gentile Christians had to be circumcised (cf. Acts 15:1 ff., Gal. 2:11-14), in the disagreement between Paul and Barnabas over "John called Mark" (Acts 15:37-39), in the alienation between the Christian slave Onesimus and his Christian master Philemon (Philem. 8 ff.), in the divisions of the Corinthian church's loyalties among Paul, Apollos, Cephas, and Christ (I Cor. 1:11 ff.), and implicitly in many another passage. Paul's response to the division of loyalties in Corinth probably expresses the most frequent reaction of earnest church people to conflict in their midst: "I appeal to you, brethren, by the name of our Lord Jesus Christ, that all of you agree and that there be no dissensions among you, but that you be united in the same mind and the same judgment" (I Cor. 1:10). But then as now that appeal was probably offered in vain. Conflict among Christians persists in every age and place, as it does in any other group of people.

The Interpretation of Church Conflict

Yet as persistent as church conflict is, many Christians seem to believe not only that harmonious agreement should be the rule, but also that the presence of conflict is a sign that those church members who supposedly brought on the conflict are sinners and do not belong in the church at all. This line of reasoning seriously oversimplifies the problem, though, in that each side of a church conflict is far more ready to ascribe sinful motives to its opponents than to itself, in that it is extremely difficult in most conflicts to say with any degree of assurance who or what brought it on, and in that precipitating conflict is not necessarily wrong. The problem is not simply how to explain a given conflict, but the need for a more adequate interpretation of conflict.

Conflict is present in the church for the same general reasons that it occurs in any other social group—reasons discussed in chapter 3. The first has to do with our created nature: a multiplicity of creatures with independent wills and desires, interacting in the midst of limited alternatives, will necessarily come into conflict. The second reason is our sin, which creates unnecessary conflict and exacerbates those that are unavoidable. In any particular conflict these two characteristics are intertwined. Sin is indeed a contribution to church (and other) conflicts, and yet we need not conclude that the sin lies only on one side of the conflict. It is likely to be expressed by all the parties in some fashion or other.

Because of this mixture of reasons for conflict, it is overhasty and overly simple to approach a church conflict with the implied question, Who sinned that this conflict arose? There can be legitimate and helpful aspects to many church conflicts, like those that occur in other groups. Which man, for example, was at fault, Paul or Barnabas, in the "sharp contention" over John Mark? Quite possibly both were offering defensible judgments on the basis of the limited evidence they had about the young man's dependability under pressure, though it is also possible that one or both were exhibiting some not entirely praiseworthy attitude in the positions they took or the way they advanced them. However that may be, they could not have dealt adequately with the problem had they not advanced their differing opinions. It is important to realize that there are "conflicts of the head"—conflicting opinions about how best to think one's way through a problem—and not only "conflicts of the heart"—conflicting loyalties underlying a conflict of opinion. We more readily solve problems if we consider alternative solutions, and we are more likely to do that if each serious alternative is stated in its best light. Education does not occur unless the learner is aware of conflicting possible answers to a question. Christians, because of their very concern with moral and spiritual questions and their acute awareness of the phenomenon of sin, desirable as these characteristics are, sometimes try to explain too much by the concept of sin. There are conflicts of the head as well as of the heart, and though the two may be inseparable, they are certainly distinguishable, so that it is unwise to try to reduce the one to the other.

In spite of the persistence of conflict throughout the history of the church, Christians have, understandably enough, not found satisfactory ways to cope with it any more than to interpret it. On the one hand, they have tended to condemn conflict and those who seem to have brought it about. On the other hand, they have often recognized that there is no easy way to avoid or eliminate it. Church leaders have, like Paul, pleaded for harmony, and yet when what they consider to be a major issue has been at stake, they have readily and often justifiably destroyed a surface harmony in order to struggle for what they deemed essential. They have spoken highly of the "one holy catholic church" and yet have—justifiably and unjustifiably—been ready to divide it on behalf of deeply held convictions.

Conflict over Social Action

Of the many kinds of church conflicts we might consider, I shall give attention only to one: conflicts over the church's role in society and the social conditions it should seek to promote. Such subjects are especially ready sources of conflict, because they raise questions about which the wider society is already in conflict and bring to the surface differences in social identification and sense of obligation of the various members. Whatever the reason, a sure way to bring on a conflict in almost any church meeting is to inject an opinion about church social action. That is a major reason why church groups often steer as far as possible away from the subject. Yet the church's mission to proclaim God's inclusive covenant in word and deed requires dealing with social issues. The church cannot responsibly avoid the subject. Neither will it do so in fact, even if it tries. As a social institution the church tends to support *some* configuration of social policies. If it does not intentionally and openly seek to affect society, it nevertheless does so unintentionally and unknowingly through such means as its not speaking of the way things are, or the way it spends and invests its money, or the subtle signals its leaders give the members about what it means to serve the neighbor. The church is always proclaiming *some* viewpoint toward society by its words and deeds; if it would have integrity, that viewpoint must express the Christian proclamation entrusted to it.

Even the question whether the church should deal with social concerns is a matter of church conflict. Edward Norman objects to the whole range of the church's involvement in social and political questions. He criticizes what he calls the politicization of the churches, that is, "the internal transformation of the faith itself, so that it comes to be defined in terms of political values—it becomes essentially concerned with social morality rather than with the ethereal qualities of immortality."[18] He is skeptical, he says, about any kind of Christian politics, whether liberal or conservative. His opposition is to any kind of corporate church social witness, though not to political judgments and actions by individual Christians. In his opinion Christianity is "by nature concerned primarily with the relationship of the soul to eternity,"[19] in a way that apparently he believes is separable from the relation of the self to the needs of other people in society. Although not many professional theologians today espouse Norman's position, large numbers of the church's laity do. Many of them are readily upset when church leaders issue statements about social problems or become involved in church social action, though ironically they are less likely to be disturbed when the church's stance expresses their own social and political opinions and their perceived interests than when it does not.

The whole direction of this book makes it obvious why I do not agree with Norman's rejection of the church's involvement in political and social questions. Most church leaders of virtually every stripe today do disagree with him on this question: those of the left, right, or middle; of this continent or that, this racial or ethnic group or that, this denomination or that, this or another theological leaning. Most believe that in some fashion the church should make a corporate witness concerning society—that it should seek to influence the way society behaves and should do so at times through church structures of some kind and not only through its individual members' actions in secular institutions. People of such divergent viewpoints as Jerry Falwell of the Moral Majority, Latin American liberation theologians, and the bishops of The United Methodist Church agree on this general idea about the church's social role. But this agreement only transfers the conflict to another level, because those who agree on this very general idea disagree deeply up and down the line about how the church should go about seeking to affect society and about the social policies it should espouse.

This is not the place to try to grapple with those issues; they call for far more space than I can take here. Church people must, of course, continually struggle with them, seeking to discern what social posture they should take and what policies they should support if they would declare God's inclusive covenant in ways appropriate to their time and place. Our question here is less complex: If we understand the church to be that special covenant entrusted with the responsibility of declaring in word and deed God's inclusive covenant made known in Jesus Christ, how can this covenantal understanding help us see how to approach internal church conflict over the church's action in the wider society?

One implication of this covenantal approach, as we have seen, is that the church has a strong and continuing obligation to be concerned with and to engage in various aspects of social action, of which I wish to mention two in particular. The church is obligated, on the one hand, to *social service*, that is, to seek to help individuals who are in serious need within the existing structures of society. It is, on the other hand, also obligated to *social change*, in the sense of efforts to modify existing social structures in the direction of greater justice for all. In both these aspects of social action, the church will sometimes find it best to act upon society through its own structures (contra Norman), and at other times through voluntary groups of Christians or through individual Christians working through other social institutions. Whatever the form Christian social action takes, it is obligatory upon the church, as part of its calling, to declare God's action in Jesus Christ in deed as well as in word. It is obligatory because the covenant love that the church proclaims is a love that understands persons as essentially social, recognizes the moral claims of everyone and not only of fellow Christians, and seeks to meet people's needs. What I shall say below would make little sense except within the framework of this first implication.

A second implication, and the one to which I shall give more extended attention here, is that in its engagement in social action the church has a strong and continuing obligation to engage in dialogue concerning that action. It has an obligation to dialogue with those outside the church, to be sure, but I wish to give special attention here to the obligation of church members to dialogue with one another concerning social action.

Dialogue and Church Social Action

By dialogue I mean a process of communication between two or more people in which they openly examine matters over which they differ as well as matters that they hold in common. Reuel Howe describes dialogue as a process "in which the being and truth of each is confronted by the being and truth of the other," and "in which there is a flow of meaning between [the participants] in spite of all the obstacles that normally would block the relationship."[20] He contrasts it with monologue, communication in which one tells others "what they ought to know," and in which "the speaker is so preoccupied with himself that he loses touch with those to whom he is speaking."[21] In dialogue, on the other hand, each participant is to some extent revealed to the other, and each is to some degree open to the possibility of change. It is important not to confuse dialogue with any particular method of communication, such as group discussion. A skillful leader can manipulate discussion so as to avoid genuine dialogue, while a lecture can be dialogical in the way the speaker takes account of the viewpoints of the listeners and elicits a free and active response on their part.

Howe identifies several goals for which dialogue is essential[22] and which, we might observe, are important in the church's social action. First, dialogue enables education to occur. Without dialogue, indoctrination or a mere reporting of what the student is expected to say might take place, but education in the sense of an enhancement of one's inner capacity to respond to one's environment will not. Second, dialogue helps people make responsible decisions, enabling them to work their way through a moral question to an answer for which they are prepared to take responsibility, regardless of which side of the issue the answer supports. Third, dialogue makes possible the revitalization of routine forms of organizational life, in that through it the members can come to renewed commitment and involvement in the life and work of the community. These contributions show that dialogue is essential in some degree to the life of any special covenant—family, political community, occupational group, church, or whatever—that would endure over time and fulfill its special obligations, both to its own members and to those beyond its membership.

Dialogue can contribute to these goals even though it is intermixed with coercive kinds of power—even though, for example, those who dialogue in one moment take a vote in the next, with the majority voting down the minority, and with coercive sanctions present that require the acceptance of a majority vote. Some forms of coercive power—voting, acts of punishment, and perhaps even recourse to arms—can constitute a further communication in an ongoing dialogue when conducted against the background of serious earlier deliberation. Although coercion can be of the sort that undercuts dialogue, the two are not necessarily exclusive. Dialogue is never wholly removed from the exercise of coercive power, even when the latter retreats far into the background.

Positive though our response to the term *dialogue* may be, dialogue as an actual process elicits mixed feelings. It necessarily involves both conflict and commonality, and as with all conflict it is not unambiguously enjoyable. Dialogue always presupposes some degree of commonality, of shared commitment and outlook, without which it would be impossible. At the same time dialogue always involves some element of conflict of beliefs and commitments, without which we would have no incentive or need to enter into dialogue. The presence of conflict in dialogue is suggested by the terms *confront, change,* and *decision,* which were used above to characterize it. The confrontation may be shaking, the change radical, the decision wrenching. Yet to the extent that dialogue rather than monologue is occurring, the common outlook and commitment constitute the more basic element in the relationship, a framework within which the participants carry on the conflict and which limits and directs the way they do so. In contrast, when the conflict becomes more fundamental than what is in common, the community is on its way to disintegration, and we can expect dialogue to be replaced by less affirming and more destructive kinds of interaction. Similarly, to the extent that dialogue diminshes in the life of the community, we can expect the shared views and commitments to become more external and less vital, and the community to become more vulnerable to external and internal threats to its unity. Dialogue is essential to the well-being of the church, including its engagement in social action, just as it is to the well-being of a marriage, a friendship, an educational institution, or a legislative body.

Even while giving lip service to the good of dialogue, some members of a community may view it as at least an inconvenience and at worst a serious threat to the attainment of their goals. Thus it happens that through the exercise of coercive power, manipulation, or simply abdication to "the way things are done," groups can seriously reduce the opportunities for significant dialogue. In the case of church social action, church leaders dialogue continually over it. The problem is that the dialogue tends to take place among those who most nearly agree, rather than among those whose Christian consciences sharply conflict. This happens at the level of the local congregation both because most congregations tend to be relatively homogeneous ("our kind of people") in their makeup and because where serious differences are present in the same congregation over the church's action in society, the members are ordinarily reluctant to discuss them with one another. When conflict over social issues comes to the surface, the outcome is often either that the dominant group subtly encourages those who hold a minority viewpoint to keep quiet or to go elsewhere, or that there is a full-blown congregational split. It is an unusual congregation that brings conflict to the surface and handles it as constructively as did the one to which Robert Lee and Russell Galloway assign the pseudonym "Christ Church" in their study of local church conflict over community organization, and few pastors show the sensitive and skilled leadership of their "Rev. Robert Sharp" in the management of congregational conflict.[23] Yet there is no reason why church leaders cannot learn and practice these skills effectively, enabling the congregation to carry on dialogue and not to have to choose between avoidance and division.[24]

Church bodies often reflect the same tendency to repress dialogue at levels beyond the local congregation, as, for example, in denominational boards and agencies and in the church's seminaries. There are, of course, significant exceptions—board staffs and faculties that over time have built into their procedures the practice of bringing serious issues out into the open and examining sharply differering opinions about them, and that in making new appointments give a high priority to competent persons who will bring perspectives that challenge already dominant ways of thinking. But this attitude toward conflict and dialogue seems to be in the minority. More often a faculty or staff will prefer new members who, for the most part, fit in with existing perspectives. Often a staff or faculty seems more interested in telling the church's grassroots laity and clergy what they should think—about a social issue or some other subject—than in seriously inquiring into their own views and examining divergent opinions. Some years ago the social action board staff of a major denomination arranged some meetings with the professors of ethics and social action from the denomination's seminaries. The agenda and attitudes of those who attended seemed to reflect that the primary interest from each side was to "be of service" to the other—a euphemism for "How can *we* help *you* see the way you should think?" Little opportunity occurred for serious deliberation about the several widely different perspectives represented. The absence of encouragement to dialogue may have been one reason why the meetings did not continue.

Interdenominational agencies have been criticized for similar tendencies. They sometimes seek to give an appearance of unanimity on major social issues that is contrary to reality. They can do this by selecting leaders who hold opinions within the desired range, or by frowning on those who attend but express opposing viewpoints, or simply by giving the opposition little or no attention. Some have accused the World Council of Churches of this problem in its conferences on social issues. Dr. Kenneth Slack of the British Council of Churches, commenting on the fifth World Council of Churches Assembly in Nairobi, Kenya, writes, "For all the vaunting of the method of dialogue as a way towards truth and understanding there is too little evidence of provision of contrasting viewpoints."[25] In stronger language Richard John Neuhaus cites the charge that "the WCC has effectively excluded from dialogue those who dissent from its establish-ment line,"[26] and maintains that the WCC is structurally disposed to encourage conformity to a particular line of social policy. Undoubtedly there is considerable dialogue over social issues within the deliberations of the World Council. The question is whether the dialogue is sufficiently open to viewpoints that are unpopular among the participants. And certainly the phenomenon can be observed among other ecumenical bodies, to the extreme that some ultraconservative groups carry on a crusade against the views of other ecumenical bodies.

It is not surprising that many church leaders and members at all levels seek to avoid threatening dialogue, even while praising it, and that they try to give others the impression that the church is of one mind on controversial issues. Many other kinds of social groups reflect the same tendency. Indeed, to the extent that a voluntary social group attempts to pressure governmental bodies toward the policies it desires, it is a standard tactic to give the appearance of unanimity, though the tactic is so widely recognized by governmental leaders that its impact is largely lost. But the question is not how groups ordinarily operate, but what is an appropriate means to the church's mission in society. Insufficient dialogue and the false appearance of agreement do not assist that mission, nor do they adequately express the members' common loyalty to Jesus Christ as Lord. They can be church-political ploys to establish or maintain dominance for particular social propos-als, whether of the right or left or center. At some point any group, the church included, must come to a decision by voting or some other proper procedure, even while differences of opinion remain. Unforced consensus is not an option for any but small groups. But decision needs to be reached on the further side of dialogue. Without dialogue our hunches, our prejudices, our deeply held though poorly examined convic-tions will not be tested to see wherein they conform to God's action in Jesus Christ rather than merely to our social groups' self-interest. Without dialogue church leaders have no chance of educating their members (and vice versa) concerning controversial social problems. Without dialogue those who are outspoken on some social issue, regardless of the position they take, will tend to cut themselves off from support by their ecclesiastical constituencies. The deeper our commitment to effective church social action, the greater the need for dialogue over the issues at whatever level of the church is involved.

Church leaders can adopt practices to encourage dialogue within the church on social action as a prelude to decision and action. In the first place they can seek to structure into their personnel and their established procedures ways to ensure that dissent can be present, that significantly varying points of view can be heard. Paul Ramsey has suggested that those who attend meetings that will speak about church and society should "take along with us in our minds a 'counterpart'—a fellow Christian we know who disagrees with us on specific economic, social, and political conclusions, whose particular 'scruples' are different from ours, but who (we cannot deny) thinks about his life and his responsibilities upon the same basis that we do."[27] That would indeed serve to moderate the presumption of church leaders that their own moral convictions are adequate without input from those who conscientiously differ with them. A more effective step, though, would be to take such people along in the flesh, and not merely in our minds—to make sure that such different scruples, arrived at on a similar basis to ours, are advanced by those who genuinely hold them. Christians have good reason to recognize the need for competing points of view—that though only one (if either) of two differing sides can be right, both can express intellectual pride. In the church, as in civil society, we need competing points of view to restrain our tendency to claim to know more than we really do.

A second way to encourage serious church dialogue is for more Christian groups to adopt the practice of coopting the services of able theological specialists in church deliberations. Roman Catholic bishops have their *periti*, their theological advisers who not only serve them in their ordinary work but who go with them to church councils—to Vatican II and Medellín and Puebla—and assist them in dealing with the complex issues that call for specialized knowledge. Protestant bishops and moderators and presidents might well emulate this arrangement, and indeed some do. It is valuable that church conferences often include theological specialists as members. It would also be valuable if in a Protestant Council of Bishops, or near-equivalents in nonepiscopal polities, there were Protestant *periti*. The accredited representatives would forgo none of their responsibilities, but the level of debate would rise markedly, and the resulting church pronouncements would have a much greater chance of recognizing the qualifications that need to be placed on overly simply moral assertions.

A third method to bring about, as well as to express the results of, serious church dialogue is for the resulting statements to embody what Richard John Neuhaus has recommended as "a pluralistic style."[28] There will be occasions when advocacy of a single position by church leaders to the churches is what is appropriate. More frequently, however, an issue will be such that the most helpful word to the churches will be to present, each with it own best reasons, several possible alternative positions that could be taken on the same issue from a reflective Christian point of view. Neuhaus argues that this style of pronouncement would prevent a process whereby those in the minority eventually drop out of the deliberations. It would also remind the churches that more sides than one are worth hearing and that when one takes a position in church social action, it should be done in awareness of the plausible alternatives. But this method will not work well without still another step.

Last, we can encourage significant dialogue in the church on social issues if we aim at church pronouncements in which the reasons for the social ethical judgments are explained. Many church pronouncements seem to be summaries of conclusions only: for example, many of the decisions of world conferences on church and society or of other ecumenical conferences, and much of the present Social Principles statement of The United Methodist Church. When pronouncements proceed in that way, they use what we might call "the submarine tactic."[29] They state theological premises and social ethical conclusions, but "go underwater" between the two, leaving out the connecting argumentation that would show how they got from one to the other and what other, unidentified assumptions contributed to the conclusions. Anyone who works from similar theological premises but comes to different social ethical conclusions would understandably be puzzled as to why the theological submarine came up where it did. There may indeed have been justifiable reasons for the conclusion, but the point is that in many pronouncements these reasons are not offered. The submarine tactic undermines dialogue in the church. It establishes no basis for rational discussion, either in agreement or in disagreement. If this tactic is intended to influence the judgment of church members, it is likely to be a failure, serving only to rally the already convinced. A better objective would be to educate the members to the process of moral reflection about the issues, rather than to seek to indoctrinate them to the "right" conclusions. Church pronouncements do not have to use the submarine tactic, and some major ones avoid it, such as Vatican II's *Pastoral Constitution on the Church in the Modern World* and the recent Pastoral Letter of the United States Bishops on war and peace. Better objectives would be to seek to sensitize, deepen, and refine the conscience of the reader, whether inside or outside the church, to move readers beyond the simplistic moral judgments ordinarily fostered in our culture, and to identify the crucial points over which sensitive moral consciences diverge, so as to promote better dialogue at those points. Church statements of that kind would take the public, both inside and outside the churches, far more seriously than those which announce conclusions only. It would be harder work; it would make for longer statements; but it would express far better the nature of the church, and it would minister better to its objectives for speaking at all.

It is strange that many church bodies deliberate less fully and air their differences less freely than the ordinary legislature or parliament in a Western democracy. Perhaps it is because church bodies do not have to rule over a body politic, perhaps because they therefore have greater liberty to speak without regard to the full implications of what they are saying. Whatever the reason, the practice misrepresents the nature of the church. If the church is truly to serve God in the world that is actually before us, its members must be prepared to dialogue with one another and with that world about the form of its service. So to dialogue is one much-needed way to embody the belief that the church is a covenantal body in which the members are responsible under God to and for one another, as well as to and for the world.

Our examination of special covenants could go on indefinitely, both to probe further into the three types discussed here, and to add others, some of which have to do with crucial aspects of our lives. Much attention needs to be given, for example, to the special covenants of economic life, the effects of which shape so heavily our common life in marriage, political community, and the church. Educational relationships, to cite another type, likewise involve a continual entrusting and accepting entrustment in special covenants, and we all participate in them, formally or informally, throughout our lives. We can also rightly speak of special covenants in the various professions,[30] in the realm of the arts, in our treatment of the nonhuman environment, and in other dimensions of sexuality and family life besides marriage, to name only a few of the more obvious possibilities. I have neither space, time, nor sufficient expertise to carry on all these inquiries here. Instead those who are reflecting seriously on these aspects of life are invited to consider them as special covenants under the umbrella of God's covenant love. When people reflect on these relationships, they are invited to ask, first, what it might entail to interpret them covenantally rather than as mere contractual relationships of essentially separate beings, or as simply the way parts fit in a whole; and second, what it would involve to seek to pattern our lives in these relationships after the covenant love of the God revealed in Jesus Christ.

Notes

1. A Covenantal Model of the Moral Life

1. H. Richard Niebuhr, *The Responsible Self* (New York: Harper & Row, 1963), p. 63.
2. Augustine of Hippo, *Confessions*, Book I.
3. Walther Eichrodt, *Theology of the Old Testament*, trans. J. A. Baker (Philadelphia: The Westminster Press, 1961), vol. 1.
4. Concerning these covenants see especially Ronald Clements, *Abraham and David: Genesis 15 and Its Meaning for Israelite Tradition* (Naperville, Ill.: Allenson, 1967); and Gerhard von Rad, *Genesis, a Commentary*, trans. John H. Marks, rev. ed. (Philadelphia: The Westminster Press, 1972), pp. 182ff.
5. Concerning covenant and the Ten Commandments see especially Brevard S. Childs, *The Book of Exodus: A Critical Theological Commentary* (Philadelphia: The Westminster Press, 1974), pp. 337-439; Gerhard von Rad, *Old Testament Theology*, trans. D. M. G. Stalker, 2 vols. (New York: Harper & Row, 1962–1965) 1:187-279; Johann Jakob Stamm and Maurice Edward Andrew, *The Ten Commandments in Recent Research* (London: SCM Press, 1970); Delbert R. Hillers, *Covenant: The History of a Biblical Idea* (Baltimore: Johns Hopkins University Press, 1969), pp. 46-71; and *Interpreter's Dictionary of the Bible*, "Covenant," by George E. Mendenhall, 1:714-23.
6. On the covenant form cf. esp. Mendenhall, "Covenant."
7. von Rad, *Old Testament Theology*, 1:193.
8. Ibid., p. 194.
9. Hillers, *Covenant*, pp. 130-31.
10. Cf. Ibid., pp. 120-22.
11. Cf. Rudolf Bultmann, "Prophecy and Fulfillment," trans. James C. G. Greig, *Essays on Old Testament Hermeneutics*, Claus

Westerman, ed., English trans. ed. by James Luther Mays (Richmond, Va.: John Knox Press, 1963), pp. 50-55.

12. The translation here is a literal one taken from Alfred Plummer, *A Critical and Exegetical Commentary on the Second Epistle of St. Paul to the Corinthians* (New York: Scribner's, 1915), pp. 85, 87.

13. Cf. the interpretation of C. K. Barrett, *A Commentary on the Second Epistle to the Corinthians* (New York: Harper & Row, 1973), p. 112.

14. See W. C. van Unnik, "*Hē kainē diathēkē*—a Problem in the Early History of the Canon," *Studia Patristica* 4 (1961):222-26.

15. Erik H. Erikson, *Childhood and Society*, 2d ed. (New York: W. W. Norton, 1963), pp. 247-51.

16. D. J. McCarthy, *Old Testament Covenant: A Survey of Current Opinions* (Richmond, Va.: John Knox Press, 1972), pp. 41-42.

17. Donald D. Evans, *The Logic of Self-Involvement* (New York: Herder & Herder, 1969), p. 75.

18. W. D. Ross, *The Right and the Good* (Oxford: Clarendon Press, 1930), p. 21.

19. William F. May, *The Physician's Covenant: Images of the Healer in Medical Ethics* (Philadelphia: The Westminster Press, 1983), p. 110.

20. For a discussion reflecting a similar idea about this point, see Karl Barth's discussion of the relation of creation and covenant in *Church Dogmatics,* III/1, ed. and trans. G. W. Bromiley and others (Edinburgh: T. & T. Clark, 1958), 42-329.

21. *Newsweek,* 4 June 1979, p. 49.

2. The Standard of Covenant Love

1. Cf. William K. Frankena's discussion of utilitarianism, *Ethics*, 2d ed. (Englewood Cliffs, N.J.: Prentice-Hall, 1973), pp. 34 ff.

2. Immanuel Kant, *Foundations of the Metaphysics of Morals*, 429 (Beck translation).

3. Frederick S. Carney, "Deciding in the Situation: What Is Required?" in *Norm and Context in Christian Ethics*, ed. Gene H. Outka and Paul Ramsey (New York: Scribner's, 1968), p. 11.

4. Gene H. Outka, "Character, Conduct, and the Love Commandment," in *Norm and Context in Christian Ethics*, ed. Outka and Ramsey, p. 40.

5. Cf. Frankena, pp. 65-67.

6. James Gustafson, *Can Ethics Be Christian?* (Chicago and London: University of Chicago Press, 1975), p. 174.

7. Stanley Hauerwas, *Character and the Christian Life: A Study in Theological Ethics* (San Antonio: Trinity University Press, 1975), pp. 227-28.

8. See especially his *Responsible Self* (New York: Harper & Row,

1963); "The Responsibility of the Church for Society," in *The Gospel, the Church and the World*, ed. Kenneth Scott Latourette (New York: Harper & Brothers, 1946), pp. 111-33; and *Radical Monotheism and Western Culture* (New York: Harper & Brothers, 1960).

9. *The Responsible Self*, p. 126.
10. Ibid., pp. 64-65.
11. *The Purpose of the Church and Its Ministry* (New York: Harper & Brothers, 1956), pp. 35-36.
12. *Radical Monotheism*, p. 47.
13. "The Responsibility of the Church for Society," p. 119.
14. Ibid., p. 120.
15. Ibid., p. 132.
16. This is intentionally the philosophical procedure adopted by William K. Frankena in *Ethics*, pp. 28-30.
17. Karl Barth, *Church Dogmatics*, 4 vols., ed. and trans. G. W. Bromiley and others (Edinburgh: T. & T. Clark, 1936–75); II/2 (1957):563.
18. Ibid., p. 566.
19. "A Treatise on Christian Liberty," trans. W. A. Lambert, in *Three Treatises* (Philadelphia: Muhlenberg Press, 1943), p. 279.
20. *Commentary on a Harmony of the Evangelists, Matthew, Mark, and Luke*, trans. William Pringle (Grand Rapids: Wm. B. Eerdmans Publishing Co., n.d.), 1:308 (his italics).
21. *Basic Christian Ethics* (New York: Scribner's, 1950), p. 21.
22. For illuminating discussions of the social nature of the self see Karl Barth, *Church Dogmatics*, III/2 (1960):222ff.; and H. Richard Niebuhr, *The Responsible Self*, pp. 69ff.
23. *Ethics*, pp. 9-11, 61-62, 79-94.
24. Anders Nygren, *Agape and Eros*, trans. Philip S. Watson (London: S.P.C.K., 1953), p. 77.
25. Gregory Vlastos, "Justice and Equality," *Social Justice*, ed. Richard B. Brandt (Englewood Cliffs, N.J.: Prentice-Hall, 1962), pp. 43ff.
26. Nygren, *Agape and Eros*, pp. 77-78, 210.
27. Kant, *Foundations of the Metaphysics of Morals*, 429.
28. Thomas Aquinas, *Summa Theologica*, I, Q. 93, art. 4 (italics added).
29. Reinhold Niebuhr, *The Nature and Destiny of Man*, 2 vols. (New York: Scribner's, 1941, 1943), I (1941):151-66.
30. Karl Barth, *Church Dogmatics*, III/1 (1958):42, 94.
31. Walther Eichrodt, *Theology of the Old Testament*, trans. J. A. Baker (Philadelphia: The Westminster Press, 1961), 1:38 (his italics).
32. H. Richard Niebuhr, *Radical Monotheism*, p. 16.
33. H. Richard Niebuhr, "Reflections on Faith, Hope and Love," *The Journal of Religious Ethics* 2 (Spring 1974):153.
34. Stephen Toulmin, *An Examination of the Place of Reason in Ethics*

(Cambridge: Cambridge University Press, 1960), p. 219 (his italics).
35. Geoffrey Russell Grice, *The Grounds of Moral Judgement* (Cambridge: Cambridge University Press, 1967), p. 155.
36. J. O. Urmson, "Saints and Heroes," *Essays in Moral Philosophy,* ed. A. I. Melden (Seattle: University of Washington Press, 1958), p. 202.

3. The Conflict of Moral Claims

1. Gregory Vlastos, "Justice and Equality," in Richard B. Brandt, ed., *Social Justice* (Englewood Cliffs, N.J.: Prentice-Hall, 1962), p. 38, n. 23.
2. "The General Rules of The Methodist Church," *The Book of Discipline of The United Methodist Church,* 1980 (Nashville: United Methodist Publishing House, 1980), p. 69 (italics added).
3. Joel Feinberg, *Social Philosophy* (Englewood Cliffs, N.J.: Prentice-Hall, 1973), pp. 26-27.
4. Ibid., p. 26.
5. Lewis Coser, *The Functions of Social Conflict* (New York: The Free Press of Macmillan, 1956), p. 8.
6. W. D. Ross, *The Right and the Good* (Oxford: Clarendon Press, 1930), pp. 19ff.
7. Quoted in Eduard Heimann, *History of Economic Doctrines* (New York: Oxford University Press, 1949), pp. 64-65.
8. See especially Niebuhr's *Moral Man and Immoral Society* (New York: Scribner's, 1932), but also numerous others of his works.
9. Cf., for example, *The Nature and Destiny of Man* (New York: Scribner's, 1951), 2:256ff., and *Moral Man and Immoral Society,* pp. xvff.
10. Cf. especially *Moral Man and Immoral Society,* p. 5 passim, and *Nature and Destiny,* 2:249 passim.
11. Cf. *Moral Man and Immoral Society,* p. xvi; *Christianity and Power Politics* (n.p.: Archon Books, 1969 [reprinted from the 1940 edition]), p. 15; *Nature and Destiny,* 2:265.
12. *Nature and Destiny,* 2:81-82; see also p. 265 and *Moral Man and Immoral Society,* p. 23.
13. Cf. *Nature and Destiny,* 2:88, 256ff., 265ff.
14. Ibid., 1:288-89.
15. Ibid., 2:68-72.
16. Ibid., 2:88.
17. Ibid., 2:262.
18. Coser, *The Functions of Social Conflict,* p. 31.
19. Ibid., pp. 38, 47-48, 125.
20. Ibid., pp. 151-52.

21. Ibid., p. 157.
22. Judith Plaskow, *Sex, Sin and Grace* (Washington, D.C.: University Press of America, 1980), pp. 86 ff.
23. Reinhold Niebuhr, *An Interpretation of Christian Ethics* (New York: Harper & Brothers, 1935), p. 9.

4. Moral Conflicts I: Self and Others

1. Cf. for example Calvin, *Institutes of the Christian Religion*, III, vii; Reinhold Niebuhr, *The Nature and Destiny of Man*, 2 vols. (New York: Scribner's, 1941, 1943), 2 (1943), chap. 3; and Paul Ramsey, *Basic Christian Ethics* (New York: Scribner's, 1951), pp. 92-103, pp. 147-52.
2. Among the psychotherapeutic theorists who have either been directly critical of theological rejections of self-love or who have presented an alternative and more positive assessment of it are the following: Erich Fromm, *Man for Himself* (New York: Rinehart & Co., 1947), pp. 119-41; Erich Fromm, *The Art of Loving* (New York: Harper & Brothers, 1956), pp. 57-63; Rollo May, *Man's Search for Himself* (New York: W. W. Norton & Co., 1953), pp. 238-46; and Carl R. Rogers, *On Becoming a Person: A Therapist's View of Psychotherapy* (Boston: Houghton Mifflin Co., 1961), pp. 87-90. Theologians who have sought to restate psychotherapists' insights about self-love for theological purposes include Paul Tillich, *Love, Power, and Justice* (New York: Oxford University Press, 1954), pp. 33-34; and Albert C. Outler, *Psychotherapy and the Christian Message* (New York: Harper & Brothers, 1954), pp. 225-33. Cf. Barbara Hilkert Andolsen, "Agape in Feminist Ethics," *Journal of Religious Ethics* 9 (Spring 1981):69-83, for a discussion of feminist concerns related to the ideas of self-love and love for others.
3. Fromm, *The Art of Loving*, p. 60 (his italics).
4. Ibid., pp. 60-61 (his italics).
5. Cf. Rudolf Bultmann, *Jesus and the Word*, trans. Louise Pettibone Smith and Erminie Huntress Lantero (New York: Scribner's, 1958), p. 116; Paul Tillich, *Love, Power, and Justice*, p. 34; Gene Outka, *Agape: An Ethical Analysis* (New Haven: Yale University Press, 1972), pp. 63 ff.
6. Ramsey, pp. 99-100.
7. Ramsey, "The Biblical Norm of Righteousness," *Interpretation* 24 (October 1970), 422, 427.
8. Søren Kierkegaard, *Works of Love*, trans. Howard and Edna Hong (New York: Harper & Row, 1962), p. 39 (his italics).
9. Fromm, *The Art of Loving*, p. 59 (his italics).
10. Ibid., p. 58.

11. Ramsey, p. 94.
12. *The Patient as Person* (New Haven: Yale University Press, 1970), p. xiii.
13. Niebuhr, 2:82.
14. Cf. John Stuart Mill, *Utilitarianism*, chap. 2, par. 18.
15. W. G. Maclagan, "Self and Others: A Defense of Altruism," *The Philosophical Quarterly* 4 (April 1954):113-14; cf. Outka, pp. 302-5.
16. Cf. Outka, p. 300.
17. Niebuhr, 2:68 ff.
18. J. O. Urmson, "Saints and Heroes," *Essays in Moral Philosophy*, ed. A. I. Melden (Seattle: University of Washington Press, 1958), p. 202. See above, chap. 2, p. 79.
19. Niebuhr, 2:88.
20. Luther, "A Treatise on Christian Liberty," *Works of Martin Luther* (Philadelphia: Muhlenberg Press, 1943), 2:337-38.
21. Thomas Aquinas, *Summa Theologica*, I-II, Q. 108, arts. 2, 4.
22. Ibid., art. 4.
23. Calvin, *Institutes*, II, viii, 56 (Library of Christian Classics ed.).
24. Luther, "Treatise on Good Works," *Works of Martin Luther*, 1:187.
25. Ibid., 1:190.
26. Valerie Saiving, "The Human Situation: A Feminine View," in Carol P. Christ and Judith Plaskow, eds., *Womanspirit Rising* (New York: Harper & Row, 1979), p. 37.
27. Barbara Hilkert Andolsen, "Agape in Feminist Ethics," p. 74.
28. Outka, p. 277.
29. Ramsey, *Basic Christian Ethics*, pp. 155 ff.
30. Paul Ramsey, *Nine Modern Moralists* (Englewood Cliffs, N.J.: Prentice-Hall, 1962), p. 136.
31. Cf. Maclagan, pp. 118-19; Outka, pp. 68-69.
32. Cf. Maclagan, pp. 116-18.
33. Outka, pp. 305-6.

5. Moral Conflicts II: Conflicting Obligations to Different Covenants

1. Cf. Joel Feinberg, *Social Philosophy* (Englewood Cliffs, N.J.: Prentice-Hall, 1973), pp. 85 ff.
2. John Calvin, *Institutes of the Christian Religion*, III, x, 6 (Library of Christian Classics ed.).
3. G. Russell Grice, *The Grounds of Moral Judgement* (Cambridge: Cambridge University Press, 1967), pp. 47 ff.
4. John Rawls, *A Theory of Justice* (Cambridge: Harvard University Press, 1971), pp. 111 ff., 344 ff.
5. James Childress makes this point in his discussion of civil disobedience; see his *Civil Disobedience and Political Obligation* (New Haven: Yale University Press, 1971), p. 109.

6. See, e.g., Leo XIII's *Rerum Novarum* (15 May 1891), where the principle of subsidiarity may be implicit; Pius XI's *Quadragesimo Anno* (15 May 1931), esp. par. 79; John XXIII's *Pacem in Terris* (11 April 1963), pars. 140, 141; Arthur Utz, "The Principle of Subsidiarity and Contemporary Natural Law," *Natural Law Forum* 3 (1958):170-83; and William Bertrams, S.J., "Subsidiarity in the Church," *Catholic Mind* 59 (August 1961):358-63.

7. Bernard Häring, C.SS.R., *The Law of Christ*, trans. Edwin G. Kaiser, C.PP.S. (Westminster, Md.: Newman Press, 1966), III, 87.

8. *Quadragesimo Anno*, par. 79.

9. Cf. Childress, *Civil Disobedience and Political Obligation*, pp. 109, 123, 131.

10. See T. Dunbar Moodie, *The Rise of Afrikanerdom: Power, Apartheid, and the Afrikaner Civil Religion* (Berkeley: University of California Press, 1975), pp. 6, 20-21, 178-81.

11. *Dallas Times Herald*, 10 June 1982.

6. Moral Conflicts III: Justice for Whom?

1. For discussions of Ulpian's formula see Giorgio del Vecchio, *Justice: An Historical and Philosophical Essay*, trans. Lady Guthrie (Edinburgh: The University Press, 1952), pp. 55, 72-73; Thomas Aquinas, *Summa Theologica*, II-II, Q. 58, art. 1; and Emil Brunner, *Justice and the Social Order*, trans. Mary Hottinger (New York: Harper & Brothers, 1945), p. 17.

2. This correlation of justice and rights appears in such contrasting philosophical works as John Stuart Mill's *Utilitarianism* (chap. 5, par. 15); and John Rawls, *A Theory of Justice* (Cambridge: Belknap Press of Harvard University Press, 1971), p. 5.

3. *Nicomachean Ethics*, V, chaps. 1–2.

4. Ibid., V, 2–4.

5. For a discussion of formal justice see especially Joel Feinberg, *Social Philosophy* (Englewood Cliffs, N.J.: Prentice-Hall, 1973), pp. 99-100; and Ch. Perelman, *The Idea of Justice and the Problem of Argument*, trans. John Petrie (London: Routledge & Kegan Paul, 1963), pp. 15-16 passim.

6. R. M. Hare's "universal prescriptivism" proposes using only this test for what is right (including, presumably, what is just); see his *Freedom and Reason* (Oxford: Clarendon Press, 1963).

7. Feinberg, p. 98.

8. Ibid.

9. Ibid., p. 59.

10. H. L. A. Hart, "Are There Any Natural Rights?" *Philosophical Review* 64 (April 1955):175; see my interpretation of Hart's position on this subject in "A Theological Approach to Moral

Rights," *Journal of Religious Ethics* 2 (1974):124-25, 130. Contrast Rawls, p. 511, and Ronald Dworkin, *Taking Rights Seriously* (Cambridge: Harvard University Press, 1977), pp. xii, 180-83, 272-78, both of whose philosophical theories of moral rights give an important place to respect for each person.

11. Cf. Dworkin, ibid.; and H. L. A. Hart, "Between Utility and Rights," in *The Idea of Freedom*, ed. Alan Ryan (New York: Oxford University Press, 1979), pp. 91 ff.

12. See articles 23–26. A critique of this concept is offered by Maurice Cranston, "Human Rights, Real and Supposed," *Political Theory and the Rights of Man*, ed. D. D. Raphael (Bloomington, Ind.: Indiana University Press, 1967), pp. 43-53.

13. Cf. Rawls's discussion of slavery in "Justice as Fairness," *Philosophical Review* 67 (April 1958):187-90.

14. William K. Frankena, *Ethics*, 2d ed. (Englewood Cliffs, N.J.: Prentice-Hall, 1973), p. 58.

15. Reinhold Niebuhr, *The Nature and Destiny of Man* (New York: Scribner's, 1951), 2:68-72, 88, 246.

16. Joseph Fletcher, *Situation Ethics: The New Morality* (Philadelphia: The Westminster Press, 1966), p. 87; cf. 93, 99.

17. Ibid., p. 95.

18. James Childress, *Civil Disobedience and Political Obligation* (New Haven: Yale University Press, 1971), p. 128.

19. Gregory Vlastos, "Justice and Equality," in *Social Justice*, ed. Richard B. Brandt (Englewood Cliffs, N.J.: Prentice-Hall, 1962), pp. 43 ff.

20. The following are a few statements of liberation theology that together reflect something of its diversity as well as some of its common themes: Carol P. Christ and Judith Plaskow, eds., *Womanspirit Rising: A Feminist Reader in Religion* (New York: Harper & Row, 1979); James H. Cone, *God of the Oppressed* (New York: The Seabury Press, 1975); Mary Daly, *Beyond God the Father: Toward a Philosophy of Women's Liberation* (Boston: Beacon Press, 1973); Gustavo Gutiérrez, *A Theology of Liberation*, trans. and ed. by Sister Caridad Inda and John Eagleson (Maryknoll, N.Y.: Orbis Books, 1973); José Míguez Bonino, *Doing Theology in a Revolutionary Situation* (Philadelphia: Fortress Press, 1975); Schubert M. Ogden, *Faith and Freedom: Toward a Theology of Liberation* (Nashville: Abigdon Press, 1979); J. Deotis Roberts, *A Black Political Theology* (Philadelphia: The Westminster Press, 1974); Letty M. Russell, *Human Liberation in a Feminist Perspective—A Theology* (Philadelphia: The Westminster Press, 1974); Juan Luis Segundo, *The Liberation of Theology*, trans. by John Drury (Maryknoll, N.Y.: Orbis Books, 1976); and Gayraud S. Wilmore and James H. Cone, eds., *Black Theology: A*

Documentary History, 1966–1979 (Maryknoll, N.Y.: Orbis Books, 1979).

21. For a helpful discussion of models of society see William W. Everett and T. J. Bachmeyer, *Disciplines in Transformation* (Washington, D.C.: University Press of America, 1979), pp. 87-108.

22. On crosscutting, or overlapping, cleavages see Robert A. Dahl, *Pluralist Democracy in the United States: Conflict and Consent* (Chicago: Rand McNally, 1967), pp. 288, 338-70; and Seymour Martin Lipset, *Political Man: The Social Bases of Politics* (Garden City, N.Y.: Anchor Books, 1963), pp. 77-80.

23. Russell, pp. 167-68.

24. Theodore R. Weber, "Guilt: Yours, Ours, and Theirs," *Worldview* 18 (February 1975):15-22.

7. Moral Conflicts IV: Wrongdoers and the Wronged

1. Paul Ramsey, *The Just War* (New York: Scribner's, 1968), p. 143 (his italics).

2. Robert McAfee Brown, *Religion and Violence* (Philadelphia: The Westminster Press, 1973), p. 7.

3. I am indebted to John Stoesz for assisting me in personal discussions in my thinking about this subject.

4. Cf. Feinberg, *Social Philosophy* (Englewood Cliffs, N.J.: Prentice-Hall, 1973), pp. 20 ff.

5. For discussion of Christian just-war theory see especially Roland Bainton, *Christian Attitudes Toward War and Peace* (Nashville: Abingdon Press, 1960), chaps. 6–8; James Turner Johnson, *Ideology, Reason, and the Limitation of War: Religious and Secular Concepts, 1200-1740* (Princeton, N.J.: Princeton University Press, 1975); James Turner Johnson, *Just War Tradition and the Restraint of War* (Princeton, N.J.: Princeton University Press, 1981); Edward LeRoy Long, Jr., *War and Conscience in America* (Philadelphia: The Westminster Press, 1968), pp. 22-33; William V. O'Brien, *Nuclear War, Deterrence and Morality* (New York: Newman Press, 1967), pp. 17-31; Ralph Potter, *War and Moral Discourse* (Richmond, Va.: John Knox Press, 1969), pp. 47-62; Paul Ramsey, *War and the Christian Conscience* (Durham, N.C.: Duke University Press, 1961); and Paul Ramsey, *The Just War*. For an extended discussion of just-war theory from a different standpoint see Michael Walzer, *Just and Unjust Wars* (New York: Basic Books, 1977).

6. Cf., e.g., James F. Childress, *Civil Disobedience and Political Obligation* (New Haven: Yale University Press, 1971), chap. 4.

7. For general discussions of the alternatives to just-war theory in the Christian tradition see Bainton, *Christian Attitudes Toward War*

and Peace, and Long, *War and Conscience in America,* pp. 33-41, 48-70.

8. Long, *War and Conscience in America,* p. 37.
9. Johnson, *Just War Tradition and the Restraint of War,* pp. xxv-xxvi.
10. Cited in Reinhold Niebuhr, *Love and Justice,* ed. D. B. Robertson (Philadelphia: The Westminster Press, 1957), p. 254.
11. John C. Bennett and Harvey Seifert, *U.S. Foreign Policy and Christian Ethics* (Philadelphia: The Westminster Press, 1977), pp. 95-100.
12. Richard B. Gregg, *The Power of Nonviolence,* 2d rev. ed. (New York: Schocken Books, 1966), pp. 43 ff.
13. Cf. ibid., p. 51; Martin Luther King, Jr., *Stride Toward Freedom* (New York: Harper & Brothers, 1958), p. 102; Charles E. Osgood, "Reciprocal Initiative," *The Liberal Papers,* ed. James Roosevelt (Garden City, N.Y.: Doubleday, 1962), pp. 193 ff.
14. It is interesting so long afterward to read Reinhold Niebuhr's prediction, written in 1932, that it would take coercion to force whites to recognize black rights and that nonviolent coercion would work toward this goal, but that violence would not (*Moral Man and Immoral Society* [New York: Scribner's, 1932], pp. 252 ff.).
15. For Niebuhr's discussions of nonviolence and pacifism and his criticisms of the pacifism-as-strategy argument, see ibid., pp. 231-56; *Christianity and Power Politics* (New York: Scribner's, 1940); and *Love and Justice,* pp. 241-301.
16. John H. Yoder, *The Politics of Jesus* (Grand Rapids: Wm. B. Eerdmans Publishing Co., 1972), pp. 245-46.
17. Ibid., pp. 15, 19, 23, 63, 99, 107 ff.
18. Ibid., pp. 163 ff.
19. Ibid., p. 158.
20. Paul Ramsey, *Basic Christian Ethics* (New York: Scribner's, 1951), p. 167; cf. pp. 38-40.
21. Ramsey, *The Just War,* p. 143.
22. Yoder, p. 158.
23. See Thomas Aquinas, *Summa Theologica,* II-II, Q. 64, art. 7; also Joseph T. Mangan, S.J., "An Historical Analysis of the Principle of Double Effect," *Theological Studies* 10 (March 1949):41-61.
24. See Walzer's extended illustration of its continuing relevance in *Just and Unjust Wars.*
25. Feinberg, *Social Philosophy,* p. 33 (his italics; see also pp. 20-35).
26. See above, chap. 3, p. 83.
27. *Pacem in Terris,* par. 127; see the translation in *The Pope Speaks* 9 (Summer 1963):38; cf. Paul Ramsey's interpretation of this statement, *The Just War,* pp. 204-5.
28. The Pastoral Letter of the United States Bishops, "The Challenge of Peace: God's Promise and Our Response," *Origins* 13 (19 May 1983):15.

29. Ibid., pp. 15, 31 n. 61.
30. Ibid., p. 17.
31. See my "Nuclear Freeze and Christian Responsibility," *Perkins Journal* 36 (Winter 1983):4ff.
32. B. H. Liddell Hart, *Strategy*, rev. ed. (New York: Praeger, 1954), pp. 338ff.; cf. my discussion of this point in "The Relation of Strategy and Morality," *Ethics* 73 (April 1963):174-75. My present position disagrees with the teleological outlook underlying this earlier article, while continuing to affirm many of its specific moral judgments.
33. Cf. John C. Ford, "The Morality of Obliteration Bombing," *Theological Studies* 5 (September 1944):261-309; Ramsey, *The Just War*, esp. pp. 148-67; Germain Grisez, *Abortion: The Myths, the Realities, and the Arguments* (New York: Corpus Books, 1970); and Ramsey, "Abortion," *The Thomist* 37 (January 1973):174-226.
34. Cf. David Irving, *The Destruction of Dresden* (New York: Ballantine Books, 1965).
35. Desmond Young, *Rommel: The Desert Fox* (New York: Harper & Brothers, 1950), p. 94.

8. Marriage

1. Thomas Aquinas, *Summa Theologica*, Supplement, Q. 49, art. 2.
2. F. E. Brightman, *The English Rite* (London: Rivingtons, 1915), 2:800, 802.
3. Ibid., p. 802.
4. This view finds expression, for example, in Jungian psychology. For a lucid discussion see Ruth Tiffany Barnhouse, "The Religious Identity of Women," *The NICM Journal* 1 (Fall 1972):7-19; and Ruth Tiffany Barnhouse, "Male and Female Sexuality Compared," pp. 62-76 of *Homosexuality: A Symbolic Confusion* (New York: The Seabury Press, 1977).
5. Paul Ramsey, *One Flesh: A Christian View of Sex Within, Outside and Before Marriage* (Bramcote, Nottinghamshire: Grove Books, 1975), p. 4.
6. Cf. Nena and George O'Neill, *Open Marriage* (New York: Avon Books, 1973), pp. 240ff.
7. Cf. Ronald Mazur, *The New Intimacy: Open-Ended Marriage and Alternative Lifestyles* (Boston: Beacon Press, 1973), p. 10.
8. Emil Brunner, *The Divine Imperative*, trans. Olive Wyon (Philadelphia: The Westminster Press, 1974), p. 357.
9. Derrick Sherwin Bailey, *The Mystery of Love and Marriage: A Study in the Theology of Sexual Relation* (New York: Harper & Brothers, 1952), pp. 21-22 (his italics).
10. Martin Luther, *A Treatise on Christian Liberty*.

11. H. L. A. Hart, "Are There Any Natural Rights?" *The Philosophical Review* 64 (April 1955):185; cf. John Rawls, "Justice as Fairness," *The Philosophical Review* 67 (April 1958):179.
12. Hart, "Are There Any Natural Rights?" p. 185.
13. Rawls, "Justice as Fairness," pp. 178, 180, 182.
14. Jessie Bernard, *The Future of Marriage* (New York: Bantam Books, 1973), pp. 145 ff.
15. Nena and George O'Neill, *Open Marriage*, pp. 253-54.
16. Rustum and Della Roy, *Honest Sex* (New York: Signet Books, 1969), pp. 109 ff.; cf. Mazur, *The New Intimacy*, esp. pp. 1-17.
17. Nena and George O'Neill, *Open Marriage*, p. 253 (their italics).
18. Ibid.
19. Mazur, *The New Intimacy*, p. 15.
20. Nena O'Neill, *The Marriage Premise* (New York: Bantam Books, 1977), p. 174.
21. Roland H. Bainton, *Christian Attitudes Toward War and Peace* (New York: Abingdon Press, 1960), pp. 98-99 (italics added).

9. Political Community

1. See Andrew Levine's analysis of this attitude in his *Liberal Democracy: A Critique of Its Theory* (New York: Columbia University Press, 1981), pp. 16-17.
2. Aristotle, *Politics*, 1253a.
3. See J. W. Gough, *The Social Contract: A Critical Study of Its Development* (Oxford: Clarendon Press, 1957), p. 4.
4. See, for example, Joseph Tussman, *Obligation and the Body Politic* (London: Oxford University Press, 1960), and John Rawls, *A Theory of Justice* (Cambridge, Mass.: Belknap Press of Harvard University Press, 1971), pp. 11-12, 16 ff.
5. See the discussion in chap. 2, pp. 61-62 above, of God's covenants with Abraham and David.
6. William F. May, "Code, Covenant, Contract, or Philanthropy," *Hastings Center Report* 5 (December 1975):30-31.
7. Robert N. Bellah, *The Broken Covenant: American Civil Religion in Time of Trial* (New York: The Seabury Press, 1975).
8. Cf. James Childress, *Civil Disobedience and Political Obligation* (New Haven: Yale University Press, 1971), p. 131.
9. Tussman, pp. 23-24.
10. Ibid., p. 38.
11. H. L. A. Hart, "Are There Any Natural Rights?" *Philosophical Review* 64 (April 1955):185.
12. Rawls, pp. 111-12.
13. Childress, p. 109.
14. Cf. H. L. A. Hart's identification of this tendency in utilitarianism

in his "Between Utility and Rights," in *The Idea of Freedom: Essays in Honour of Isaiah Berlin*, ed. Alan Ryan (Oxford: Oxford University Press, 1979), p. 79.

15. For a recent sensitive discussion of this subject by a political scientist, see Stanley Hoffmann, *Duties Beyond Borders: On the Limits and Possibilities of Ethical International Politics* (Syracuse, N.Y.: Syracuse University Press, 1981).

16. Jeremy Bentham, *The Principles of Morals and Legislation*, chap. 1, iv (italics his).

17. Talcott Parsons, *The Structure of Social Action* (New York: Free Press of Glencoe, 1964), p. 59.

18. Ronald Dworkin, *Taking Rights Seriously* (Cambridge: Harvard University Press, 1977), pp. 272-73.

19. Ibid., p. 273.

20. Contrast, for example, the approach of Robert Nozick in *Anarchy, State, and Utopia* (New York: Basic Books, 1974).

21. Cf. Childress's definition of civil disobedience, p. 3.

22. See Robert A. Dahl, *Pluralist Democracy in the United States: Conflict and Consent* (Chicago: Rand McNally, 1967); V. O. Key, *Politics, Parties, and Pressure Groups*, 3d ed. (New York: Crowell, 1956); V. O. Key, *Public Opinion and American Democracy* (New York: Alfred A. Knopf, 1961); Seymour Martin Lipset, *Political Man: The Social Bases of Politics* (Garden City, N.Y.: Anchor Books, 1963); E. E. Schattschneider, *The Semisovereign People: A Realist's View of Democracy in America* (New York: Holt, Rinehart & Winston, 1960).

23. Schattschneider, p. 14.

24. Lipset, p. 2.

25. Dahl, pp. 270-81.

26. (New York: Harper & Brothers, 1956.)

10. The Church

1. F. W. Dillistone, *The Structure of the Divine Society* (Philadelphia: The Westminster Press, 1951), p. 231.

2. Ibid., cf. pp. 39-40, 72, 161-68, 215-16.

3. Ibid., p. 84.

4. Ibid., p. 37.

5. Ibid., p. 213.

6. Ibid., p. 216.

7. See, for example, the Westminster Confession, chapter 7.

8. Cf. Karl Barth's identification and criticism of this viewpoint in the federal theologians Musculus and Szegedin, in *Church Dogmatics*, trans. G. W. Bromiley (Edinburgh: T. & T. Clark, 1956), IV/1, 58-59.

9. Cf. ibid., pp. 55ff.
10. See Perry Miller, *The New England Mind: The Seventeenth Century* (New York: Macmillan, 1939), pp. 377ff.
11. Paul Minear, *Images of the Church in the New Testament* (Philadelphia: The Westminster Press, 1960).
12. See above, pp. 28-29.
13. Minear, pp. 67ff.
14. Barth, *Church Dogmatics*, III/1 (1958), 97.
15. *The Documents of Vatican II*, ed. Walter M. Abbott, S.J. (New York: The America Press, 1966), p. 15.
16. Karl Rahner, *The Christian of the Future* (New York: Herder & Herder, 1967), p. 81 (his italics).
17. Gustavo Gutiérrez, "Faith as Freedom: Solidarity with the Alienated and Confidence in the Future," in *Living with Change, Experience, Faith*, ed. Francis A. Eigo, O.S.A. (Villanova, Pa.: Villanova University Press, 1976), p. 43.
18. Edward Norman, *Christianity and the World Order* (New York: Oxford University Press, 1979), p. 2.
19. Ibid., p. 80.
20. Reuel L. Howe, *The Miracle of Dialogue* (New York: The Seabury Press, 1963), p. 37.
21. Ibid., p. 32.
22. Ibid., pp. 56-65.
23. Robert Lee and Russell Galloway, *The Schizophrenic Church: Conflict over Community Organization* (Philadelphia: The Westminster Press, 1969), pp. 75-90.
24. Among studies of conflict-management in the local church and other local community groups, see James S. Coleman, *Community Conflict* (New York: The Free Press of Macmillan, 1957); Speed Leas and Paul Kittlaus, *Church Fights: Managing Conflict in the Local Church* (Philadelphia: The Westminster Press, 1973); Paul A. Mickey and Robert L. Wilson, *Conflict and Resolution: A Case-Study Approach to Handling Parish Situations* (Nashville: Abingdon Press, 1973); and Lyle E. Schaller, *The Change Agent* (Nashville: Abingdon Press, 1972).
25. Cited in Norman, p. 26.
26. Richard John Neuhaus, "Toeing the Line at the Cutting Edge," *Worldview*, June 1977, p. 17.
27. Paul Ramsey, *Who Speaks for the Church?* (Nashville: Abingdon Press, 1967), p. 56.
28. Neuhaus, pp. 21-22.
29. See my "Some Reflections on the 1972 Social Principles Statement," *Perkins Journal* 28 (Fall 1974):35.
30. See William F. May, *The Physician's Covenant: Images of the Healer in Medical Ethics* (Philadelphia: The Westminster Press, 1983).

Index of Scripture References

325

Index of Subjects and Authors

329